FILTERED BY TIME

A TRUE STORY OF SUCCESS IN VIETNAM

Robert Faulkender

SECOND EDITION

Filtered by Time
A True Story of Success in Vietnam

ISBN: 978-1-61005-049-4

Copyright © 2010 by Robert Faulkender

All rights reserved. No part of this book may be used or reproduced by any means, graphic, electronic, or mechanical, including photocopying, recording, taping or by any information storage retrieval system without the written permission of the author except in the case of brief quotations embodied in critical articles and reviews.

Filtered by Time
Is Dedicated

To the men and women of the United States armed forces who fought in the Vietnam War and to their wives and families who suffered, uniquely, in an ignoble home front.

To my grandchildren: may this story from the Vietnam era give you an understanding of America's contribution to world stability better than the accounts given by most historians.

Acknowledgments

I have accomplished nothing in life without the assistance and support of others. This book is certainly no exception. First and foremost I am deeply grateful for the support given me by my wife, Luanne. Without her love and encouragement, this book would not have been written.

I want to acknowledge Valerie Clark, who pushed and guided the development of the story and was instrumental in the organization of material. I must further acknowledge the support and technical critiques provided me by Holly Bayendor, Vanessa Ratliff, Jennifer Bailey, and Tony Simon. This eclectic little group provided an outstanding sounding board for character and scene development.

Next, I wish to acknowledge those who provided advice and critiques on content and story line. I am most grateful to Patsy Flint, longtime friend and master editor. Thanks to my military advisors Gary Webster, air force; Sam Focer, army; and Don Beatty, navy, for their special view of the work. I owe a special *thank-you* to the professional organization, the National League of Pen Women, whose members, Mimi Gould, Francis Statham, and Polly Craig contributed their time and professional coaching on the publication industry.

Lastly, I cannot express how fully I appreciate the expertise and thoroughness of Peggy Green, who read and critiqued every page—twice—corrected my broken French, and saved the protagonist from looking like a total klutz.

PRINCIPAL CHARACTERS

AMERICAN

Tra Vinh Province Advisor Team

Major Joe Bass	Senior Advisor, Tra Vinh Province
Captain Bob White	Intelligence Officer
Captain Ramsey Hartmann	Assistant Team Leader, Tra Vinh Province
Captain Lenny Khrol	Logistics Officer
Jake Ledbetter (wife Letha)	Foreign Service Officer, State Dept.

Vung Liem District Advisor Team

Captain Edward W. Skillman	Team Chief, Vung Liem District
Captain Nails Hopkins	Forward Air Controller, IV Corps
Captain K. C. Flint	Assistance Team Chief, Vung Liem
Sergeant First Class William Kuntz	Operations Sgt. Advisor, Vung Liem
Master Sergeant Jose Santana	Medical Advisor, Vung Liem
Private First Class Peter de Groot	Radio/Telephone Operator And Driver

Vietnamese

Vung Liem Vietnamese Officials

Daui (Captain) Nguyen Tranh	District Chief, Vung Liem District
Ong (Mr.) Hoa Hoang	Asst. District Chief, Admin
Ong Than (Sergeant retired)	House Manager to the Americans
Daui Sau, (Commander)	Regional Force Company, Vung Liem
Sergeant Khe	Vietnamese Interpreter, Americans
Lieutenant Vu	Operations Officer
Lieutenant Van Le	Communications Officer
Ong (Mr.) Pham	Civil Affairs Officer

Vung Liem Vietnamese Civilians

Father Phan	Catholic Priest, Village Ap Chanh
Sister Lan	Catholic Schoolteacher/ Midwife
Co (Ms.) Mai	Vietnamese Schoolteacher
Tien Van Quan	Monk from Hanoi
Duc To Ngoc	Blind Monk from Hue
Ong Phan Dinh Chi	Rice Mill Owner, Ap Lin
Ong Loc Van Lang	Rice Mill Owner, Vung Liem

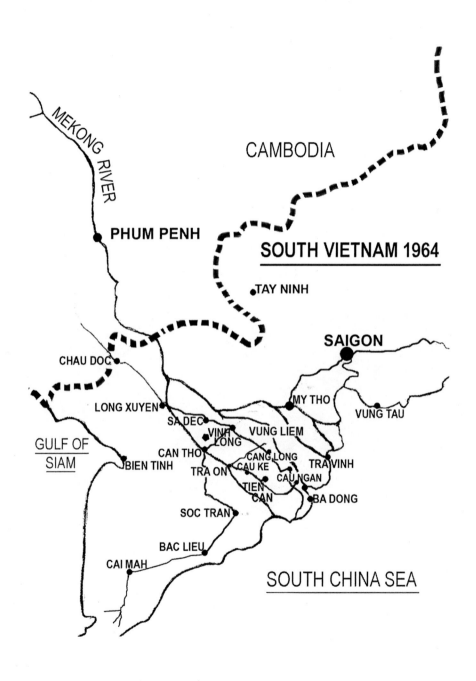

The only sure bulwark of continuing liberty is a government strong enough to protect the interests of the people, and a people strong enough and well enough informed to maintain its sovereign control over the government.

—Franklin Delano Roosevelt

BACKGROUND

Dominoes

THE FRENCH INFLUENCE IN Indochina began with Catholic missionaries in the seventeenth century. It ended in 1954 with military defeat in the mountains northeast of Hanoi. The disaster at Dien Bien Phu translated into the Geneva Agreements, which called for an end to the fighting and the separation of the combatants into North and South Vietnam. The agreement also called for a free election in two years to settle the political future of the country.

The French military completely abandoned Indochina after Dien Bien Phu. But even before the last legionnaire departed the country, North Vietnam began a concerted effort to destroy the government of South Vietnam. In the ensuing years both the Russians and the Chinese significantly aided the North, creating steady pressure on the American containment policy toward communist expansion.

By mid-1963 the American media began to take a closer look at the steadily escalating events. Respected journalists, such as David Brinkley of the National Broadcasting Corporation and Walter Cronkite of the Columbia Broadcasting System, brought the dilemma straight into the living rooms of the American people. But they did so initially in the context of a struggle to contain the relentless expansion of Communism around the world; that is to say, the Cold War.

President John F. Kennedy, to be sure, did make efforts to reduce direct tensions with the USSR following the Cuban Missile Crisis. But JFK's desire to reduce these tensions with the USSR in no way meant the United States was backing away from the basic principle of containment, first enunciated in the Truman Doctrine. Khrushchev had still publicly declared that the Soviets would support "wars of national liberation," wherever they occurred in the world. Since President Kennedy firmly believed in the "Domino Theory" (as he told David Brinkley in September 1963), the idea of backing away from containment was impractical from a national security standpoint, let alone political.

For these reasons alone, holding the line in Vietnam was essential. It was President Kennedy who increased America's troop strength from five hundred to sixteen thousand. He repeatedly insisted that while Vietnam might be, "in the final analysis, their war," American troops were nonetheless not there "to see a war lost," and that he totally disagreed with those who were suggesting a pullout of US personnel. "I think that would be a mistake," he said to Walter Cronkite in October 1963.

The role played by Vietnamese Buddhism was not fully understood by the press or by military analysts in those days. All advisors knew at the time was that wherever there was trouble, a monk seemed to be in the wings. As I researched the Buddhist movement for this book, I learned that in late 1963 the Vietnamese monks began concerted and determined efforts to undermine the South Vietnamese government, and those efforts continued until mid 1965. Historians strongly suspected that these very byzantine activities included collaboration with the National Liberation Front, the political arm of the North Vietnamese.

In this book I created a history for individual monks in order to capture the facts of the Buddhist activities of the day: the history of Japanese occupation, the riots in Hue, the Buddhist convention in Saigon, the monk suicides by self-immolation; things that only surfaced when filtered by time.

—Author

CHAPTER ONE

Knight Errant

LOOKING PAST THE DOOR gunner as the helicopter banked and climbed out of the flight pattern, I could see that, even in 1964, Saigon lived up to her history. In the old days, she was called "the Pearl of the Orient." She was a gem from the sea, symbolizing wealth and beauty and mystery. She certainly seemed that way to me, Ed Skillman. I had been there just a week, and now I was headed to my new job as advisor to the civil guard battalion in Tra Vinh Province.

The chopper reached cruising altitude and took a southerly heading toward the Mekong Delta, which was two or so hours away. I settled back, and, for the first time since I'd left San Francisco, began to reflect on all that happened in the past seven days. It seemed like a month.

From the moment we had disembarked from the contract Boeing 707 at Tan Son Nhut Airport, nothing occurred that met our expectations. We were a fresh planeload of army officers newly assigned to advisor duty in Vietnam. The anticipation of what to expect had been building over the last nine months of preparation.

There was the Military Assistance Training Advisor (MATA) course at Fort Bragg Special Warfare Center: better than three months of intense training in everything, from simple Vietnamese words and phrases and basic social etiquette, to survival skills against an unidentified enemy hiding in a civilian population. Then we spent another three plus months in French language school at the Presidio of Monterey, California: a cram course in spoken French—no reading or writing skills, just speaking.

With that, the army pronounced us ready for deployment. All our training had not only prepared us for the role of advisor in a hostile environment, but it built self-confidence; and that confidence was, perhaps, more important than the training itself. It didn't, however, eliminate altogether the healthy fears lurking in the back of my mind.

Still, the events of the year ahead could not have been further from anything I had imagined.

The first unexpected event was the pretty American stewardesses on the contract Pan Am flight out of San Francisco. Combat pay began the moment we left Travis Air Force Base in California, but it hardly seemed like we were flying into a combat zone.

In retrospect, the refueling stop in Anchorage felt more like a combat zone than the first week in Saigon. An earthquake hit the Alaska region just days before our arrival. The quake registered 9.2 on the Richter scale, and dropped the landing strip forty feet, more or less, below the surface of the surrounding terrain. The aircraft descended into the earth's newest canyon and landed on the intact Anchorage strip—not your everyday occurrence.

By contrast, Saigon's Tan Son Nhut Airport was, unexpectedly, very normal. It was a split-use facility with the military on one side of the field and a civilian terminal, lively with business, on the other. The show of security seemed minimal. There were one or two armed guards with rifles, but it was no more threatening than in Rhine-Main at Frankfurt, Germany.

When we loaded onto the bus headed for downtown Saigon, apart from the grenade screens on the school bus windows, the ride revealed a bustling, cosmopolitan city without the slightest sign of violence. It could have been anyplace in the Orient. It was, simply, not what I had pictured. I grew up with an insatiable appetite for all those old action movies with Gary Cooper and Humphrey Bogart and John Wayne. So far, this wasn't measuring up to French foreign legion adventure.

The lifestyle of all foreigners in Saigon, Americans included, deepened the surreal feeling of my arrival in Vietnam. The army leased two floors of the Majestic Hotel for the use of military in transit. The Majestic Hotel was a fine old French hotel, ten or so stories high, overlooking the corniche along the Saigon River. The rooms were small, but the top floor boasted a lovely restaurant with a splendid view of the lush jungle vegetation that escorted the Saigon River down to the South China Sea. The ceiling-to-floor glass panels could slide open for the better part of the day, giving patrons the advantage of the balmy, subtropical climate. By evening, the panels closed and the focus of attention became the adjoining bar and cabaret.

The nightly feature at the cabaret was a four-piece Vietnamese band playing American sixties music. The jewel in the crown was a five-foot-nothing Vietnamese songstress with a dynamite rendition of "I Left My Heart in San Francisco." And that was *definitely* not what I had expected. It wasn't just the unexpectedness of the girl and the music that choked me up. It was the rush of remembering the tearful good-bye to my wife and my three-year-old daughter at the Denver airport, kidding ourselves that a year wasn't all that long.

Suddenly, the chopper banked a little west of due south. The countryside below changed from predominately jungle laced with waterways, into cultivated fields outlined by tropical foliage. The paddies were flooded this time of year, reflecting the blue-white sky. It was early April and a new rice crop was just being planted. The water from all the paddies, canals, and rivers blended together, only to be carved up by narrow dikes and tree lines along canal banks. Green clusters here and there marked villages and hamlets. It struck me as monotonously flat.

My thoughts drifted, again, to yesterday and the tailor shop I visited on Tudo Street. I was seven years out of West Point, and my first tailored uniform had lost its sharpness—or perhaps I had changed shape. My wife took it as a personal challenge to get me a little less lean and a little less mean. She was winning on the lean side. Either way, the old uniform no longer appeared tailored, and I rationalized that investing in a new uniform was the right thing to do.

As a last act before leaving Fort Carson I dropped by the quartermaster store and bought a kit of material, padding, and buttons with the intent of finding a good tailor in Saigon.

The briefing officer last Wednesday morning recommended a shop, suggesting that if I wanted a nicely tailored uniform, this was the place to visit; so, professional that I am, I stopped, made a deposit, and was measured for a top-of-the-line class-A uniform.

I was comfortable with the briefing officer's recommendation of a tailor, since the same man had also recommended two, truly outstanding, French restaurants. The French onion soup at La Petite Auberge was better than any I could recall, even in France. This place wasn't called French Indochina for nothing.

"We are approaching Tra Vinh, Captain," a voice came through the headset. "Ten minutes out. I've radioed the MAAG House we're coming in, so there will be someone down there to meet you."

I gave the pilot a thumbs-up acknowledging the transmission. My heart pounded like it had when we landed in Saigon. Every one of us on that plane was ready for unarmed combat as soon as we touched the ground. It seems a little silly after the fact. But now, it was the same, except this time I was armed with a .45-caliber pistol. The adrenaline was up.

The chopper dropped to a thousand feet, and circled downwind. The door gunners were alert. The pilot flew a short base leg, then turned back into the wind and rapidly descended.

★★★

Major Joseph Bass was the team chief of the Tra Vinh Province military advisor team. Joe had four commissioned officers and three noncommissioned officers assigned to his team. All lived in a large French villa across the street from the province chief's residential compound. He was a stocky, barrel-chested man, and as long on patience as he was on experience. He had received a battlefield commission in Korea and never expected to be promoted beyond the grade of captain. The five rows of decorations on his class-A uniform gave visual testimony that he was combat tested and battle wise.

"Copy, Tiger 36." Bass acknowledged the chopper's transmission, and then hollered to his Vietnamese driver, "Bring my jeep around, Tom!"

The Military Advisory and Assistance Group Headquarters, or MAAG House as it was called, was the center of American life in the province capital. Each assigned officer had his Vietnamese counterpart. Most of the duty hours were spent with the counterpart observing, sharing, and advising on the functions of the particular job. Today, Major Bass was about to meet the new advisor to Tra Vinh's civil guard battalion.

"Airstrip, Tom. The new civil guard advisor has just arrived."

The driver's name was Tuan, but around the Americans he was Tom, and he liked it. Tom pulled the jeep out onto the dusty century-worn cobblestoned street and turned left toward the northern edge of town. They raced by the gardens that constituted the backyard of the province chief's compound and passed the tennis club. The club wasn't used much now, but in the old days it was the social center for French and Vietnamese aristocrats in the province.

In the year AD 40, the Trung Sisters led a successful insurrection against the Chinese. Internal civil strife continued for several centuries as various regions struggled for dominance. In 1627 a French missionary adapted the Vietnamese language into the Roman alphabet, making way for French cultural dominance and establishment of an Indochinese aristocracy.

In 1787 French missionaries with the backing of Louis XVI established Nguyen Anh as emperor and supported his control of the country. Catholicism, accompanied by French language, French bread, and French wine developed into a powerful cultural part of the Vietnamese society.

For more than four centuries, the Vietnamese aristocracy derived its political and economic power from France. In 1925, Parisian-educated Bao Dia became theoretical emperor, but did not assume the throne until France backed him in 1932 in exchange for religious and economic concessions.

About five hundred meters past the tennis club and just out of town, Tom turned left onto a dirt road that led through an old banana grove. Another five hundred meters and the jeep pulled onto the end of a grass landing strip. The banana trees outlined this end of the field, but the far end of the field stretched away from the tree line into the surrounding rice paddies. A lonely wind sock marked the middle far side of the strip.

The chopper came over the rice paddies on a steep glide path: no sniper fire from the rice paddies for this pilot. As the bird settled down, Joe Bass watched me toss my duffel bag out the chopper door and replace my soft cap. He noticed, too, that I had my pistol holster unsnapped and probably wondered if that was a sign of preparedness or of oversight. The chopper pilot waved to us on the ground, then pulled pitch. The aircraft looked like a stallion pivoting on its hind legs before it gallops off. Tom drove the jeep up toward me.

I delivered a smart salute before the jeep came to a stop. The major responded from his seat with a far more casual salute. "Joe Bass." He stuck out his hand. I shook what was more like a paw—broad and rough and a firm grip which the old soldier held, along with a steady look in my eyes.

"Welcome to Tra Vinh Province. We've been looking forward to your arrival. Dump your gear in the jeep. You're in time for lunch."

The ride back to the MAAG House was uneventful. Feeling really foolish, I surreptitiously snapped my holster flap back in place. Major Bass did all the talking, and I tried to pay attention, but the sights and scenes were captivating. Now, it really was like something out of an old French foreign legion movie.

Bass continued, "In addition to the MAAG House, the United States leases another of these mansions for the Foreign Service officer assigned to the U.S. Overseas Mission (USOM) in Tra Vinh. Jake Ledbetter and his wife, Letha, live in that house just on the other side of the province compound."

The jeep pulled into the drive of the MAAG House. It was a two-story building with a porch across the front. I could picture legionnaire Gary Cooper leaning against one of the front porch columns smoking a cigarette. We drove down the drive alongside the house and stopped in front of a small, detached building that was connected to the main villa by a covered walkway. What had once been the servant quarters was now the kitchen and storage for the MAAG team.

A veranda ran across the full width of the villa. It overlooked the backyard, which was the exact size of a volleyball court; in fact, it was a volleyball court. What was probably green lawn in the old days was now as sandy as any California beach, and the regulation-size court was outlined neatly in yellow engineer tape. High evergreen hedges enclosed the yard and insured privacy as well as stoped rogue balls that failed to fall in court bounds.

Like many middle-class American homes, the functional entrance to the MAAG House was not the front door. Major Bass pointed me through the screened double doors, located in the center of the back veranda. As one entered a spacious anteroom, to the right, against the far wall, a large open staircase led to the second floor.

"Tom will get your duffel upstairs. There's a small lavatory under the stairs." Bass pointed. " We can wash up down here. You never can tell who'll show up for lunch. Half the time you're out with your Vietnamese counterpart doing whatever he's doing. The rest of the time we spend trying to figure out what and why things are happening the way they are—and of course reporting that to higher headquarters."

A wide hall out of the anteroom stretched straight to the front of the villa. Off the hall to the left was the dining alcove with just one man sitting at the large, fully set table.

"This is Captain Bob White, our intelligence officer." Bass indicated for me to sit. "Make yourself a sandwich."

White was about my age. He had a friendly face and eyes that were a little too far apart, which gave him an interesting and disarming look. White passed the plate of cold cuts. The conversation was the usual introductory exchanges establishing everyone's credentials and linking up do-you-know networks. Listening to the conversation, it could have been a lunch break at the Fort Benning officers' club. But it wasn't. It was a MAAG House in the Mekong Delta. I was beginning to let go of a little of the paranoia.

The Major finished his instant iced tea and announced he had a meeting over at province. He turned to me. "Get yourself unpacked and settled in. White here will show you your bunk and how the housekeeping works. Volleyball at 1630, happy hour at 1830, dinner at 1900, and movie at eight. We'll start the rounds tomorrow."

He turned into the hall. "Tom. Crank the jeep."

Tra Vinh Province is sometimes known as Vinh Binh Province and appears that way on many maps. The Ca Chien River, which is a major artery of the Mekong River Delta, borders the northeast edge of the province. The Hau Giang River, a second major artery, is the southwest boundary of the province. The South China Sea winds around the coastline connecting the banks of these two great arteries. The South China Sea is the southern border of Tra Vinh Province. Long Toan is the southernmost district in the province, on the seacoast.

The northern boundary of the province is a canal connecting the Ca Chien River with the Hau Giang River. The canal is about 150 kilometers inland and up the river delta from the sea. Technically, Tra Vinh Province is an island.

Over three hundred years ago Cambodians, mainly fishermen, drifted down the Mekong and settled along its banks. It was through the spread of their brand of Buddhism that they developed enough influence to change the name of the province from Tra Vinh to Vinh Binh. The South Vietnamese Government restored the Vietnamese name, Tra Vinh.

Over the centuries the Cambodians and Vietnamese lived side by side but separately, for the most part. In some districts the Cambodian dominance was so complete that the population still does not speak Vietnamese. Nor do the Vietnamese in these areas speak Cambodian.

At the end of three days of orientation, I had come to a couple of conclusions. First, San Miguel beer from the Philippines was, perhaps, the best beer I had ever tasted; second, my counterpart had a lot more on his plate than he was staffed to handle. It looked like I was going to supplement the commander, not just shadow and advise him.

And, it started the next day. Ramsey Hartmann, the assistant province team chief, and I took a little trip down to Cau Ngang District. The VC had hit a watchtower on a canal bridge two nights before, and Bass wanted someone to go down and assess the situation. The size of the force was vague: although there were no friendly casualties, the bridge was reported as seriously damaged.

Ramsey Hartmann was a senior captain of infantry. He had bright blue eyes and an infectious little-boy smile that totally disarmed friend and foe alike. His frame was stocky, which foretold weight battles in the future, but, for now, he was muscular and fit.

Ramsey had spent most of the previous evening telling me about the province's history and explaining the anomalies of the guerilla war in Vietnam. Now the two of us were speeding along Highway 8 south to Cau Ngang. We were riding in the jeep issued to me by the civil guard commander, Captain Nguyen Tung. The driver, Diem—pronounced *Zim*—came with the jeep and spoke a little English.

"With the canal network so interconnected across the province, Ramsey, what's the big deal over one bridge out?"

Ramsey leaned forward from the backseat. "The bridge connects the fishing village by road with the district town. The frustration is that the people in Cau Ngang have a hard time getting fish into the inland marketplace. When the bridge is out, the fishermen have to work their way inland to market by canal, which is a hassle and wastes a lot of time. Plus, it demonstrates the government's inability to provide security for the people." Ramsey turned to the driver. "We're going to Cau Ngang, soldier. Turn off at the next left—by the road markers."

Ramsey never tried to learn the Vietnamese names. He just called every one of them "soldier." With his twinkling blue eyes and that boyish smile, no one ever seemed to mind that their name was not used. It did not occur to them that "soldier" was anything but a term of friendship. They might have been surprised to learn that Captain Hartmann had not a clue as to any of their names.

The driver slowed for the turn. The side road was dirt, but it was well engineered. The quality of road nets in Vietnam was one of the supporting factors in the decision by the United States to take its stand in this part of Indochina. Between Cambodia, Laos, and Vietnam, Vietnam was believed to have the best road network.

Cau Ngang was about two kilometers down the road running between rice paddies. The paddies were lightly flooded. It was just enough mud to make it easy for the farmers to plant. And they formed the quintessential scene of the Orient: the rice farmer in conical hat and black pajamas rolled up above his knees, ankle deep in muddy water, placing rice plants in rows beside the paddy dike.

The jeep pulled through the district town to the far side of the marketplace and stopped at the small villa with the Vietnamese flag on a pole in front. Ramsey jumped out from the backseat and motioned for me to follow.

"You always want to check through the local chief before you go into his area—an international courtesy—but you'd be surprised at how many people don't seem to honor that."

A small, weathered Vietnamese in uniform stepped out onto the porch of the villa. He smiled at Ramsey. "*Chau, Daui.*" Hello, Captain.

"*Chau*, Chief. Got someone here I want you to meet. This is our new civil guard advisor, Captain Skillman."

After brief introductions, Ramsey began asking questions about the incident that occurred the night before last. He learned that the three-man outpost had, indeed, been overrun by the VC. Seemed the defenders fled before being captured. The bridge was damaged, but the chief was able to temporarily repair it the next day.

"Is OK today, but need more longtime repair pretty soon."

Ramsey asked, "Are the defenders back on site?"

The chief nodded. "Yes."

"Was any artillery used?"

"No. Post have no radio."

"All right." Ramsey looked at me. "Let's go see what it looks like. You want to come with us, Chief?"

The chief smiled nervously, "I there all day yesterday. I catch up here."

Ramsey hopped into the back of the jeep as I slid into the right front. "Head out on the river road, soldier."

As the jeep broke out of the tree line at the edge of the district town, we could see the next village about five hundred meters in the distance.

Ramsey leaned forward from the backseat. "Not using the artillery is a problem. Something you can take a look at in your job. Your counterpart should be able to get a radio net down here. Training the troops to use artillery is not that hard, assuming they have reasonable intelligence."

The driver slowed down as we entered the next settlement of thatched houses. A group of children stopped their play as the jeep passed. They shouted and waved from behind a fenced dirt yard that did not display one green blade of anything. The driver hustled on through town and back into the countryside. The next hamlet looked to be another half kilometer down the road.

Just as the jeep approached the hamlet, the road curved to the right along the edge of the tree line and, after thirty meters or so, curved back to the left and into the town. The settlement consisted of half a dozen thatched houses and one small stucco building that was some sort of community house. No need to stop. There were no children around, and the adults all seemed to be out in the fields. About fifty yards out of the village, however, the driver did need to stop—suddenly.

A light tree branch stretched out across the road. Zim just stared.

"OK. Hold the phone here," said Ramsey.

At that moment I heard a crisp staccato sound. In one fluid movement Ramsey went over the side of the jeep into the ditch. Soldier Zim dropped out of his seat and down beside the jeep. I heard a second and third CRACK and a couple of THUMP sounds, and the Fort Benning rifle range flashed into mind. I watched the dust kick up in little puffs, and it dawned on me: someone was ... *holy shit* ... firing at me.

How could that be? I'm a nice guy. I'm here to help. More dust spouts. A stop action moment ...

If I could have just jumped up three feet, that would have all gone under me ...

Ramsey's shout broke the spell. "Get your ass down, Skillman." I hit the dirt and rolled into the ditch next to Ramsey.

My mind was out of body. Here I was ... *Knight errant to the Court of Camelot, on assignment for a just and noble cause, and those sumbitches were shooting at me—and what's more—they made me muddy up my fricken fatigues.*

"NOW, Skillman. Now's the time. Get your goddamn pistol out," yelled Ramsey. He laid three rounds along the tree line to the right of the road, but the target was pretty much out of pistol range. Didn't matter. I was mad and fired a couple of two-round bursts. Then we heard the thump of three more shots, but without the preempting crack.

"We're getting supporting fire," yelled Ramsey. "Hell, looks like the guard tower is alive and well-- if not swift."

"That the watchtower to the left of the road?" It seemed to me all shooting had stopped.

"Yeah. Soldier, clear that branch carefully, and let's get going." Ramsey and Zim both walked slowly and carefully toward the branch.

"Any trained enemy would have hooked up some sort of explosive device to this branch, but either they don't have any grenades, or they don't know any better—probably both." Ramsey grabbed one end of the branch, and Zim took the other. Together they dragged it off the road.

Ramsey hopped into the jeep and motioned for Zim to drive on slowly. "Those little guys are long gone by now. They are not very sophisticated, and they don't have much staying power, but you can't let that reality fool you. These little fellers can kill you deader than a door nail; and that's the truth."

Ramsey seemed to sense that I was not altogether in touch with reality.

As we approached the tree line, I could see that the trees actually defined the edge of a canal bank. The road continued over a bridge to the far side, but Zim turned left onto a short driveway leading up to the edge of a three-sided fort.

The walls of the fort were made of packed mud about six feet high and a lot thicker at the bottom than at the top. Barbed wire ran along the top. Each wall was about one hundred feet long, more or less, and formed an equilateral triangle. In the center of the triangle was a concrete watchtower, maybe thirty feet high. Three soldiers in black pajamas and sandals were standing tall outside the barricaded entrance—big smiles on their faces.

"These guys are Cambodian," said Ramsey. "You can tell by their larger size and coloring. Their coloring is a more brownish hue, where the Vietnamese have the yellow hue and are smaller and more delicate in stature. The Camboats are pretty fierce fighters."

I surveyed the soldiers and then did a double-take. Was I seeing just one rifle? And what was the other guy carrying? So help me god, was that a samurai sword?

"It sure looks like a samurai sword." Ramsey was shaking the rifleman's hand. Everybody was speaking sounds that no one understood—except of course, the universal language of a victory.

"The thing that's really scary is that the middle guy doesn't even have a weapon." Ramsey turned to Zim. "Ask this man where his rifle is."

Zim and the soldier exchanged words, and the soldier answered with a big smile. "He say he carry the ammo for the rifle."

"Well, how much ammo does he have?" said Ramsey. Zim and the soldier exchanged words at length.

"He say he only carry three bullet. But now he has no bullet. They shoot VC."

Ramsey turned to me, "What we have here is a watchtower with one Indochina rifle, one not so sharp sword, and three rounds of ammunition. It's a wonder the bridge is still standing. Let's take a look at it."

Our eclectic little party walked back to the road and up to the bridge. It was a well-constructed bridge spanning high over the canal with plenty of clearance for boat traffic. Clearly the charges placed by the VC were inadequate to blow down a bridge this well built. But the district chief was right: it would take more repairs before it could carry much more than a water buffalo and cart. Vehicle traffic was out—at least as it concerned my jeep.

Ramsey nodded. "We got the picture. Might just as well head back. Bring up the jeep, soldier."

He walked over to the man with the rifle and shook his hand again. "Thanks for your help this afternoon. You did real good. I will tell the district chief you were very brave. Thank you."

We climbed into the jeep. I told Zim to make sure they knew we were grateful for their help and that we would tell the chief they needed ammo.

Zim sang out a few phrases, smiled a big smile, then headed the jeep back down the road to the scene of the live fire exercise. We hastily drove on and were halfway through the village when we realized that no adults were in town. There were children playing beside the road. No one spoke. No one waved, not even the children.

"Something tells me these folks had an idea what was going to happen here," said Ramsey. "And that's the VC victory. The villagers had to know something bad was about to go down. They could see the roadblock. But they didn't tell anyone. They knew, and they just let it happen. And it is not because they support the VC or believe that Communism is a better form of government or any of that crap. They simply don't trust the district chief to protect them from retaliation if they report the activity. It comes right down to safety."

Zim was already accelerating before they had cleared the tree line when I noticed, in passing, the Vietnamese monk wrapped in the saffron yellow robes of his Buddhist order. The monk stood in the underbrush a few feet down the footpath toward his pagoda. He watched the American jeep race down the road toward the village headquarters. The look on the monk's face was unreadable. It might have been disgust or discouragement or just frustration; it was hard to tell. I saw him turn and walk back to the pagoda.

We drove along in silence until the jeep pulled up in front of the district headquarters. Both of us dismounted and hustled into the villa. Ramsey dropped down into the chair next to the chief's desk.

"You got bad guys running loose in your yard, Chief." The chief looked a little confused.

I translated that Ramsey meant a couple of VC had fired on us that afternoon just south of the canal watch tower. The chief showed a blank expression. I asked him straight out if there was some way to get a couple more rifles out to those men in the tower—at least some additional ammunition. Three rounds hardly seemed sufficient.

The chief looked at Ramsey, who looked away and spoke with exasperation, "You explain it to him, *Daui*. I get confused." Old blue eyes got busy cleaning the mud off his boots.

The chief turned back to me. "The watchtower is to watch bridge and report danger. He shoot three bullet for danger and protect self. Only take one gun. More gun and more ammunition make the tower a target for capture gun and ammunition. Now target is bridge. We fix. VC win nothing ... no gun, no ammunition."

"Well, you may want to get them three more rounds before dark. We thanked them and you, for their help today." Ramsey headed for the door. "Crank it up, soldier."

I stood and shook the chief's hand. "Nice to meet you today. We'll be back soon. I am going to see what I can do about getting some radios down here for direct communications with the watchtower."

The chief smiled, said something in Vietnamese, and walked me to the jeep.

The trip back to Tra Vinh was driven pretty much in silence.

I thought about the events of the day.

I had actually been in a firefight. Some people had really tried to kill me. Bullets were flying…

Tower guards armed with a lousy three rounds…

And the only emotion I had registered was anger over getting my fatigues muddy.

This was just not what I had expected. Where was paranoia when you needed it?

CHAPTER TWO

The Vietnamese

Bob White was a distinguished graduate of North Georgia Military College, which meant he was pretty smart. By graduating in the top 2 or 3 percent of the military students, he had earned his professional regular army status. Not all North Georgia students were military, and not all were offered a regular army commission. Bob had been. He was perfectly suited as the team's intelligence officer.

As White explained it to me, part of my job was to keep resupplied a Special Forces camp located in Long Toan District on the China Sea. The supplies came through Vietnamese channels. We simply saw to it that materials and air support actually got to the camps in a reliable fashion. I had yet to experience one of these resupplies, but White was quick to say that he went on most trips in order to get firsthand information on the situation in Long Toan. Tomorrow morning would be my introduction.

Morning came with the blast of painfully whiny, screeching music booming over a PA system. It put the reveille cannon at West Point to shame. Asian music is an acquired taste, and ten days is insufficient acquisition time. I had never experienced a wake-up call like it, and for the entire period that I lived in the Tra Vinh, I never quite got used to that tuneless whine masquerading as music.

Outdoor public-address speakers were mounted on poles throughout the town. The government billed it as a public information service. It was a means of communicating with the town's people in the event of an emergency—or on any other occasion deemed critical. Included in that service was the five-day-a-week broadcast of Vietnamese music and news at the crack of dawn—the Vietnamese equivalent of your morning news and traffic report.

An hour later White and I waited beside the airstrip for the arrival of an H-21 helicopter. I still was unclear as to how the Special Forces operated and coordinated in the province. The SF camp was just outside the district town of Long Toan, which was the southernmost district in the province and stretched out into the South China Sea. The coastline consisted entirely of mangrove swamp. The swamp was a two- to three-kilometer strip spreading inland from the sea. The district town was nearly inaccessible by roads.

I asked White how it was that we were supplying this camp directly when there was no other contact with their operations.

White sat down on the artillery shell boxes that the ammunition officer delivered to the airfield. He pulled off his sunglasses and began cleaning them with a handkerchief. Odd: no one carried a handkerchief, much less a khaki-colored one.

"Besides the civil guard forces, there are three other military organizations overseeing the basic province security. First, the Army of the Republic of Vietnam, called ARVN, is the active-duty army of trained and seasoned troops. They deploy in offensive operations against VC concentrations as identified by intelligence sources. They blow in and out of Tra Vinh every couple weeks to stand down and resupply." White finished cleaning his glasses and was now pinching a diagonal corner of the handkerchief between the thumb and forefinger of each hand. What on earth was he doing?

He continued, "Second, the U.S. Army maintains active teams of the Special Forces, which operate in-country, but they are strategically directed out of Fort Bragg. These are highly specialized teams trained to operate independently and in direct support of the Vietnamese local governments at the grassroots level. They go into contested areas to recruit the locals, and they train them to defend themselves against guerrilla elements attempting to intimidate the population."

The man was swinging the handkerchief around like a skip rope between his fingers, and I watched in dumb fascination as he tied the roll around his neck—a sweatband; son of a gun.

White finalized the knot on the bandana, "There is a third level of operations which you will run into from time to time. The Central Intelligence Agency guys have spooks who run around in the field and occasionally drop by to request some kind of support ... never anything big. Then they disappear. Weird."

The sound of a couple of choppers came into range. The Vietnamese sergeant barked at his ammo detail. Bodies stood up and unlimbered. The choppers came into view, only it was just one helicopter with two rotors. No wonder it was nicknamed the flying banana. That was exactly what it looked like. The skinny fuselage angled upward from the midsection at about thirty degrees. A rotary wing was on each end. The beast flew through the air rather like a scorpion with its tail up in the rear and blades spinning.

"That doesn't seem like much 105 ammo." I was looking at the intended cargo.

White put his sunglasses back on and stood to hook up his field harness. "Well, they only have two tubes down there. They use them for preplanned fire mostly. The 105 howitzer gives them a long reach into the swamps and around the outer villages if VC gets too frisky. The local security forces won't go out to fight: strictly defense. The artillery wards off the enemy and builds confidence among the locals."

We followed the ammo detail onto the chopper, and the door gunners motioned everyone to settle down. Instantly the craft left the ground. We made a long, low run out over the rice paddies before slowly climbing to cruise altitude.

From the air, the Long Toan district town was hardly definable. It looked more like a large cluster of thatched buildings scattered among the tropical foliage. Two American uniforms appeared along the tree line as the chopper eased down on what was, no doubt, a soccer field. About a dozen Vietnamese dressed in black pajamas followed at a distance behind the two Americans.

I felt a jolt of paranoia.

Bob offhandedly mentioned, "Sometimes it's hard to tell the local security boys from the VC. As you no doubt noticed, everyone down in the districts wears the same peasant dress, black pajamas. But take a look at the footgear. The best clue is that Popular Force guys are in standard-issue ankle-high canvas shoes … usually."

"No kidding." I tried to sound casual. I took special note that these black-pajama guys were wearing ankle-high canvas shoes that looked a lot like old-time tennis Keds, only they were olive drab. I followed White out of the chopper.

One of the waiting Americans, a captain, spoke first. "Just in the nick of time, Bob. We're about out of everything." He turned my way. "And you must be the new civil guard advisor. Meet Master Sergeant Leo Klazinsky. I'm Mike Frickey."

Sergeant Klazinsky could have been the recruiting poster for Special Forces: big, square shouldered, with a Dick Tracy jaw. By contrast, Captain Frickey was lean and wiry and more typical of Special Forces troops. Frickey had intense black eyes with sort of a cobra look. In fact, he looked mean as a snake. I recognized that look. Back in ranger training there was an instructor on the hand-to-hand combat committee who demonstrated, conclusively on several occasions, that he was capable of killing an enemy with his bare hands.

During the running of the bayonet training course the ranger trainers positioned themselves along the course to give "encouragement" to the candidates. It was not enough for rangers to run the course just once. Rangers must run the course until they could no longer run—or until a lane grader said stop. And ranger instructors were there to see how many trainees they could wear out before someone said stop.

On my umpteenth lap, this same killer sergeant jumped in front of me as I approached an obstacle consisting of a series of two-foot railings spaced about four feet apart along the trail like hurdles. There were four railings in the series, requiring you to high-step through the obstacle. As trained, I gave a textbook thrust at the sergeant without any serious attempt to actually stick the man. After all, the bayonet was unsheathed.

The next time around the same sergeant at the same location again jumped in front of me. I gave the same textbook thrust, except the son of bitch parried my thrust, stepped inside my extended arms, and actually grabbed at my rifle. Conditioned response kicked in. My vertical butt stroke broke his grip: I had hoped it broke his arm.

As I came around the next time, I'm mad, and I really want to hurt the man. We go through the dance; only this time he has a solid grip on my rifle, which is across my chest, and I am using it to push him into the railing. Lucky for me he was sideways to the knee-high railing—he either turns toward me or breaks his knee over the obstacle. He turns facing me and falls over backward; I fall on top.

The fall knocks off my steel helmet, which drops smack onto my adversary's nose. Lane graders rush in to pull us apart. I am directed back on the bayonet course, but not before I see my enemy has a really nice bloody nose between his snake eyes. I grabbed a quick look at the name tag on his fatigues—Frickey. *Oh my god …*

★★★

I offered up something like "Good to meet you guys," and, with an awkward laugh, "I guess I will be your go-to man for the next cycle." I shook hands and stared into Frickey's lifeless gaze as long as I could. *No sign of recognition on his part—that was good.* The man seemed completely at home in this jungle. We walked along a dirt road that was obscured by the vegetation. The road angled at a half left toward the built-up area.

Long Toan district town was much larger than it appeared from the air. The dirt road from the soccer field ran past a school and a line of thatched houses, then past a larger building constructed more permanently with rough boards and corrugated-steel roofing.

Further down the road, we came to the centerpiece of the village. It was a marketplace consisting of an open-air pavilion covered by corrugated steel mounted on concrete pillars over a concrete slab floor. It was the most permanent structure in the town. Various shops and stalls selling specialty services and hardware items, lined the outer edge of the road that formed the perimeter of the market place. Frickey led us to a large thatched stall with four tables arranged around the swept dirt floor.

"Have a seat," said Frickey.

We sat. Instantly, a Vietnamese man wearing black pajamas and *rubber sandals* appeared through the passage in the back wall.

White quickly laid his hand on my arm. "The 'issue shoes' thing is just a rough guideline for identifying friendlies." Almost apologetically he said, "Most peasants are barefoot or in rubber sandals. What would you like to drink ... tea, sausi, or beer?"

I had no idea what a sausi was, and a beer just didn't seem right. "I'll take tea."

Frickey held up two fingers and in Vietnamese said, "Two teas," then held up one finger and said, "bier." *Interesting how beer is "beer" in almost every language.* He looked over at Klazinsky.

Klazinsky stood. "I'm going back and check on the unloading. I'll catch up when everything is stowed."

As Klazinsky turned to leave he waved to a Vietnamese soldier who had just walked into the market square from the other end of the road. The soldier smiled and angled toward the restaurant.

Frickey leaned over in conspiratorial way. "This is the new district chief; been on the job about three months. Seems a little green to me; maybe a little slow to take charge. We'll see."

The Vietnamese officer smiled and saluted as he approached. The insignia on his fatigues indicated the rank of captain. Introductions were made, and after a time, the conversation turned serious. I watched and listened, noting how well Bob White did his intelligence job. Frickey and Klazinsky had a handle on what was happening along the seacoast, and it did not always match up with what the Vietnamese were getting through their own channels.

"Province indicates not much activity down here lately," said White. But it was more of a question than a statement.

"Whenever did Province know what was going on until after the fact?" said Frickey. "If you hadn't shown up today, we'd be flat out of artillery rounds by morning. Been popping on these guys every night for ten days. Seems VC imported a few troops, since they can't get any recruits out of the area. They're running around in the swamp staying clear of the villages but interrupting canal traffic. Possibly trying to collect taxes."

The district chief spoke in halting English. "No one complain yet about VC taking some of their fish."

White said, "What do you think they are up to, Chief?"

"I think they maybe passing through … maybe head north to Tra Vinh."

"Why wouldn't they just go up the river to Province?" asked White.

Frickey said, "Not a bad idea for them to approach Province from the inland—that is, if raising hell on Province was their mission. But I don't think so. I tell you, something is building down here, and I'm not sure yet what it is."

The restaurant owner arrived with two helpers to serve the tea. He himself served Frickey the beer. With a flourish he set a liter-size tumbler down in front of the captain. It was filled with chunks of ice. The proprietor poured half the rich amber beer over the ice. He finished by placing the brown liter bottle next to the glass.

Now this, again, was totally unexpected. That there was beer in this place was startling enough. But here, in a place where no roads could enter, where the population lived in short supply of all commodities, where VC threatened all lines of communication … here in the middle of a mangrove swamp on the South China Sea, this guy can get ice … no ammunition, but plenty of ice. *Unbelievable.*

Frickey looked at me over his beer—*still no sign of recognition.* "Had any of the local beer?" He pointed to the bottle with La Rue printed in yellow diagonally around its side.

"No, not yet. Had San Miguel; pretty damn good, but they tell me that it is Pilipino."

"Well, this La Rue is not too shabby either. Maybe the only thing the French do well when they colonize is introducing the population to French bread, French wine, and French beer. Have a taste."

What the hell, maybe this wasn't the same "Frickey"; it had been six years …

I took a sip and was surprised at the rich, stout taste. It would clearly take a lot of melted ice to dilute that flavor. "You're right. I'm just surprised to see ice here in the middle of nowhere."

"Ah, that's no big deal. Comes down from My Tho or Saigon in big blocks on a sampan. Even the VC like ice. It gets through." Frickey laughed. It had seemed like a big deal to me but what did I know? So far, nothing I had seen was what I'd expected.

The waiters disappeared through the door in the back wall and the conversation picked up again.

"How much Popular Forces have you got these days?" asked White, looking at the chief and then to Frickey. The chief blew on the hot tea and took a sip.

Frickey said, "We've got about fifteen trained irregulars at our base camp that we can count on, and another five or so that show up from time to time. Gives enough to run small operations every couple days. That's how we picked up on the new VC in the area." Frickey turned to the chief, "Those boys we trained last month seem to be earning their pay this month."

The chief smiled. "Yes, preplanned artillery target very good. Popular Force soldier better able to protect people."

"Yeah, well, you need to recruit more of those boys," said Frickey. "You still got villages that don't know how to call for artillery support."

He turned to me: *dead eyes*. "The chief's Popular Forces are pretty poorly equipped. Some security posts only have three men assigned, and they don't leave their post for any reason. Their job is to defend a little triangular fort strategically placed for the protection of an assigned bridge or a canal junction. And they do that by rifle fire only, never by going out in pursuit of the VC. That's where the artillery comes in. It gives the PF the ability to chase the VC."

Still no sign of recognition.

"The fire is already planned to hit a selected target area. When the VC come near the target area, the men in the fort radio a planned fire request. Back at the guns they already know the settings for the area and respond immediately. Then, by adjusting the fire, they chase them back into the swamps."

Frickey continued his discussion of the PF. "Between the small arms fire from the fort and a couple of artillery rounds, the VC are kept from destroying the terrain feature assigned for protection. Teaching the PF how to fire the tubes on the one hand and how to call for support on the other is one of the things my boys do."

I recognized the classic Special Forces mission: an "A" team made up of five cross-trained specialists comes into an area; recruits, organizes, and trains the indigenous population to first defend itself and then take offensive actions to capture or kill guerrilla forces bent on disrupting the functions of government.

I asked him, "Are we winning?"

Frickey again turned his snake eyes on me ... *Was there a glimmer of recognition?* "Depends on what you mean by winning. If you mean is my team able to do its job successfully, then absolutely. If you mean are we neutralizing the VC and making the land safe for democracy, no."

Sergeant Klazinsky returned to announce that the supplies had been off-loaded and moved to the base camp.

"Thanks, Leo," said Frickey. "Your chopper pilots are going to get antsy if they sit too long on the ground. Let's go."

Everyone shook hands with the chief, and he left in a different direction. Frickey dropped a bill on the table, and the group moved back to the aircraft. White and Frickey walked ahead.

I was curious about the oddball frame building beside the road on the way to the soccer field and asked Klazinsky about it.

"That's a rice mill, sir. These folks do a lot of fishing, but as you could see when you flew over, there are miles of rice paddies defining the edge of the swamp. Most of their livelihood comes from rice."

The moment the party broke out of the tree line, the chopper blades turned over. Children, now out of school, lined the schoolyard fence to see the white Americans pass by.

"Vietnamese have beautiful children," I observed to Klazinsky.

He glanced at the kids and turned back to me. "You got any kids at home, Captain?"

"Yeah, a three-year-old girl." The picture of Kelly Jayne with that long auburn ponytail flashed in my mind's eye ... How I loved to comb it—*Sit still, you wiggle worm.* I was smiling.

"Well, kids are kids any place in the world. My two are in high school already; hardly know them." The sergeant pulled up beside Frickey. "We'll be seeing you again, Captain." He flipped a friendly salute to us. Frickey waved, and the two disappeared into the jungle. The light loaded flying banana snapped into the air and headed north.

★★★

By the time we had returned to the MAAG House, the volleyball game was into its third round. They didn't need any new players. I followed White to the front room of the house. The front room stretched across the entire width of the house. Slow-twisting fans hung from the ultra-high ceilings like something out of the movie, *Casablanca.*

At either side of the room there was an alcove formed by two columns dividing the room into thirds from front to rear. A four-foot-high divider ran between the column and the front wall. Another similar divider ran between the second column and rear wall. This alcove had been neatly remodeled into a bar. The alcove at the other end sported a large movie screen that could be seen from anyplace in the room.

Bob White pulled two San Miguels out of the fridge behind the bar. "Now's the time for a beer." He set them on the bar top. "So what did you think about today?"

Captain Ramsey Hartmann came into the room. "Mark one up for me, too," said Ramsey. "And, what, *overall*, do you think by now, Captain?"

"I have to tell you guys. I've been in-country for not quite three weeks, and nothing I have seen is anything like I expected."

Ramsey teased. "Expected to come out the chopper door guns blazing. dincha?"

"Well, not exactly …"

If the full truth were known, I hadn't volunteered for assignment in Vietnam. I was plenty happy running a rifle company at Fort Carson, Colorado. But I was a professional soldier, and I was genuinely eager for the chance to ply my skills in real action. I certainly believed the mission of stopping the spread of Communism was in the best interests of America. And I was certain that the things we were doing for Vietnam were noble and worthy of sacrifice. I could see that-- even after a few short weeks in-country. I was pumped up for the challenge. But I didn't say that out loud. It was embarrassing.

"Don't feel bad, buddy. We all come with that same expectation." Ramsey smiled knowingly.

CHAPTER THREE

Suffer Not the Children

THE NEXT MONTH OR so was more of "settling in." I was given an office at the armory. The armory doubled as the civil guard battalion headquarters. I checked in almost every day, but my counterpart, Captain Tung, never seemed to be around—either he was gone, or he was just on his way out or just in and too busy to talk. Most of my time was spent shadowing Bob White or Ramsey, seeing what was going on in their areas. It seemed that activity was heating up in the southern part of the province around Long Toan.

Finally, after almost two weeks, I had the opportunity to recommend to the guard commander that some radios be issued down in Cau Nang District. The commander seemed enthusiastic about the idea, which made me wonder how many other watchtowers were out of touch with their district headquarters. I decided that answering this question would be my first project. I would inventory the radios in the province and bounce it against the total number of watchtowers. The difference would identify shortages, but the challenge was to find more radios. I would pass the idea by Major Bass tonight.

However, the major and the intelligence officer were late coming in for dinner. Normally, the team returned to the MAAG House around five o'clock for a couple of reasons, other than the end of the workday. The main reason was that beginning around 1730 or 1800 hours, depending on the season, the Regional Force soldiers, or "rough puffs" as they were affectionately known, began setting up roadblocks for the night. This practice was designed to keep VC from using the road net during the hours of darkness. Anything or anyone moving on the roads after dark was likely to be shot. Considering the Regional Force's training status, it was not a good idea to leave one's destiny to the good judgment of a rough-puff soldier who was, likely, more frightened than was the tardy traveler.

The second reason for the early call to quarters was that, with the natural flow of daily events, dinnertime became the time for an informal staff meeting. Events of the day were shared around the table. The major made comments and issued guidance, and generally the team coordinated future events. Thus, when the boss was late to dinner, something was in the wind.

Joe Bass dropped his pistol belt on the hall chair and stepped into the room. He plunked into the seat at the front corner of the square table. The Vietnamese cook flew in behind, gathering up empty and half-empty bowls for refilling. White sat down next to the boss.

"Such a day we're having." White sighed. He passed the rice to the major, who busied himself piling the stuff on his plate. "Looks like the VC in the mangrove swamps are more than the Long Toan District boys can handle." White took the rice back and began a pile on his plate.

Bass spoke. "Special Forces guys say they can keep peace, but they can't tell what's going on out in the swamps—if anything. District chief thinks there is a small buildup of guerrillas along the Cau Nang border." He took the fresh bowl of creamed chicken and spooned it liberally over the rice.

Everyone at the table went into his own thoughts. I regretted that I had not pushed for the radios sooner, since it looked like the watchtower bridge in Cau Nang might be hit again.

Ramsey surfaced first, "What's the colonel have in mind, boss?" The province chief held the grade of colonel in the ARVN.

Joe Bass took another bite of his dinner, "Can't we ever get something besides rice? Have these guys ever heard of a potato?" He smiled sheepishly at his verbalizing the complaint; then continued.

"I don't know what the colonel thinks, but I'll tell you what I recommended. He has two Regional Force companies in Cang Long and two in Vung Liem. Looks to me he needs to take one of those four down to the swamps. Skillman, when is the last time you were able to pin down your counterpart?"

"I caught up to him today. He was very receptive to getting radios down to Cau Nang. I can't believe he hasn't equipped these watchtowers before, because it seemed like a brand-new idea to him."

"It's 'cause he hasn't got radios. Now that you have suggested it, he'll come back to you in a few days asking for your support in getting them issued. He barely has enough working radios for his companies. That's how the watchtowers usually communicate. They piggyback on the Regional Force company when it's positioned in the district."

"Well, is there a way we can get some for him?"

"Nah. All military supplies get to them through Vietnamese channels. They actually supply us, just like with your jeep; comes out of their hide. Best thing is we talk to the USOM guy, Jake Ledbetter. USOM buys cheap walkie-talkies off the American market, and then they ship them to Vietnam for distribution in key locations. The radios aren't waterproof and don't have much range, but they ought to do the job for the watchtowers. Besides, Letha Ledbetter likes to have a couple of us over for dinner from time to time. New men get priority. I'll get us invited. You can mention it at dinner."

The table conversation eased into casual talk and turned to the title of the evening movie. New movies came on a mail plane from Saigon every couple of days. Sometime during the week, the team switched out films with the boys in Vinh Long. Since Vinh Long was the home base for all helicopter aircraft supporting the Delta region, swapping movies wasn't a big deal—only sixty-eight kilometers up the river from Tra Vinh.

However, the resupply plane that came every ten days, more or less, *was* a big deal. And it was dicey for a big C-130 cargo plane to land on the grass strip at Tra Vinh. The problem was not the length of the runway, nor was it the grass surface of the field. It was the long, low approach to landing and similar climb-out at takeoff that puckered up the pilots.

Understandably, they wanted some assurance that the approaches were secure in a five-kilometer radius of the field. But, even a new hand like me realized, early on, that the probability of "no armed VC" within five clicks of *anywhere* in the province was uninsurable. Too often, the ground loading crew experienced a sinking feeling as they watched the approaching cargo plane suddenly pick up air speed and altitude, and turn to the north. Real or not, the pilot perceived ground fire and passed Tra Vinh by.

Lenny Khrol, the team supply officer and logistics advisor, was the man in charge of coordinating these resupply flights. Right or wrong, when the plane turned around, it was clearly Lenny's fault, according to Joe Bass. Bass loved to ride Lenny. And the supply plane was his favorite saddle.

"We're out of San Miguel beer, Lenny … When we going to have steaks again, Lenny? … We got a flight coming in tomorrow, Lenny?"

Lenny's salvation was the Canadian-built De Havilland aircraft known as the Caribou. It was a high-wing aircraft that looked a lot like the C-130 except it had two engines, not four. It had a smaller payload and flew much slower than the C-130, but it had one single advantage over the C-130. It was flown by Australians. That was not a reflection of Lenny's attitude toward American pilots. The Americans were highly qualified technicians. It was just that the Aussies were cowboys.

When Lenny heard his radio transmission sign-off with the words, "Roger, Mate," he knew he was going to have a good day. The Caribou would pass over the field at about two thousand feet and begin a tight circle, spiraling downward and ending up high over the end of the runway. At that point the plane would "slip" by pointing a wing tip toward the ground and continuing straight ahead, causing the craft to lose altitude very quickly. Then at the last possible minute, the pilot would straighten up the aircraft and pull back on the stick so that the plane flared out and settled down on the runway, like a duck on a lake. Steaks and San Miguel tonight …

Two days later, after Major Bass made his recommendation to the province chief, I found Captain Tung in his office. Tung motioned me to come in.

"*Chau, Daui*, hello, Captain."

"Morning, Captain Tung. What's got you stirred up this morning?"

"We are planning an operation down south," said Tung. He had my attention.

The captain laid out a plan for moving a Regional Force company out of Cang Long District to Long Toan; just as the major had recommended. It was not that big a deal as a military operation, but logistically it was a major move for the soldiers and their families. The captain explained the plan. They would motor-march in trucks to the border of Cau Nang and Long Toan, where the company would dismount and move by foot to Long Toan district town. The movement would sweep the edge of the swamp in search of VC activity.

Two more mornings and I sat in the cab of a three-quarter-ton truck loaded with Regional Force soldiers. We were headed south. We had just passed the turnoff to Cau Nang district town and were about thirty minutes from the dismount point.

I'm ready for combat. This was the real thing. The VC were stirring up unrest in the area, and the Special Forces were unable to seize the initiative with the local Popular Forces. A strong new presence of additional soldiers in the area should bolster the sense of security for the local citizens and reduce the VC to defensive operations.

The trucks entered the dismount area. As I approached, Captain Tung was busy deploying his units into the swamp. The soldiers looked a little ragged, to say the least, but they were dressed in fatigues and wore a sort of olive drab tennis shoes. That was reassuring.

The captain motioned me to follow him. Walking and talking, "We move along the rice fields to the district town in order to be there when the soldiers close in. We be faster. I want to talk to the district chief, and you, maybe, want to talk to the Americans there."

I acknowledged, now conscious of a couple of soldiers standing by me. I looked askance at the captain.

"They are your security." And he set off down the paddy dike. I, with my security team, followed.

By late afternoon we pulled into the Long Toan district town. The march had been hot and muddy but otherwise uneventful. Neither Captain Frickey nor Master Sergeant Klazinsky was anywhere to be seen, but the district chief came up to me with a salute and a smile.

"*Chau, Daui*. Hot."

I wasn't sure whether that was a comment on the weather or how I looked, but in either case I responded in the affirmative.

"Come." The chief led the way into the marketplace and over to the café where we had gathered on my first visit. The same little man in black pajamas appeared from the back of the room and smiled when he saw me.

The chief sat down. "Beer?'"

I said, "You bet," which did not translate, but my smile said everything, and the chief gave instructions to the waiter.

"You have meal with my family tonight. My wife make beef for you."

That startled me a little. I had not thought about meals and sleeping arrangements. I had expected to shadow Captain Tung, but evidently that was not to be. Over the beer, I learned that Tung was staying with a relative. In fact, most of the troops would billet with local families until their own families closed into the village—if, of course, the family chose to move, and if separate houses could be acquired or built. This whole process of moving a civil guard company was a bit more complicated than just moving soldiers.

The general activity in the marketplace seemed to have a little more bustle than when we visited earlier. There was more energy in the community, and I was about to ask the chief if my observations were real or imagined when Captain Tung came in and sat down.

"The troops are still pulling in: nothing eventful to report." The proprietor appeared from the back and served Tung a beer.

"The chief here invite you to dinner?" Tung looked at the chief, who nodded slightly.

"You will be comfortable in the mill tonight. I send alert before we leave in the morning."

I don't know what I expected, but what I did not expect was to be sleeping in a rice mill while on operations. Sleeping in the mill tonight was hardly roughing it. Evidently, a test of hardship was not to occur this evening.

Captain Tung stood. "Got to check a few things; see you in the morning."

"You got it."

The chief finished his beer. "I show you mill now. You leave things there while we go dinner."

We walked down the road to the soccer field. I scanned the marketplace. Clearly there *was* a new energy in the town. We approached the wooden structure, which stood out from the other thatched buildings along the road. It was the same building I had asked Klazinsky about that first day—a mill, he had said. I looked more closely as we approached. It was bigger than it appeared from the road. The chief went around the side to a small door. He opened it and led me into a large room with a hard dirt floor.

"This very dry and no noise. There lantern for you. You be very safe here. Can leave your pack, too."

I looked around the huge room. Off center was a thick slab of stone in the form of a large squat cylinder perhaps ten feet in diameter. It was overshadowed by some sort of mechanism hanging from the ceiling. The room was very clean. And the two large posts supporting the pitched roof would be the perfect place to string up the MATA hammock.

At the Special Warfare Center at Fort Bragg, all attendees had been issued a piece of newly developed equipment known as the MATA hammock. It was a marvelous piece of equipment designed to improve the welfare of the American fighting man under the most difficult of circumstances. With this MATA hammock and issued rations, I was prepared to face and survive the most severe challenges. The rice mill was a piece of cake.

"OK, Chief, very nice. Thank you."

We walked back through the center of town together. The chief's English was not bad as long as we talked about military things, but pleasant conversation was difficult. I tried out my French, and there were some terms that worked, but not so many as to hold any hope for an interesting night of conversational exchanges.

I could smell the roast beef even before I knew where we were headed. It smelled wonderful, the more so because it was not a smell common to the environment. The chief introduced his wife, who was very small and probably looked much older than she was. She smiled nervously and bowed in Buddhist fashion. We exchanged greetings entirely by body language, and she led us into a small room containing a table and two chairs. Little children's faces peaked around the doorway that led, it seemed, to a cooking area.

The chief motioned for me to have a seat and then sat down across from me.

"Americans like eat beef, yes?" His face showed clearly some last-minute concerns that he might have made a mistake about the eating habits of his guest.

"Absolutely. Yes. Certainly." I watched relief wash across the man's face. He spoke to his wife, who smiled and disappeared, only to reappear with a large plate of warm, thick-sliced roast beef covered in thick brown gravy. She set the plate in the center of the table and turned to the small child behind her to receive the meal plates. The child lingered, wide eyed watching this American. The little girl broke into a bright smile and a "tee-hee," which resulted in a sharp word from the mother and a hasty exit by the daughter.

The aroma was magnificent. The hostess served me a large cut of very well-done beef about a half an inch thick. She spooned out a portion of gravy and poured it over the serving. She then returned to the kitchen. The thought now occurred to me that this man and his wife had gone to great lengths to make my visit as pleasant as they knew how. I was duly impressed and touched. The hostess returned with a pot of hot tea and two cups. She poured a cup for each of us. She bowed ever so slightly and left. Now, if only I had eating utensils, I would do them the honor of devouring this offering.

The chief's plate was empty, and I asked if he was going to have some.

"Beef is not for me," he said sipping his tea. "You enjoy. *Bon appétit*." He smiled. Small faces appeared around the doorway behind the chief.

I had no idea how they expected me to eat the slab of beef. Evidently they had no clue as to how *anyone* ate beef. I reached into my pocket and pulled out my Swiss army officer's knife—something no professional soldier is without. I opened the small blade and cut off a strip of the beef. Eyes at the doorway widened. With index finger and thumb I artfully dipped the strip into the gravy and popped it into my mouth. Magnificent ... chewy, but magnificent ... but very chewy. It seemed like hours, and it was definitely two and half pots of tea later, before I actually finished the beef. I had eaten all but one small strip, which I dutifully, according to custom, left as an indication to my hostess that I had been served more than enough.

With my best body language I thanked the chief and his wife for the delightful special meal they had prepared for me. And now, I sat in the mill on the edge of the millstone in the light of the kerosene lantern. I had my hammock laid out on the floor. It was about ten feet long and easily three feet wide. There were two aluminum stays that fitted into sleeves at the ends of the canvas. These stays insured that the canvas bed remained spread apart while the occupant lay in the center of the hammock.

State-of-the-art nylon cords extended from points about six inches apart along the edge at the narrow ends of the canvas. These cords were about twenty inches long and gathered on a metal ring where they tied off. Also looped through this ring was a heavier nylon line. The hammock was hung by tying the heavy line to a post or tree at one end and stretching the hammock out toward a second post or tree, and then tying it off with a similar heavy line on the second end.

What made this hammock so special was the mosquito net that hung by a line stretched above the bed of the hammock. In theory a man could climb into his hammock, pull down the mosquito net, and seal himself in with the VELCRO strips along the outer edges of the canvas bed. Additionally, there were storage pockets for personal items, and on top of it all, it was waterproof—truly an engineering marvel.

But, I was tired and just wanted to string it up and get some sack. Besides, you really needed a field manual to put the sucker up correctly. I tied off one end of the hammock high up on the roof support post. One thing I knew from ranger training: this nylon line was like a rubber band. If you didn't tie off high enough you could be sleeping on the ground after it stretched out under your body weight.

The second post was about twenty feet from the first. The good news was that the hammock had plenty of line for just such situations. I tied it off at eye level having pulled it as tight as I could get it. I stepped back to examine my handiwork. Clearly I could have done a better job. The hammock was neck high in the middle of the room. Nowhere were there implements or furniture to use as a stepladder for getting up onto the bed of the hammock.

I pulled down on the center. Yes, I had stretched it plenty tight. If I pressed down hard and jumped up into the bed, I might just be able to stretch out and call it a night. It was worth a test run. I threw my arms up over the canvas and put my weight into the pull down. I sprang onto the flat of the hammock and wound up lying face down and cross ways. Worse, the momentum of my leap carried me right on over the other side, turning the hammock upside down and dumping Captain Edward W. Skillman, U.S. Army, and school-trained professional soldier, smack dab on the floor—face up.

Apart from the surprise and the loss of breath, the very gods themselves were laughing at me.

Only the laughing was more like giggling, the kind that comes from the glee of little children. I sat up slowly. The walls of the mill had eyes—little eyes—so little as to peer through the cracks in the wood siding of the old frame building: the village children.

Now, who could not be infected by such abandoned laughter? I pulled myself up, acknowledged my audience, and took a magnificent stage bow. It brought another round of laughter. Chuckling, I walked over to the lantern, lifted the carriage and blew out the flame. The audience sounded its disappointment with a soft moan.

I untied the hammock and laid it out on the dirt floor. Still chuckling into the darkness, I wrapped up in my blanket and stretched out on this wonderful MATA hammock.

The events of this day would never be a scene in a movie like *Guadalcanal Diary*...

Maybe *South Pacific*...

But certainly, never *Sands of Iwo Jima*...

Tien Van Quan walked along the paddy dike leading north to the next village. Yesterday, he had watched the convoy of trucks deliver government troops to Long Toan District. It seemed like a good time for him to get back on the road. He walked along in the hot sun and wished for just a little cooling breeze off the river.

Quan was a long way from home and his childhood days on the outskirts of Hanoi. His father had been a tradesman, and little Quan had been expected to follow in his footsteps. As a young factory worker, he became active in the newly forming trade unions. When the Japanese marched into Vietnam, Quan developed an intense hate for the foreigners who attempted to run the industrial base.

After the French returned following World War II, it seemed to Quan, the only change was the language the foreigners spoke. He became so outspoken against the French that he joined the Viet Minh rebels which was his introduction to Communism.

The path he walked along descended off the dike into the tree line. He passed by a thatched home with a large crock of fresh water standing on the porch. With greetings of peace to the little boy standing in the doorway, he begged a dipper full and, without waiting for the boy's reply, helped himself. He let the cool water slide slowly down his throat. The little boy watched with big black eyes. The child smiled shyly, and the monk blessed him. A wife and children were things that Quan would never have …

But this was his choice. After being captured for burning French and American flags in 1951 and subsequently tortured during a three-year imprisonment, his hate for the French was so etched in his heart that it consumed his every emotion. Only his religion had helped him survive prison, and upon his release, he made his way to a monastery for recuperation. Eventually he donned the robes of a monk and traveled south in search of a new beginning.

Quan passed through the village, giving and receiving wishes for peace, and, again, made his way along the checkerboard dikes, zigzagging always to the north. Quan had come ashore a couple of weeks ago off a large sampan from Saigon. The boat carried big blocks of ice packed in wood chips and sawdust covered over by huge tarps. It headed straight down the South China Sea coast to the Delta region. Quan and a dozen or so Vietcong joined the crew of the sampan for the direct trip to Tra Vinh Province.

From Tra Vinh the sampan began its return leg, trading some of its ice for fresh fish from the small coastal villages. Eventually, the sampan made its way back into Saigon with a load of fresh catch on ice. Quan never asked the Vietcong about their business in Tra Vinh, nor did they show much interest in what he was doing. Whatever they were up to, he concluded, these additional guerrillas in Long Toan had prompted the deployment of government troops which he'd watched yesterday.

In spite of the heat, Quan was glad to be back in the Delta. Here had been his "new beginning" after prison. The people of the South were friendlier, and the pace of rural life represented the kind of change he sought. Traveling and teaching in the countryside was rewarding, but before long, it became clear to him that Buddhism was being challenged by the Catholic Church. Under Diem, the current president of South Vietnam, the Catholic Church was encroaching on traditional Buddhist populations.

Diem, and the Americans who supported him, had even imported whole villages into the South. And now the Saigon government was removing local Buddhist administrators for no apparent reason other than to make room for Catholic administrators. The rebel in the heart of Tien Van Quan bubbled up like a cauldron … even hotter than before.

It was time to join up with his mentor.

CHAPTER FOUR

The Hierarchy of Needs

Joe Bass sat alone in the dining room at MAAG House absentmindedly drinking a cup of coffee. It was less than three weeks since the province chief had redeployed the Regional Force company down to Long Toan: not nearly enough time for them to have a handle on the area. But there it was. Military Advisory Command of Vietnam (MACV) had just informed him about an hour ago that the Special Forces (SF) camp was to be turned over to the Regional Force (RF). The American SF team was to be redeployed to the Cambodian border.

It made sense from the SF point of view. The VC were increasingly active along the Cambodian border, and it was the correct application of Special Forces teams. It made perfect sense for them to provide early warning and to interdict, where possible, enemy activity along the Ho Chi Minh Trail. It made perfect sense for SF but not for Tra Vinh Province.

Joe walked over to the coffeepot for a warm-up. It certainly was going to anger the province chief. Long Toan District was fragile right now. The Regional Force had the capability to do the security job, but the local people needed confidence that their own soldiers would acquit themselves well in battle. The Regional Force soldiers had to demonstrate that fact decisively.

Joe looked at his watch. *The "cows" will be coming home soon,* he thought in anticipation of his team's evening rituals. *People need to feel secure before they acknowledge their desire to be free. Let's hope the Regional Force has convincingly demonstrated that their boys can keep the peace. Three weeks is pretty short.*

★★★

At the same moment, I was headed back to the MAAG House from the Tra Vinh docks. Following the Long Toan operation, life for me became a series of trips to the various district towns checking this, that, and the other thing. Sometimes it was just me and my driver, Zim, and sometimes it was with the intel officer, Bob White.

Even the assistant team chief, Ramsey, would ride shotgun from time to time.

It was strange the way things just turned up; like late yesterday afternoon. A Caucasian American showed up at the house totally unannounced. He was in civilian clothes of sorts—like a truck driver in gray work pants and shirt, except he had on government issue combat boots. He said he was with the U.S. Agriculture Department with some nondescript title. Said he had hitchhiked into town and wanted to make contact with some named Vietnamese, allegedly in the Vietnamese Department of Fisheries.

What he needed was a lift on the regional force's gunboats. Bob White became his self-appointed escort and spent most of the evening in conversation with the man. By the end of the night it had been arranged that I would take the man down to the docks and introduce him to whatever boat captains were around. White would go with us, but it was up to the stranger to arrange his own piggyback ride.

Actually there were six gunboats in the fleet, but Captain Tung never had more than four running at any one time. Besides he only had four qualified boat commanders, so it worked out well. Two of the commanders were drinking tea at a sidewalk café when I spied them from the far side of the harbor.

The driver threaded the jeep through the street traffic, made up mostly of pedestrians finishing up the morning marketing. By the time we reached the café, the two commanders were paying their bill. Before they could leave I jumped out of the traffic-bound jeep and caught up to them. I was already explaining the situation to the captains when Bob and the civilian joined me.

As soon as the civilian was introduced, he began speaking in fluent Vietnamese. We were dumbfounded, but the stranger carried on as though it was the most natural thing in the world. Until he walked away with the boat captain, he did not speak English in our presence again.

Now, heading back to the MAAG House, I reflected on the day. Apart from the mystery of the stranger, things had worked out rather well. We found the man a ride, we toured the boat pens, and I had a better idea of how these boats were employed. Best of all, the commander of one boat made me a present of thirty sandbags.

Sandbags were unbelievably scarce in this part of Vietnam. There was plenty of barbed wire, so much so, that a four-foot wall of wire, still on the spools and stacked like cinder block, fenced the backyard of the province chief's villa; but no sandbags. Now the advisor team could pack the floors of their jeeps with filled sandbags. It wasn't a total defense against the blast of land mines, but it certainly was better than plain sheet metal.

Yes, it was a good day.

The jeep pulled around to the back of the MAAG House where the major was waiting on the veranda. Bob and I dismounted as the major motioned us to follow. Ramsey was already in the dining room when we entered.

"We got some adjustments to make." Bass dropped with a sigh of patience into his corner chair. "Fort Bragg has redeployed their SF teams to surveillance missions along the Cambodian border. That means as we speak the Long Toan camp is being turned over to the Regional Force company that we put in place three weeks ago."

"They're not ready," blurted Ramsey. Bass ignored him.

"Did they take out the two 105 howitzers?" asked White.

"Yes, they did. And that's our immediate concern. I have recommended to the province chief that he deploy a mortar platoon as soon as possible. I am sure he will do it, but ASAP sometimes has a different urgency when translated into Vietnamese."

I was trying to think ahead. "Maybe I can stir the pot over at the armory by checking for mortars in operating condition and prepped for deployment."

"That's good ... and check on a basic load of ammunition while you're at it," said Bass. "Ramsey, call Vinh Long and see if we can get some chopper support day after tomorrow. As soon as the chief gives the command, we want to be able to fly the mortars and ammo in the same day they're ready."

"Got it. Do you think the Regional Force can handle this, boss?"

"They're going to have to, aren't they?"

★★★

The UH-1D helicopter, better known as the Huey, was the workhorse of army aviation in the sixties. It was a cargo ship. It was a troop transport ship. It was a medical evacuation ship. And it was a gunship when the occasion demanded, which it often did in any one of the above situations. The pilots who flew them were incredibly courageous men as a matter of routine.

I was standing with the mortar section leader watching the Huey settle down onto the grass. Two mortar tubes and their basic load of ammunition were stacked beside us. Before the pilot had feathered the rotor blades, the two-man loading crew was already moving toward the aircraft with the first ammo boxes. The Huey door gunner unhooked his gunner belt and jumped down to assist the loading crew. Six trips and the chopper was loaded. The section leader and I hopped on board as the loading crew backed away from the aircraft.

Some thirty minutes later the chopper circled Long Toan district town. The pilot took his time coming in, and the door gunners were on high alert as the craft hovered over the rice paddies.

I hit the press-to-talk button on the intercom. "The soccer field on the edge of the town is the landing area."

"Roger. I'm looking for signs of friendlies before I commit to landing," was the response.

Door gunner: "Three uniforms coming down the road. They look friendly."

The section leader motioned to me that those were his people. "Section leader recognizes the party."

"Copy." The chopper touched down.

The section leader jumped to the ground and greeted his people. I unbuckled my seat belt and began moving ammo boxes across the floor to the edge of the door. Both door gunners assisted as I slid the boxes to a point where the people outside could grab hold. Everyone focused on getting the cargo off the aircraft.

I could see a crowd of villagers gathering about fifty feet from the aircraft. They were just watching the unloading, and I didn't pay much attention to them. I was concentrating on getting the bird unloaded. But, in the back of my mind it registered that they were not smiling or waving.

"What the *hell*? Who are these guys?" screamed the gunner on the door away from the village.

Three of the villagers had hopped up into the aircraft and were taking seats. I had not asked Captain Tung if there would be return passengers. I just assumed there would not be—a dangerous assumption. I looked out at the section leader who was trying to stop the crowd of villagers as they rushed the chopper.

"Get the bastards off my ship." The pilot was revving up the engine. By now the villagers were mobbing us from both sides, and once they got hold of the airframe, they would not let go. As fast as the door gunners pushed them off, more would pile on. I was dealing with those who had pushed through the door and were trying to hook up seat belts. It was outright hand-to-hand combat. The chopper was bobbing up and down trying to escape gravity.

"Get the fuckers OFF," screamed through the headset. "They're overloading the ship. I can't get lift."

The chopper rose a few feet, but those villagers who were still outside hung on to the skids for dear life. The chopper dragged them across the ground.

The gunners were now grabbing people and pushing them out the door: men, women, made no difference. A mother on the ground tried to hand her child up to the gunner. I grabbed two people by their clothing and threw them to the door gunner, who continued their forward motion right out into space.

The gunner on the other side of the plane was now down on the skids stomping on hands. A villager grabbed the gunner's boot and he would have pulled him out of the aircraft if not for a long gunner's belt. The plane was hovering at four or five feet.

Now both door gunners were stomping on hands. I was wrestling with another villager of unknown gender. The pilot had the chopper out over the rice paddy at ten or fifteen feet and climbing. I threw the villager right past the door gunner and hoped the fellow landed in the soft paddy mud. Unbelievable: certainly not what I expected.

Unfortunately the chopper pilot took the whole episode personally. Perhaps he had every right. A mob under any circumstances is a scary thing. In this circumstance no one saw it coming, and that made it worse. Maybe I should have anticipated the problem. But something like this never came up at Fort Bragg, and it sure wasn't like anything Cary Grant ever faced in *Gunga Din*. It was more like Bob Hope in *Road to Morocco*.

But at dinner that night Joe Bass soaked up every detail of the day. He asked me to expand on everything. How many men were in the crowd? Did a woman really try to hand off her child? Did I think anyone was hurt? How much water was in the rice paddies?

And after a long stare into his beer glass, Bass said, "I guess that answers the question about Long Toan."

"What do you mean?" asked Ramsey. "What question?"

"The answer to the question is that departure of the Special Forces has not been balanced in the minds of the peasantry by the arrival of more Regional Force troops; that the people of Long Toan have not yet gained confidence in the regional force's ability to protect them; and that the citizenry will first start withholding information, and then slow their support for the commander down there." Everyone sat in silence making up his own scenario for the future of Long Toan.

"By the way, Ed, you, Ramsey, and I are having dinner at Ledbetter's a week from tomorrow—eight o'clock civilian time."

✯✯✯

Lenny heard the chopper circle the MAAG House. This was not a scheduled flight, nor were any visitors expected, but someone was coming. He called out the back door for Tom to bring up the major's jeep while he pulled on his web belt and pistol.

By the time he got to the airstrip, the chopper was already lifting off, and a single soldier was by the wind sock sitting on his duffel bag. Lenny pointed Tom toward the soldier.

A mature staff sergeant pulled off his sunglasses as he stood and rendered Lenny a smart salute. Lenny returned the greeting and stepped from the jeep.

"Welcome to Tra Vinh, Sergeant. Toss your gear in the back."

"Thank you, sir." The man was average height but heavier than he had appeared from a distance. He looked to be in excellent physical condition, with biceps that fully filled the rolled-up sleeves of his fatigues. He replaced his sunglasses over pale blue eyes and then protected them further by repositioning his cap low on the forehead.

"What brings you our way?" asked Lenny as Tom headed the jeep back to the house.

"I'm on leave. Just hitched a ride with that chopper on his way south to Soc Trang."

"I see." Everyone was authorized two weeks R & R (rest and recuperation) during his or her one-year tour of duty. Most traveled out of country on whatever military flights they could catch to wherever they were going. Most popular places were Hawaii and Bangkok. A good number went to Hong Kong and some even to Australia. But no one ever came to Tra Vinh. There were in-country R & R sites like Vung Tau and Nha Trang, but no one—no one in his right mind—came to Tra Vinh.

"Would it be any trouble for me to spend the night at your house this evening? I'll be moving on tomorrow."

"Don't see any reason why not. We'll check it with Major Bass, the team chief, but there should be no problem."

As soon as they arrived at the house, Lenny found the sergeant a spare bunk, pointed him to the sinks, and gave him the evening routine. *There is something very, very strange here*, he thought. He went to find the major.

Looking smart in a fresh set of *starched* fatigues, the guest sergeant appeared at the team happy hour. Captain Leonard Khrol stepped up to make the introductions: first to the major. Lenny had already briefed Bass who quickly endorsed Lenny's hospitality.

"It is a pleasure to meet you, Major Bass. Thank you for allowing me to lay over a night," said the staff sergeant.

Lenny became conscious for the first time of an East European accent in the sergeant's speech … *curiouser and curiouser.*

"What brings you to Tra Vinh for R & R? It's not exactly the first choice vacation for most soldiers," asked the major, a little sarcasm creeping into his tone.

The soldier offered a slight smile. "Oh, I have many old friends in this part of Vietnam."

"Really. Were you stationed here before?"

"Yes, in 1954."

Lenny approached with Ramsey in tow and a bottle of San Miguel in each hand. "Sergeant, this is Captain Ramsey Hartmann. Care for a beer?"

"Welcome to Tra Vinh. Lenny tells me you are down here on R & R, and I tell Lenny, 'Introduce me to this nut case.'"

"It's true." The sergeant's thin smile grew to a grin.

Bass was still processing the fact that the sergeant had been down here in the midfifties, "The sergeant was stationed here in 1954; came down to see some old friends."

Bob White stood on the edge of the group listening to the conversation. "Welcome, Sergeant. I'm Captain White." He shook the sergeant's hand. "Fifty-four would have put you here before there was any formal American military presence, if memory serves me."

"That is probably true. I would not know, as I was in the French foreign legion at the time."

Dead silence gripped the little discussion group.

Lenny announced that dinner was on the table, and with that all activity shifted to the dining room. Conversation was the usual table talk. Eventually everyone introduced himself to the guest, and the meal passed pleasantly without the normal business exchanges. The sergeant shared all the news and scuttlebutt from Saigon. But thinly veiled beneath the light conversation was the mystery of who this guy really was. Lenny gave the five-minute call for the movie to start, and the film buffs moved back to the social room.

Joe and Bob remained. Bob poured the visitor a refresher cup of coffee.

"How on earth did you get from the French foreign legion to the U.S. Army?" asked Joe.

"Oh, it is a long story. I was not quite fifteen at the end of World War II. I was a German soldier without an army and a boy without a family. My home village was in the north of Germany along the Polish border. The Russians took all the German soldiers they could capture or arrest and were sending them to Siberia as slave labor."

"Wasn't there anyone at home you wanted to return to?" asked Bob.

"There might have been, but the whole region, Latvia, Estonia, Lithuania, and Poland were all under Russian authority enforcing their Marxist stuff on people. The probability that I would be arrested and sent off to Siberia wasn't worth the chance. I thought I might be safe in Czechoslovakia. I figured to get some kind of work and start a life … maybe later see if anyone I knew was left back in my village."

"Why didn't that work out?" Bob continued to press.

"The Russians kept coming even after Germany was defeated. The president of Czechoslovakia jumped from his office window rather than turn his country over to the Russians. I figured Russia had the same fate planned for all of Eastern Europe. It looked like the Legion was a place for me when there was no other place."

He studied the coffee in his cup, taking time to recall the events that had led him into an organization where a man's history was of no interest and he could begin fresh simply as a number. Then he took a swallow.

"So that's what got you to Vietnam?" Bass put in.

"Well, not right away, but yes, eventually my outfit was sent into Indochina. We operated mostly in northern Vietnam and Laos. It was then I met a Vietnamese family who treated me very well."

The sergeant paused and looked across the table. "You know of course the outcome of our efforts. It all ended at Dien Bien Phu. After that the Legion began to pull us completely out of Indochina. The only family I had ever really known became refugees, and the Americans helped them relocate to the Delta region."

"The United States Navy?" asked Bob.

"Yes, hundreds of thousands of North Vietnamese families were transported by the United States Navy to resettle in the South. One of your army officers, Colonel Lansdale, was one of the first Americans helping the Vietnamese. He played a role in the massive movement of nearly a million North Vietnamese Catholics into the South. The Catholics were fiercely anti-Communist.

"Before I was shipped back to Algeria, I was able to travel to Vinh Binh to visit my friends one last time. I promised them I would return someday."

The three Americans noted individually that he had used the old name for Tra Vinh.

"And this is someday?" White took the plate of cookies from the major and passed it to the sergeant.

"Yeah, you could say so." He helped himself to a cookie.

"How'd you get in the U.S. Army?" The major intercepted the dish before the sergeant could hand it back to White.

"The Legion was clearly not ever going back to Vietnam, and I could never afford to take myself back, so I did not reenlist after ten years of service. Instead, I traveled back to France and approached the first American unit I could find. The recruiter enlisted me as Sergeant E-5 based on my soldier record."

"And then what? Volunteered for Vietnam?" Bob reached over for one more cookie before the major ate them all. The boss was a blatant cookie fanatic.

"Not exactly. I *am* a professional soldier. I served in Germany for a tour, which got me to the Seventh Army NCO Academy in Munich and a promotion to Sergeant First Class. On my reenlistment I requested Vietnam, which was just beginning to show up on the assignment offerings."

"Tell you what," said White, taking on a businesslike tone. "We haven't been over to Cau Ke District for some time. The Regional Force company hasn't been checked out for a while. Wouldn't hurt to be seen around the town and countryside. Why don't Skillman and I just take you with us in the morning—save you a miserable ride in a Lambretta. You did say it was Cau Ke that your family settled in?"

White glanced over at me and I nodded assent. The sergeant caught White's eyes. "I'd appreciate that, sir."

The major snapped up the last cookie, and the three eased into the social room to catch the end of the movie, which they had all seen before.

The evening conversation picked up again the next day on the way to Cau Ke. Captain White asked about the family being visited and learned that the main attraction of the family was the oldest daughter. The father was a schoolteacher, and the family was literate in French. Both parents had traveled in France.

"How do you know your young lady is not married?"

"No guarantees, but, if you never really had a family, and you find one that takes you in like a son, then this is just coming home to visit. If the girl is still single, then it's a gift."

After nearly an hour and half, we approached the district town of Cau Ke. The countryside looked like everywhere else in the province. But to me the monotony of the rice fields, by now, held a beauty and charm that I knew I would forever remember and relish.

This morning Cau Ke rose up like an island out of the watery fields of late spring. As in most district towns, the grade school was on the edge of the built-up area next to a grassy lawn designated as a soccer field. And like most soccer fields, the Cau Ke soccer field was utilized for everything from playground to chopper pad. As we approached the school, we could see children playing in the soccer field.

"Captain, could you let me out here?" the sergeant asked.

White signaled the driver to stop. "Are you sure that's what you want? Would you like us to carry your gear into town?"

"No … no, this will be fine. Thank you very much, sir." He sprang easily out of the jeep and snapped his duffel onto the road as if it weighed nothing. He again caught the captain's eyes and held them.

"Ah, what the hell, Sarge." White stepped out of the jeep. They shook hands. "I thought I was a goddamn romantic, but you got me beat by a country mile."

The legionnaire stepped back and rendered a crisp salute, then picked up his duffel and, without another word, moved smartly on down the road toward the schoolyard. We sat and watched as the sergeant approached the children. He must have said something they understood because they scattered. Three or four ran to him and the rest ran to the schoolhouse.

The children pulled him along the path to the building, but before he arrived, an older Vietnamese man walked through the school doorway. The man stopped abruptly, then brought the palms of his hands together on his chest in Buddhist fashion. He remained there, transfixed, until the sergeant came near enough to reach out and place both hands on his shoulders. The old man appeared to be trembling.

"Head into town, Tom," said White. "We'll check in on the district chief, run by the Regional Force headquarters, and see if we can get out of here before the welcome home party begins. In a couple of hours this town will belong to that man."

★★★

Jake Ledbetter was a career Foreign Service officer with the State Department assigned to the U.S. Overseas Mission (USOM). Although USOM was a State Department entity, it was manned by an eclectic collection of government employees with special talents that served the United States government's political mission in Vietnam.

In the early days of American involvement, the State Department, including USOM workers, were permitted to have their families in-country if they chose. Most of the families lived in an enclave inside Saigon, which might have been suburban Washington if not for the palm trees. With no discredit to other wives, but with credit to her, Letha Ledbetter stood by her man and relocated with her two-year-old daughter to Tra Vinh Province where Jake was assigned.

Jake had an undergraduate degree from Princeton and a master's degree in international affairs from someplace, but nobody seemed to know or remember where. USOM was a good career move for Jake, and he was ambitious. Letha Ledbetter was a Vassar girl. She had been taught that her highest calling was to support her husband's career. If it meant living in the middle of the Mekong Delta, teaching English in a Vietnamese high school, and raising her two-year-old daughter, all in a hostile environment, then so be it. She could have lived in the American compound in Saigon with the rest of the Foreign Service wives. But Letha chose not to.

There is no such thing as fashionably late in the professional world. The dinner guests arrived promptly at 2000 hours. The hostess, Letha, was lovely, and her daughter, Sarah, was precocious to say the least. After the little girl met the guests, which included crawling up into Captain Hartmann's lap, her Vietnamese nanny took the child upstairs to bed, and the group moved into the spacious dining room.

The old French Colonial homes, like the MAAG House and the Ledbetter's house, were built before electricity had come to the region; hence, the wiring was external to the walls. Cables were introduced through the ceiling.

The first evidence of power was the fan that hung from the fifteen-foot ceiling. Fluorescent lighting was also mounted to the ceiling. The fixtures were usually flush-mounted, but in the case of the Ledbetter dining room, the fluorescent lights were at the juncture of wall and ceiling on all four sides of the room. The starkness of the room was neutralized and made cozy by the two large candelabras dressing the dining table.

"Do the blue eyes work for you on women of all ages, Ramsey?" asked Jake, referring to his daughter's instant take to this young officer.

Ramsey flashed his little-boy smile, "Well, I don't know. I haven't tried every age yet."

"Is there a Mrs. Ramsey Hartmann?" Letha sat down as Joe held her chair. "Thank you, sir."

"No, ma'am. There is not, nor has there ever been."

"Why, Captain, you sound like a confirmed bachelor."

"No, ma'am. Just haven't met the right girl, and I do so much enjoy the search."

She chuckled and turned to the rest. "I know you men get your share of steaks, but quite unexpectedly, I found this beautiful beef roast at the commissary in Saigon. I thought you would appreciate the change."

A question flashed through my mind as to the source of "unexpected" beef at a Saigon commissary. I had learned from Captain Tung several days after the Long Toan deployment that my roast beef dinner was, in fact, water buffalo. An animal had died a few days before the operation, and I had been the beneficiary. I forced the thought out of my head.

The range of table conversation was wide. College days, past assignments, families and children: everyone traded his best story, and eventually the conversation came to local events. Someone made reference to my experience with the Long Toan village mob.

Letha's eyes grew wide, "That must have been frightening. What happened?"

Never one to miss an opportunity to tell a story, I repeated the blow-by-blow of the event—omitting only the obscenities. Not until I saw Letha's eyes tearing up did I break off the account.

"Those poor people," she said.

"They were mobbing the plane," Ramsey put in.

"Shouldn't someone have talked to them?" She dabbed her eye with her napkin.

"It didn't appear that the section leader on the ground was having much luck at doing that," I said.

"Neither fear nor panic are good grounds for negotiation," offered Joe.

"Still, it seems awfully cruel ..." She was back in control now.

I changed the subject. "Jake, we have a communications problem in Cau Nang, and it's common in many of the districts. Unless there is a Regional Force company in the vicinity, the watchtowers are not able to radio the district towns in the event of trouble."

Ramsey recounted their experience. Jake listened intently.

"Yes, from time to time we do procure specialty items off the U.S. commercial market. This sounds like a situation we can handle. I'll look into picking up some radios. We may even still have some in inventory. This is the kind of thing we can do. It meets a need expeditiously. But I would rather spend money on projects that stimulate the economy. Get enough economic projects, and we can win this war without guns."

Joe Bass came alive. "Don't you think, Jake, that security has a little higher priority? Economic projects have a whole lot better chance of success when villagers are not worrying about whether they will live through the week."

"Of course security is important. But if we can get people making so much money they haven't got time to fight, we have won the war."

Joe swirled his wineglass and took a sip. "You familiar with Maslow's Hierarchy of Needs?"

Maslow rang a faint bell in my head, and I was trying to get my memory up to speed while these two debated. I recalled that Abraham Maslow began studies in the midfifties and by the sixties developed a hierarchy of needs to explain the motivations of human beings in their struggle for fulfillment.

The most basic need according to Maslow was the physical—food, water, shelter, and sex. The next as I recalled was security—safety, health, and stuff like that. Only after those needs were met did humans seek friendship and status. On top of that was esteem—position and recognition—and then ultimately came self-actualization, being the person one wants to be.

Bass was making his point. "Jake, do you really think you can have any kind of prosperity without a secure environment?"

"Well, I think the jury is still out on that ..."

As dinner and the evening progressed, I found it a surprising pleasure just to be in the company of a round-eyed woman who entertained four men with equal charm for all. I was suddenly disappointed that it was about to come to an end. The boss gave up on Jake and was making his exit speech, and then the rest of the niceties began. Indeed, it had been a very pleasant evening.

Walking back across town demanded everyone's attention to security concerns, but once we were in the MAAG House, my mind returned to the evening events. I thought of my own lovely wife and her carbon-copy daughter and how I missed them. Strange how Letha felt sympathy for the villagers before she felt concern for the five soldiers whose lives were in immediate jeopardy.

I wondered what had spooked the villagers so badly. Joe Bass was right. Panic doesn't know reason. When individual fears cross the line into collective panic, mob mentality takes hold, and people do things they otherwise would never consider if they thought about it.

CHAPTER FIVE

The Wrong Side Is Right

A FORWARD AIR CONTROLLER (FAC) is a pilot of small, fixed-wing aircraft. His job is to circle the battlefield and respond to the requests of ground forces as a communications link to the big boys who bring in heavy ordnance. In the early days of the Vietnam effort, the FAC was an army pilot flying an L-19: the military equivalent of a high-winged Cessna with a souped-up single engine. Most of his missions were spotting enemy movement, but every now and then he might run an artillery fire support mission or guide in an air strike.

By the middle of 1964 the air force was taking over the mission with their new aircraft, the OV-10, designed just for this type of mission but with added capabilities. It was a twin-engine turboprop, but still capable of slow flight. It carried its own ordnance, which was used for marking targets. The rules of engagement permitted the pilot to directly engage the enemy, if, and only if, it became necessary to fix the target until the big stuff arrived. In fact, with its twin tail assembly it looked a lot like the WW II Curtis P-38 fighter, and the boys who flew them had the same fighter pilot attitude: I'm indestructible.

Nails Hopkins was the quintessential fighter pilot. Known as Stanley Hopkins in his youth and Stan in his college years, he became "Nails" as a result of his attitude toward flight cadets in his days as an instructor pilot. He was hard as nails. Now, sitting in the dining room of the MAAG House in Tra Vinh, Captain Nails Hopkins, United States Air Force, was expounding on the virtues of his new, soon-to-arrive OV-10. That plane, with him at the throttle, was going to singlehandedly win the Vietnam war effort.

"What brings you down here to Tra Vinh, Nails?" asked the intel officer.

"Got some time to kill until the plane arrives, so I thought I'd like to get a ground view of the terrain I'm going to cover. Besides, it's good to know the people you're supporting, and it can't hurt for you to know the guy who's supporting you … a little male bonding, so to speak."

Made sense to me. "Want to go with me tomorrow? I've got to travel up north to Vung Liem for some coordination with an ARVN battalion that just pulled into that district."

The ARVN battalion had just broken contact with the Cu Long I, a Vietcong regiment. The VC generally operated much further north of Tra Vinh in the province of Long Xuyen on the Cambodian border. White and I needed to hear firsthand what the ARVN boys knew about VC changes in behavior. Hostilities could accelerate quickly if this organized VC battalion linked up with the local guerrillas. White was already anticipating an increase in local activity. This might even be in conjunction with the drift of guerrillas north from Long Toan on the South China Sea. White needed more information. Plus, there was an American advisor with the ARVN unit, which would make it easier to understand the story.

Nails was in. "You bet. What time, and where do I draw a weapon?"

"We'll go over to the armory right after lunch and draw you a carbine. And we better find you a steel helmet. Nobody drives out of town without a steel pot. We'll kick off first thing in the morning. That work for you, Bob?"

"Count on it. And just for you, Nails, the movie tonight is *To Hell and Back*, with Audie Murphy. It just doesn't get any better than that."

★★★

Next morning the PA system, featuring the Vietnamese equivalent of *Good Morning Vietnam*, brought Nails to his feet with the carbine locked and loaded. He sailed downstairs with nothing on but his skivvies. "Good Lord. What *is* that?"

"Stand down, soldier. Save it for the road trip," said Bob over his bananas and corn flakes. "It's commuter news and weather, Vietnam style. You get used to it."

I'm thinking, *some people get used to it, but not everyone*. I helped myself to the cereal. I had decided to take two Vietnamese lieutenants from Regional Force operations with us today. They needed to get out more often, and see what was going on.

Bob poured out three cups of coffee, "I got two lieutenants with me also. Nails, you ride with me."

Nails seized the coffee. "I'll go up with you and back with Skillman—get to know everybody. What do you think?" We all nodded agreement and sipped the coffee.

Thirty minutes later the two-jeep convoy headed north out of Tra Vinh on Highway 8. Vung Liem district town was about an hour away if the driver could average forty-five miles an hour. It was not that traffic was so heavy. It was that traffic was so slow. The two-lane highway was well constructed, but it was narrow. Passing a Mercedes bus or truck required steady nerves if the driver was to avoid the shoulder. The good news was that the road *had* a shoulder.

Most of the traffic was what one expects in a farming community: two-wheeled carts drawn by water buffalo, bicycles, occasional small cars, and the ever popular Lambretta. This little three-wheeled vehicle was the public transport of choice for most rural Vietnamese. It was a motor scooter with a two-wheeled carriage built onto the back of the driver's seat. Two benches, one facing the other, stretched down the six-foot length of the carriage and formed the wheel wells. Six Vietnamese could fit in the little truck, which also had a roof over the carriage strong enough to carry baggage.

"Nifty little sucker," said Nails as they passed a fully loaded Lambretta. "Good thing the terrain is flat. Loaded like that, they couldn't pull a 2 percent grade."

"Well, you're right," said White. "That one is a little crowded, but you would be surprised at the power the thing has. I've seen heavier loads."

Nails sat in the backseat of the jeep with two little Vietnamese lieutenants sitting on the tire well at either side of him. The canvas tops on the jeeps were up to mitigate the glare of the tropical sun. Nails looked out over the rice paddies. "Man, this is one flat piece of real estate. Is the whole area under water?"

"Yeah." White continued, "Welcome to the Mekong Delta. These paddies are being fully flooded now that the rice planting is about over. The canals, like the one running along the left side of this road, bring river water into the fields. The farmers use the dikes to flood the paddies so the plantings remain under water. The rainy season keeps the paddies wet. As the plants take hold and grow above the water, the fields turn green. By early fall, the fields look like Kansas summer wheat. The dry season comes, and the paddies turn to mud about the time harvest begins."

The hardtop highway angled off to the left of a fork in the road. The route straight ahead became a dirt road into tropical surroundings leading to Vung Liem district town. In the Y of the road was a small vacant building in the French colonial style with a tile roof in sorry disrepair. In the front yard of the building was a locked gas pump, 1920s vintage.

The little convoy continued straight ahead along the dirt road. A hundred yards farther, the greenery on the right opened up on a grassy meadow containing one grazing water buffalo. Barbed wire along the top of a foot high wall separated the meadow from the rice paddy beyond.

"That official-looking building coming up on the right is the local schoolhouse," said White. "And don't let the water buffalo fool you. That is a soccer field there next to the school."

The pilot took off his sunglasses. "Look at those coconut trees. They're lined up like soldiers."

"Well, they are. This was a coconut plantation, and the short palm trees are banana trees. It was a two-crop experiment—coconuts on top of bananas—kind of overgrown now. That's a pagoda back in there amid the scrub."

Both jeeps continued into town until we pulled up in front of a gated compound to the left. To the right, across the road, was an open field with two 105 mm howitzers. The tubes laid out to the southeast.

I dismounted. "Let's go see who's home."

I was already through the double gate when the soldier in fatigues and tennis shoes stepped out from behind a sandbag barricade, and gave us a rifle salute after we entered. Nails and Bob joined me as I talked to a Vietnamese Army captain.

I learned that the district chief was not in town right now, but the American and the ARVN battalion commander were at a local restaurant.

Bob turned to Nails. "You are now about to experience how business is conducted in Vietnam." We started out of the compound and turned toward town. I waved over my driver, Zim, and one of the Vietnamese lieutenants to join me.

"We're going into town for a little while. You guys snoop around here. Get to know these guys a little better. Ask them what their problems are. Listen to all the gossip, but keep the jeeps in sight so we don't have to look for you when we head back. Zim, turn the jeeps around and park them next to the compound walls."

I had to smile at myself. I sounded like John Wayne in *She Wore a Yellow Ribbon*.

The town of Vung Liem was like most towns in the Delta. The center of all activity is the marketplace. In the case of Vung Liem, this was a very respectable marketplace. The district was at the juncture of the Ca Chien River and a Trans-province canal that connected the Ca Chien with the Hau Giang River, both major arteries of the Mekong Delta. The road that entered town and passed by the district headquarters compound also headed straight into the marketplace, where it ended at the edge of the canal.

A group of soldiers gathered at a sidewalk restaurant across from the market. We headed over when I heard someone in the group shout, "This is not the Hudson River, you know. You lost, soldier?"

I spied the American uniform. The face looked familiar. "Sam the man. I see they didn't dare return you to civilization."

Captain Sam Banister. Last time anyone heard of him, he had been assigned as a ranger instructor in the swamps of northwest Florida. It wasn't unusual for those guys to drop out of contact for years. But here he was.

"What in the world you doing here?" I said.

"I asked for a cushy assignment, so they upgraded me from lane grader to ARVN advisor. Haven't had it so good in years."

"That's what I love about you, Sam. You're overwhelmingly, consistently full of horse hockey."

"I have missed you too, Buddy."

Bob White and the two Lieutenants he brought with him were doing their intelligence gathering ... working the crowd. Nails tagged along. I sat with Sam and spent a few minutes catching up and telling war stories, but then got down to the business of the day.

"What's going on, Sam? What brings the Cu Long I this far to the southeast?"

"Well, we don't know why, but we do know that they are floating a lot more stuff down the river from Cambodia. We're not allowed to chase them across the border, but every now and then we get *lost*, you know."

I questioned Sam further on life in the ARVN outfit and where they expected the next operation to take them. Bottom line, Sam didn't know what was next. Looked like they were parked here for an indefinite period; a lot of resupply and some serious downtime.

White joined us. "We probably should be heading back. Hot volleyball game tonight, and it's Tuesday ... clean sheets on Tuesdays."

Sam grimaced. "Whatever happened to soldiers like Sergeant York and the *real* infantry?"

According to plan, Nails Hopkins loaded up with me for the return trip. As we approached the jeep, Zim jumped in the vehicle, started the engine, and then quickly dismounted to allow the FAC and the two Vietnamese officers to load in the back. A student of body language might have noticed that the driver was agitated. But I didn't pick up at the time.

Zim took the lead down the dirt road past the school, past the soccer field, and past the gas pump out onto the highway. As soon as the jeep hit the highway, Zim hit the accelerator. We were sailing down the road and closing fast on the bus in front of us.

About this time of day, nearly every day, a Mercedes bus came down from Saigon to Tra Vinh. The same bus left the next morning from Tra Vinh for Saigon. Zim was now feverishly attempting to pass the bus.

"Take it easy. We're not in that big of a hurry." This would have been a good time to ask Zim if he had learned anything while he was waiting for the Americans to return from the marketplace, but I was more concerned with driving safely than why Zim was driving recklessly.

Zim said nothing. But he *did* fall back a few yards and followed the bus until the next village. When the bus pulled over to the side to exchange passengers, Zim geared down to second then jammed the accelerator to the floor and zipped around the bus at a reckless speed. I grabbed the safety bar on the dash in front of me. "Cut the crap, Zim, and settle down, damn it!"

"Is this volleyball game the world championship or something?" asked Nails. He was thinking about White's excuse for heading back.

I turned halfway around, inward toward the driver, so I could look back at Nails. "It's no championship. That's just Bob's story for getting us moving. Did you get a feel for life in the country?"

"Yes, I did. This was a good thing to do. I have a feel for what you guys are up against. I don't know that it will help me be a better forward air controller, but it sure makes me want to do my best."

"That's good to know." I could see the two lieutenants each sitting, on top of one the jeep wheel wells. They were holding on for dear life to the suspension rack for the jeep's canvas top. Nails had both arms outstretched to his sides gripping the same steel bars. I was immediately aware of the speeding and looked over at the speedometer. The needle was clear off the scale pointing straight down at *per* in miles per hour: and Zim was driving down the left-hand side of the highway, slipping on and off the shoulder of the road.

"Damn it, Zim. What's the matter with you? I can see that it's clear ahead, but this speed is ridiculous. Slow down, mister." I was pissed. Zim was normally a pretty responsible driver.

"Very dangerous here, *Daui*." The first words Zim had spoken since we left the district town. He did not look at me but drove with a vengeance.

The highway was a long straight stretch running for a couple of clicks, and indeed, it was totally devoid of any traffic. No one noticed that the two jeeps were the only traffic that passed around the bus or that the bus was still in the village.

However, anyone intimately familiar with the region might have noticed that there was, in fact, no traffic at all: no bikes, no carts, no farmers walking to and from their fields—no one—just rice paddy, road, canal, and tree line all the way to the next village straight ahead. The flooded rice paddies were on the left shoulder of the road, and a canal was on the right. Foliage outlined the far side of the canal and marked the canal bank.

"Let me tell you. The way you're driving is dangerous, too. Slow your ass down, and get on the right side of the damn road."

"Very dangerous, *Daui*." Zim took his foot off the accelerator. The needle slowly restored itself to an acceptable position on the scale. But Zim did not return to the right side of the highway. Instead he hugged the left lane, occasionally slipping off the shoulder.

I was now fully attentive to the bizarre behavior of an otherwise sensible driver. "What in hell is going on, Zim?"

As if in answer to the question, there came a deafening ... KABOOM!

The right side of the highway blew up.

Incredibly, while the blast was on line with the jeep, it was not under it. The vehicle, being as loaded as it was with two Americans and three Vietnamese and with all the sandbags packed on the floor, was not blown up but rather, sideways off the highway onto the shoulder.

In an instant Zim flew halfway out of the jeep. He hopped along the ground on one foot while the other foot was standing on the brake. Both of his hands clung to the steering wheel.

At the same instant I was blown into the driver's seat. My immediate reaction was to jam down the accelerator. And I also clutched the steering wheel like a man in a death grip. With Zim's foot on the brake, my foot on the accelerator, and four hands on the steering wheel, the jeep hopscotched down the road like a Kansas jackrabbit. In thirty yards or so it finally stalled.

Good training and conditioned responses went to work. People do what they are trained to do. In any ambush, the immediate action drill is to get out of the kill zone which the enemy has just defined by detonating a land mine. I raced the jeep forward, dragging Zim along with it. Bob White's driver slammed his jeep into reverse, and it shot backward fifty or so yards. But there was no follow-up enemy fire.

Zim was absolutely livid. He grabbed his carbine and began firing in all directions.

"Zim, what the hell are you doing?" I was screaming.

Zim fired at a bicycle rider coming out of the village, driving him into the rice paddy. He was now shooting far out into the paddy at the farmer who seemed to be ignoring everything. I raced around the jeep and snatched the carbine out of Zim's hands. "Have you gone crazy?" I'm still screaming.

Zim screamed back, "They know bomb here, *Daui*. People know."

"Well, we're not killing any of them today. Put your weapon down." I slammed the carbine back into Zim's chest and turned to the jeep. "Everybody OK in there?"

The explosion had placed torque on the jeep frame, which shattered the windshield. The glass had blown past me. My head was down, so my steel helmet protected me from flying glass. The men in the back were not so lucky. My heart leaped. Three faces looked out at me, covered in blood. Fortunately, it looked worse than it really was. The bits of glass had scored a lot of small cuts, and the bleeding looked pretty bad … until you blotted it off. Nails was quiet.

I walked back to the crater. Bob White was on the other side of a twenty-foot hole, ten feet deep. The miner had dug the explosives in under the shoulder of the road. He dug about as far as he could, but it still only reached under the right side.

He had wired up the detonator and strung the wires across the canal so no one could get to him without first crossing water; by then he'd be out of Dodge. All he had to do was wait for the American jeep to cross his aiming point, touch the wires to the battery, and run.

"You guys OK?" asked White.

"What?"

"You guys OK?" White shouted.

"Seem to be." I started to laugh. *The sumbitch shot at me and missed.* I laughed harder. The mind has remarkable defenses. *The sorry bastard worked his pea-pickin' ass off and missed.* I laughed even more. It was hysterical. *That little sucker did everything right, and he blew it. Now that was funny.* It seemed to me, it was funniest thing I had ever experienced. I laughed till the tears came.

CHAPTER SIX

Lead People, Not Systems

THERE IS NOTHING MORE thrilling than to be shot at and missed, as I can attest. A little further down the thrill scale is being shot at and only slightly hit with no pain. Unfortunately, Nails Hopkins, if not in real pain, was certainly in great discomfort. The windshield glass had blown back into his eyes. The irritation was worse than something caught between the eyelid and the eyeball.

Small lacerations around the eyes created more show of blood than actual damage, but some of the splinters had gotten to the eyeball before the eyelid closed. According to the medical world the eyeball does not sense pain but you would not convince Captain Stanley "tough as nails" Hopkins of that.

The two jeeps raced down the road to Tra Vinh in the late afternoon sun. Lenny was the only officer at the house when the party arrived. Seeing the handkerchief soaked in sweat and blood tied over Nail's eye was enough to spur him into immediate action. Nails looked like something out of the "Spirit of '76" painting, and Lenny needed no further urging for him to fire up the radio for an emergency medevac.

"Where's the boss, Lenny?" I asked.

"He's over at Province Headquarters."

"What?"

"He's with the province chief," answered Lenny adding a few decibels.

"Sorry ... ears still ringing, Lenny." I needed aspirin—a lot of aspirin. "Where's that aid kit of ours?"

"The outfit is in the boss's office. If you don't find anything, I have some."

"Thanks, Lenny." I went to the office and found the aspirin. At the bottled water dispenser in the dining room I washed down four tablets. Holding my head I settled gingerly at the table. *What a day I'm having. I run into Sam Bannister, who should have been in the Florida swamps eating snakes. I get my FAC blown up by a land mine when he should have been in airplane. And I sped along the left-hand side of the highway when I should have been on the right-hand side—which blew up. Not even Chuck Connors, the Rifleman, could have pulled that off … Man, what a headache.* I walked upstairs and stretched out on my bunk. I'll let Bob tell the boss what happened.

★★★

Down in the dining room a half hour later, Joe Bass listened intently as Bob recounted the day's events. The mine incident was of course the center of discussion, but the information gathered on the excursion to Vung Liem was of more enduring importance. Bass waited until Bob finished. He asked a couple questions on details.

"All right, I want you, Bob, to write up the mining incident right now, while it's fresh in your mind. Ed was too much in the middle of everything to give a very objective analysis of what happened. There is no actionable information from Vung Liem, so we'll write that up formally tomorrow."

The sound of a chopper came through the window. Bass yelled up the stairs. "Nails, your taxi's here."

Nails, with his face cleaned up and a clean handkerchief tied over his eye, came down the stairs with a duffel bag over his shoulder. Washed and dressed, the injuries did not look nearly as disastrous as when he first walked in the door. Lenny was right behind him with a small carry-on bag.

"Sorry it all came out like this," said Joe.

"Yeah, me too. Me and my OV-10 were going to save your bacon, Major. Good news is I'm still walking, even if I may not be flying for a while. Tell Ed good-bye for me. I didn't want to wake him." Everyone shook hands around. Lenny loaded Nails and his gear into the jeep, and they moved on down the driveway.

Joe grinned to himself. "Good man … for an air force type, that is."

★★★

The Vietnamese news and weather broadcast that blasted from the PA speakers down the street were less annoying than usual the next morning. I lay there still fully clothed from yesterday afternoon. Seemed I hadn't moved. I tried to piece together the events just prior to sleep. The headache had subsided, but was still there.

How was Nails? I rolled over and sat up on the edge of the bed. A shower and a good breakfast would fix me up. I stood up—perhaps a little too quickly. I was steadying myself on the night table when I noticed the pillow. There wasn't a lot of blood, but I clearly saw blood on the pillow. I felt around my neck and ears. Blood had coagulated in both ears.

I walked hastily down to the sinks. The reflection in the mirror confirmed the source of blood on the pillow.

Joe Bass was a decision maker if he was anything. He took one look at me and shouted for Lenny.

"Get me a chopper down here, Lenny. Don't jack the medics around with an emergency, but this man needs to be checked out by a doctor today. Book him straight into Saigon." Then to me, "Pack a bag, son."

By mid-afternoon I was sitting on an examination table at the Saigon Medical Facility. For a nonemergency, the move had been remarkably swift.

The doctor on duty was examining my ears with his funky little flashlight. "Sweet Jesus, both your eardrums look like they were poked out by a paper punch. What happened to you, Captain?" The doctor turned his light off.

I gave the short version of the event. "I think someone tipped off my driver, and the kid was smart enough to disobey my orders. At least, I prefer to believe we had more friends than enemies."

"I'd say you should count your guardian angel among the *friends* crowd," the doc volunteered. "Look, you need special attention requiring expertise that is not at this facility. I'm cutting you orders to Clark for further treatment."

"What's a *Clark?*"

"Clark Air Force Base. They have a full-fledged hospital there."

"Where's there?"

"Clark is in the Philippines just north of Manila. Nonemergency medical flight goes out every morning from Tan Son Nhut. You'll be on it."

"So I'm on the town till morning, so to speak?"

"So to speak. Come back this evening to pick up your orders and medical file. Be on the flight line not later than 0600 tomorrow."

The doc fussed a little more with my ears, cleaning and applying some kind of antiseptic. It did not hurt—except for the headache—but it sure was uncomfortable, and it sounded like Hell. A couple of handshakes, and thirty minutes later I was on the streets of Saigon hailing a cab to the Majestic Hotel.

A blue and dirty white little Renault rolled up. I climbed in. The streets of Saigon were teeming with people and traffic. It made moving in traffic an adventure all in itself. Unlike the Lambretta in the countryside, in the cities the small Renault was the taxi vehicle of choice. There were hundreds of them; in all states of repair, always blue with a dirty cream-colored top, always in search of the rich Westerner for a passenger.

I became aware that the vehicle was moving strangely. It was traveling rather like a small sailboat tacking its way upwind. Must be a Vietnamese maneuver to avoid congestion. I was absentmindedly thinking about how to fill the hours till flight time and thought about stopping off at the tailor on Tudo Street. We were close, and it was a short walk from the tailor to the Majestic.

I began absorbing all the details of driving through Saigon. The streets were crowded with every conceivable mode of transportation: rickshaws, bicycles, mopeds, Lambrettas. The rickshaws were particularly scary. Unlike the turn-of-the-century version of the sedan chair pulled by a runner, the 1964 version was a bicycle with the chair mounted on the axle between two wheels in the front. The driver pedaled the bicycle from the seated position behind the handlebars, and the passenger rode in front of the handlebars. It was like riding on the front bumper of a car—real exciting. The dominant vehicles on this street were bicycles and motorbikes.

My subconscious broke into the consciousness. The driver had just cut off those three bicycles. I sat up to take a closer inspection of the cabby, and for the first time I noticed that this Renault had no steering wheel. The driver was holding an adjustable wrench clamped to the steering column. He was guiding the cab as though he had a boat rudder in his hand; only the rudder was at the front of the vehicle and not the rear.

"Drop me on Tudo Street, please." The driver grinned many teeth and, without looking either way, wrenched the cab "hard to lee" into a left-hand turn. The motorbike to the left rear ran up onto the sidewalk ... nearly pitching the biker over the handlebars. Totally oblivious, the cabby pulled up to the curb. I paid the man and then walked around the corner and toward Tudo Street. *This was my second close call in a vehicle in as many days, I'm thinking. I am truly one lucky son-of-a-bitch.*

★★★

Almost everyone was in the dining room at some stage of breakfast when Lenny came bursting in. "Boss, guess who's coming to dinner."

"I don't know... Raymond Burr ?" Lenny looked blank. "For crying out loud, settle down, Lenny. Who?"

Lenny said, "Who's Raymond Burr?"

Ramsey's impatience showed through. "Perry Mason, a criminal lawyer on TV."

Lenny looked hurt. "Very funny." Then to Bass, "General Westmoreland; I just took the message."

"OK, you got my attention. Better let me see the entire message." Bass took the yellow paper and studied it. He looked up. "Seems the man is right. We got VIP for brunch tomorrow: Bob, get those cleaning boys in here this afternoon. And Lenny, have the cook go down to market and pick up some of those French pastries first thing in the morning, and not the day-old ones this time."

The MAAG House operated logistically more or less like your basic fraternity house. There were certain housekeeping chores that were assigned to the occupants. Some chores were rotated by roster, and others were permanently assigned. The permanently assigned functions were contracted out of the house. The cleaning crew was a couple of Vietnamese men who came regularly to wash down the tile floors, clean the sinks, and generally perform the heavy cleaning needed to meet military standards of health and cleanliness.

The house hired a Vietnamese cook under the supervision of a noncommissioned officer. Two Vietnamese women picked up one laundry bag per man on Thursday and returned it clean on Monday or Tuesday.

The officers and NCOs themselves financed these services. Staple food was supplied by the military and distributed on the aircraft runs. But fresh foods and pleasantries such as French bread and pastries were procured off the economy.

An assigned officer as treasurer presented each man a consolidated house and bar bill at the end of each month. It was ridiculously cheap even with the San Miguel beer. Although a visit from the commander was a big deal, it wasn't a really big deal. By 1000 hours the next morning everything was in place for the VIP visit.

General Westmoreland was a tall, lean man with salt-and-pepper gray hair. He had those bushy eyebrows like Orson Welles and dark eyes with a very intense gaze. He was an intense man. Westmoreland was a graduate of the Citadel and of West Point.

At West Point he graduated as First Captain, the highest-ranking cadet in the Corps of Cadets. He had fought in both World War II and Korea, and to go with that experience, he looked the way a general should look. He had a command presence that would match General George Washington.

Now, here he was, sitting casually, in the social room of the Tra Vinh MAAG House. The dining room table had been moved into the social room to serve as a conference table. The dining room was set up as a reception area for coffee and pastries. The general traveled with a small entourage, who remained in the reception area while the general met with the team—officers and noncommissioned officers alike.

After briefly praising the work of the Tra Vinh team, the general went straight to the subject on his mind. "I don't need to tell you that the pacification program is not progressing as well as we had hoped. I'm here to get your thoughts on why that might be and what we might do better. I also want to get your feelings on some things we plan to do in the near future." He opened the conversation to the table.

Joe Bass had been around almost as long as Westy, and he wasn't worried about how much longer his career would last. He could retire tomorrow and be very comfortable. Therefore, his conversation was a little more candid than the rest of the men's might have been, but he was sure he spoke for all of them.

"It seems, General, that we are never able to exploit our successes. Every time we see progress someplace, before it gets consolidated, the resources get pulled to some other area. It's like we need a quarter, but we only get twenty cents, and if we are successful anyway, we have to give a nickel back."

The general studied Joe Bass. Westmoreland might have said *I sometimes feel the same way, only the stakes are higher,* but he didn't. "Hopefully we can change that. I think we are about to add to your resources and extend your capabilities. We have plans on the drawing board to extend the province advisor teams down to the district level. You men are doing an outstanding job, but your effect needs to get down to the lower levels faster. We think that district teams can make that happen. What are your first thoughts on that, anyone?"

Never the shy one, Ramsey asked, "How will these teams be organized?"

"Good question. We envision a basic five-man team—two officers and three enlisted men. The team leader is a captain from the combat arms, second officer a captain or senior first lieutenant. The enlisted personnel are an operations sergeant, a medic, and a radio/telephone operator. Teams may be expanded with specialists or additional hands, depending on the situation at any given time."

Bob White asked, "And every district will have an advisor team?"

"Not every district. Just those that we determine are the most likely to meet the strategic needs of the province."

Joe asked, "Who will these teams work for, and where do they get their guidance?"

"These teams are under the direct control of the province senior advisor. That's you, Joe. However, since there is no USOM representation at the district level, the district teams will get input from the province USOM advisor."

"And will that include some of his funding?" asked White.

Westy smiled. "That will have to be worked out by province through USOM. But I can not envision USOM not taking advantage of the advisor on the ground to monitor and assist with their programs."

The tall man stood up. "I know you've not had time to think about this. We in Saigon are much further along in our thought processes. If you have suggestions on how we can make this thing work, don't hesitate to send it up the line." Everyone stood up. "Joe, thanks for the hospitality. Those pastries were particularly nice."

"Our pleasure, sir."

The party moved out on the veranda, and the jeep drivers sprang into action. Lenny radioed the pilots of their impending return. Joe stood on the bottom step of the veranda and saluted the departing vehicles.

★★★

Tudo Street was a clean, attractive tree-lined avenue; wide by old Saigon standards. It was lined with shops and restaurants. Every block had a least one lounge frequented by all manner of expatriates, but most notably Americans. I found the tailor shop with surprisingly little trouble, although I had only been there once. The proprietor recognized me right off and profusely welcomed me.

"You like fitting?" he said as he moved to the back of the shop.

"You got that right. How are things?"

"No problem," he said, which was probably a lie. From the looks of the shop I might be the only customer the little guy had.

We chatted as the little man held out the trousers to try on. I was surprised to note my waist was an inch smaller than at the time of the initial fitting. "I think you should leave it a little loose." It felt good to get back to lean and mean.

The fellow was quick and applied the same guidance to the fitting of the blouse. A few pins and some chalk, and in less than a half hour I was back in the street on the way to the Majestic Hotel. I had just enough time to register, drop my bags, and make the round-trip to pick up my orders at the hospital. I was already looking forward to a long hot shower and a nice French meal on the top floor of the Majestic.

★★★

It had been almost thirty days since I arrived at Clark Air Force Base. The hospital had checked me in immediately and reviewed my medical file. Then came the doctors. Each new doctor looked at my ears, ooohed and aaahed, and called on his colleagues to come look. Finally one of them scheduled me to see the specialist the next day.

The specialist doctor had not been hopeful. He had decided to ship me back to Walter Reed Hospital stateside where there were more experienced surgeons. I begged the man to at least try something here at Clark before they sent me back. In the end the doc reached into the ears and reopened the blood clots forming around the wounds where the eardrums had been blown away.

He sealed up the ear canal with cigarette paper soaked in antiseptic. The doctor tucked the edges of the cigarette paper into the wound so the scab would form on the paper. The idea was to have the scar tissue form on the paper and grow into a new facsimile eardrum. For the procedure to be effective, I didn't dare yawn, cough, or sneeze, or do anything to change the pressure and blow out the cigarette paper.

It actually worked, although the doctor had to refit the cigarette paper five times. Each time the scar tissue was a little closer to closing up the ear canal. However, even after the scar tissue did grow into an eardrum, the doc would not let me fly for another two weeks for fear of blowing it out again in an altitude change by an airplane. The last two weeks, therefore, had been very boring. I knew the bartender at the officers' club by name. I saw every movie on post. I even had my teeth cleaned at the base dental clinic.

One afternoon I ran into Nails in the hospital cafeteria. Nails was sitting with another patient. He was wearing the appropriate inpatient garb plus a patch over his eye. Initially I walked right by without recognizing him.

"Is that Lucky Ed the ground pounder?" came across the dining room.

It took a moment for the scene to register on me. "Son of a gun. Is that a disguised fighter pilot I see?"

Nails practically vaulted over the tables to clap me on the back. He dragged me over to the table where his friend remained sitting. "This is the guy I was riding with when the jeep blew up."

The friend stood. "So you're the guy who grounded Sky King here."

"Well, I can't take the credit or blame, as the case may be. That goes to a little fellow in black pajamas who has probably had his ass chewed and placed on half rations for missing the target." I took the chair that was offered.

We had just got seated and begun to relive the adventure for the benefit of the new audience when an air force colonel approached the table.

"Captain Hopkins; been looking everywhere for you."

Nails popped up. "Good morning, Colonel Jack." Nails proceeded to introduce the men at the table to his unit commander. The two men stood. When Nails got to me, he made particular mention that I was the "other man" who, like himself had cheated death nearly a month ago. The colonel's smile immediately faded. He walked around the table straight into my space.

"You know, Captain, the operative word in Forward Air Controller is *air*. What in the hell were you thinking about, taking your Forward Air Controller on a *ground* escapade? A plane without a pilot is no good to anybody, any more than a pilot is without a plane. They are a *system*. And this *system* is now out of action."

This was so unexpected that I could not register any reaction but surprise.

"Do you have any idea of the cost of the system you have disabled with your little joyride—not to mention a resource that now sits on the ground? You ought to have your goddammed head examined."

He fired a look over to Nails. "Doc says you're about to break out of here. Very first thing you do is come see me." He then strode away.

We were all struck dumb. Finally Nails broke the silence and sat down. "Don't know what got into him. He's usually pretty laid back. They even call him "Smiling" Jack 'cause he never gets ruffled. Ed, you may be the first man in recent history to actually piss off Smiling Jack."

I thought about that. What kind of commander thinks of his command as *weapons systems*? Smiling Jack certainly wasn't Gregory Peck in *Twelve O'Clock High*. I needed to be where men commanded men, not *systems*. It was time to get back.

✯✯✯

In between the C-130 flight back from Clark and the Huey flight down to the Delta, I got in a kamikaze cab run to the tailor for another fitting. This was going to be one fine-fitting uniform.

The chopper flight back to Province turned out to be routine, but surprisingly pleasant. The paddies were turning green as the rice plants broke up the light reflections from the paddy water. I watched the thunderstorms building out over the South China Sea.

"Look long range at ten o'clock" came over the intercom. A waterspout spiraled down out of the cloud like the index finger of God in Michelangelo's painting in the Sistine Chapel, only it energized the sea instead of Man. The Huey continued on, dodging thunderstorms, and finally touched down in Tra Vinh. It wasn't home, but it was good to be back.

I noticed there were two new faces at the volleyball game that evening. The new captain claimed the title of best spike-man. He had skill along with his six-five frame. He was thin, too, which made him look even taller than he was. His name was Captain K. C. Flint, but nobody seemed to know what the K and C stood for because he went by "KC." He had big, expressive brown eyes and could slip from cultured discourse to salty descriptions in the blink of those brown eyes. In a word, he had a short fuse.

Private First Class Peter de Groot was also new to the team, but the formal introductions were not executed until happy hour. And it was well into the happy hour before Joe Bass arrived. He grabbed a San Miguel and, as was often his habit, added a small can of tomato juice to the freshly poured mug. After greeting one and all, he pulled me aside.

"Let's go sit in my office. Let me bring you up to speed." He led the way.

"We've had about six weeks of activity in the month you have been gone. By the way, good to have you back."

"Thank you, sir."

Bass proceeded to tell about Westy's visit and how, shortly after the visit, Tra Vinh was alerted to implement the district program ASAP with the emphasis on *soon*.

"Private de Groot was the first to arrive. You, Ed, will lead the team into Vung Liem. KC will be your assistant team leader. Your medic and operations sergeant are in the pipeline. So is the equipment ... What do you think so far?"

"Holy mackerel."

"Is that your estimate of the tactical situation?" Joe's weak attempt at humor.

"What do they know in Vung Liem?" I asked.

"The word is going down Vietnamese channels—hopefully on a need-to-know basis."

"How much of our tactical equipment is on board?"

Bass studied his fingernails. "None."

"Do we have the jeep?"

"No." He picked a piece of invisible lint off his trousers.

"When will the medic and ops sergeant come in?"

"I actually don't know, but it couldn't be more than a week ... or two, maybe."

"When are we expected to move in?"

Bass looked me in the eye. "Day after you arrive back in Tra Vinh."

"Tomorrow?"

"Tomorrow."

"Holy mackerel ... and that *is* my estimate of the tactical situation."

CHAPTER SEVEN

The Boy Scout Motto

TWO DAYS AFTER MY return to Tra Vinh, the Vung Liem district advisory team—minus two—with all their gear, loaded onto a Huey, and set forth on their new mission. There had been more details and longer lead times than Major Bass expected, hence the extra day.

I went over to the armory to see what I could scrounge up in the way of defense materials such as mines, trip flares, and grenades. Captain Tung was as helpful as he could be. I walked away with as many trip flares as KC and I could carry. Private de Groot familiarized himself with the radio communications equipment, also, there at the armory.

Peter was a friendly little guy. He was about five foot four with a quick smile that exposed even white teeth. He had dark hair and a spark in his dark eyes, and, although he was quiet, he was not shy. That was probably a very good trait for the dynamics of the team, since it was clear from the outset that Captain KC Flint was neither quiet nor shy. Peter struck up a relationship with the Vietnamese operators to whom he would be talking whenever he broke into their radio net. We did not know when our radios would arrive, so the plan was to make a daily situation report on the Vietnamese radio net. The province operators would pass on the Vung Liem status to the American advisors.

Now was the moment of truth. The Huey lifted off on a northwest heading. Everything was still new to KC and Peter. This was only their second flight over the Delta, and for them the view from the air was spectacular. The only clue that the green paddies were underwater came when the chopper flew directly over the field. Only then could the reflected light be seen from the vertical angle. It was grand.

I was thinking ahead to the situation at Vung Liem. The ARVN battalion was still in place, so I could expect to see Sam Banister again. That was good, since Sam could give us an up-to-date briefing on the tactical situation in Vung Liem.

The chopper was cruising at about two thousand feet and traveling parallel to Highway 8. I looked for the site of my jeep ambush but could not identify the exact spot. Clearly the road had been repaired, and life went on down there, just as it did for me. Out to the front I saw the highway angle off to the left. I touched the pilot's shoulder and pointed straight ahead to the district town.

I pressed the push-to-talk button on the intercom. "See the point where the highway angles to the west and the dirt road continues straight into the town? There's an old gas station in the fork of the roads."

"Roger," he responded.

"To the right of the dirt road halfway into town is a schoolhouse with a soccer field beside it."

"Got it." The Huey swung out to the right over the rice paddies and flew a little way north of the town. The pilot then banked left for a short base leg and then again for the final approach. He brought us in low over the rice paddies that bordered the soccer field and the southeast edge of town, and landed in the center of the field. Pete and KC grabbed their gear and exited first. I pressed the intercom.

"Thanks for the lift, guys. Now you know. We're down here."

"And that *is* good to know, just in case. You got a radio frequency?" Both pilots turned in their seats.

"Not yet, but it's coming."

"Well, if you need a pickup or anything, just throw out a Day-Glo orange air panel. Vinh Long Army Airfield is only thirty clicks to the northwest. First chopper that sees the panel on his way home will come in for a pickup."

"Thanks. That's especially good to know too." I pulled off my headset. "Happy trails." The pilot grinned, but I wasn't sure he was old enough to know who Roy Rogers was. I handed the earphones to the door gunner as I pulled my gear from the bird. Peter and KC watched me hustle toward them.

The chopper carefully pulled pitch and eased on back, and then swooped out over the rice paddies. We stood there watching our lifeline withdraw to the east.

"All right, men, here we go: looks like we walk into town." I picked up my gear. The other two followed me toward the road. There was a three-strand barbed wire fence around the perimeter of the field. A double-wide entrance in the middle of the fence along the road provided access into the soccer field. I stepped out onto the road.

"What kind of palms are those across the road?" asked KC. "Looks like a plantation."

"Well, it *is* an old plantation, but clearly it's not being cared for these days. You can see where they had two crops growing here. The tall ones are coconut palms and the low ones are banana palms."

"What's that back in the trees?" asked Pete.

"That, I think, is a Vietnamese pagoda ... Whoa, looks like we're in luck." Coming up the dirt road from the gas station was a Lambretta, and it was empty. I stood in the center of the road and waved the fellow over.

"*Chau, Ong.* Hello, sir," and that was as far as my conversation went. The rest was done in arm and hand signals but effectively nonetheless. We loaded onto the Lambretta with all our gear, and surprisingly everything fit-- barely.

"This little scooter moves most smartly," said KC, his arms and legs carefully folded like blades on a pocket knife.

"You bet." I tapped the driver on the shoulder as we approached the district headquarters. "OK, boys. Take a look at your new digs."

"Nice to see a little security on the front gate," said KC.

"Why are those howitzers placed across the street?" asked Peter.

"They are here to support the night ambush patrols with preplanned and interdicting fire on suspected VC movement," I said as I paid the Lambretta driver five piaster for the ride. The man was a happy camper.

★★★

The sound of the helicopter was incredibly loud. It seemed as though it would land right on top of his pagoda. The old man was not afraid; fear had no hold on him. Being blind, however, did leave him disoriented when unfamiliar sounds overwhelmed his known universe. And right now he was concerned about his young novice. The lad had gone to beg rice over an hour ago. He should have returned by now. He should be telling him, right now, what was happening outside his pagoda door.

Duc To Ngoc had long ago accepted his blindness. He saw it as a blessing which gave him powers of perception that other sighted individuals could appreciate but never fully understand... Where was that boy? The sound of the helicopter welled up again, but then, drifted away, seeming to move toward the sea ... silence.

What an infernal sound that is. Thanks for the return of peace. Ngoc's mind drifted back to his childhood memory of quiet times in the fields around the monastery. He had been born in Hue, an ancient religious center of Buddhism in Indochina. His parents were deeply religious, and their son gravitated to the teachings of the many monks in the area.

The family resented the encroachment of the French Catholics into Vietnam. The country, even today, was 70 percent Buddhist with higher percentages in Hue. Although less than 10 percent of the population was Catholic, over half the administrative positions in the country were occupied by Catholics.

Duc To Ngoc was intensely, actively angry at the Catholics, the Diem government which supported them, and the Americans who supported the regime.

Ngoc smiled to himself as he reflected on the firebrand he'd been in his younger days: how he had entered the Resistance against the Japanese, how he rebelled, how he got himself thrown into prison, how he was tortured. He was mad then and violent and young ... The sound of a Lambretta out on the road to town brought his senses back to the present. Perhaps it was the boy coming.

He continued to sit on the straw mat with his legs crossed in the lotus position. Where was that boy? His mind drifted again. No, he wasn't mad with frustration and violent without direction. Those were the days of his youth and of the torture which quickly made an old man of him. The torture had developed medical complications which went untreated and eventually resulted in the blindness—blindness that settled him down and drove him to self-pity.

After the war and his release from prison, he found his way home to Hue. That was his bitter period. He might have ended his life in those days, had he not met the brilliant master, Trich Tri Quang, who encouraged him into the saffron robes.

Light steps were coming up the path; it was the boy. In seconds a skinny lad of perhaps fourteen rushed through the recessed doorway that blocked direct entrance into the main room. Ngoc knew he was wrapped in the yellow robes of a Vietnamese monk.

"Master, Americans have arrived in town." He was excited. "They came in the helicopter, and they are alone."

"How many are there?"

"Three, Master. They are at the district chief's villa."

"Americans are nothing new; they come and go. Are we able to have a meal?"

The lad held up a cloth bag of rice in front of the old man's dark glasses—as if he could see the prize. "I shall prepare a meal now, Master."

✯✯✯

As we entered the compound, a few Vietnamese in black pajamas gathered along the road and watched. Apparently there was no one present in any official capacity to welcome us.

KC and Pete peered into the villa courtyard. The outer compound wall was about twenty feet high and maybe ten inches thick. It was most probably made of local bricks plastered over with stucco. It was painted a cream color. The compound was rectangular with the double wooden gate entrance in the center of the front wall opening on to the road. The villa sat to the right of the gate and centered on the long axis of the compound. It had a square-shaped footprint with a front porch extending out into the courtyard. On the other side of the courtyard, opposite the front gate and along the back wall, was a series of apartments side by side. They were relatively low and dedicated to specific functions including living quarters.

I directed Peter to look straight ahead to the back wall. "The radio equipment is located in the apartment immediately in front of the main gate. The radio operators live in the apartment. As soon as we settle in, that's where you go to send back a report to Province." Pete nodded understanding as he scanned the back wall.

I explained to both KC and Pete, "At the left and right of the com shack are additional apartments that you can see extend along the back wall but not all the way to the ends of the compound. The end units are larger than the ones you're looking at. On the end behind the villa is a large apartment, which is arranged as a kitchen area. At the other end to your left is an even larger apartment, which houses a series of small offices and a conference hall or classroom about thirty feet square." I led them into the compound.

"You lost again, soldier?" The voice of Sam Banister preceded the man as he walked out the villa front door. His right arm was through the shoulder strap of his backpack.

"Hey, Sam. Heard you were still in town."

"Not for long. Just hanging around till you got in."

"What do you mean?"

"Well, apparently someone decided that Captain Ed Skillman and two good American fighting men were the equivalent of one ARVN battalion. We're moving out."

"No kidding ..." The three of us walked up on to the porch, and I made the introductions.

The porch was about twenty feet square with steps coming up from the left side. We dropped our bags, and went into a large front room in the villa. An extra-wide door opened from the porch into the front room. Two interior walls ran from front to rear dividing the villa into thirds. Another wall ran from side to side one-third of the way in from the exterior back wall. The floor plan was like a tic-tac-toe board with one horizontal line missing in the front.

I spied an upholstered chair and sat down. "OK. What do I need to know?"

The front room was furnished with a three-seat couch upholstered in vinyl and two matching chairs. There was a long low table in front of the couch and a small, round end table to the side. The matching chairs were placed at either end of the table in front of the couch. Sam sat on the end of the couch. He returned to my question. "Nothing has really changed since you were up last month. The VC are actively operating further to the north around Ben Tre. We have had no contact at all. It has been a good rest for this hard working bunch."

"So, it's just time to move back into the fray?"

"I'm not sure, yet, where we're headed. I need to catch up to my *Daui* counterpart. I just held back in hopes of touching base with you; just about gave up."

"Glad you didn't. Thanks." I began to feel a little exposed. "Is the district chief around?"

"Haven't seen him in two days. His truck is here, but his little green Peugeot is gone." Sam rose and moved to the porch. "I have got to go, men. There are three back sleeping rooms. Two are for the Americans—the center and the south side. This side of the villa is the private quarters of the Chief, which include the third back room."

Sam indicated the north side of the villa. "There are three other entrances into the villa, one in the center of each of the other exterior walls. The north door is the private entrance for the Chief. The south side room opens toward the kitchen and is a common area for houseguests—that's you. And this room is a common room for joint business with visiting leaders and representatives. That's about it."

I followed Sam out on the porch. "How reliable is the local security?"

"Well, you see that guard post at the front gate? He has a large triangular piece of steel like a bent train rail. After the hours of darkness the guard gets into his sandbagged guardhouse with his rifle and bangs that triangle every thirty minutes to prove he is awake. There is a guard post just like this one on the backside of the compound. When the guy in the back hears the guy in front bang his triangle, the guy in the back bangs his piece of iron. Now each of them knows that the other is awake. Any questions?" Sam slung his backpack over one shoulder and headed to the gate.

"You're kidding, of course?" I forced a smile.

"Wish I were, Buddy. Keep your head down." And with the precision of a practiced team Sam's driver pulled up to the gate before the captain said a word. I waved as they sped away.

Back in the villa, K. C. Flint was inspecting the quarters. KC was the kind of person who placed great value on quality of life and living. He had lived eighteen good years in a very successful entrepreneurial family outside Philadelphia. It was said that KC had the same physical characteristics as his father; tall, thin, big brown eyes with a quick mind and a tongue to match. The wealthy father was a self-made man, and had drilled personal responsibility into his son from the day the boy got his first dog.

KC graduated from the University of Pennsylvania and received an ROTC commission in the Transportation Corps. As was the army practice at the time, officers commissioned in combat support branches, like the Transportation Corps, would serve first in a combat arms branch for five years before taking up their assigned branch. That way every support branch officer knew firsthand how to really support the combat branches.

KC was assigned to the infantry and served his first tour of duty at Fort Lewis, Washington. When he'd put on those new captain bars three months ago, he believed he was ready for Vietnam. If KC lost any self-confidence standing in the front room of an old French villa in Vung Liem, Vietnam, it certainly did not show. He was a survivor.

"The sleeping rooms have five cots, all right—there are three in the end room on the left and two in the center. The end room on the right is locked. There is a back entrance off the center bedroom," KC reported as I returned from seeing Sam off.

"Good. Peter, go over to the communications room and see if you can get a message out to our boys at Province that we are in place. Ask for an acknowledgment to test the system."

"Roger that, sir." Pete was out the door.

I motioned to KC to sit down and took a seat myself. "All right, doesn't seem that anyone here knew that we were coming. No district chief around, so we'll just squat here like that was the plan. It's late afternoon, and we need to see to our security before it gets dark." I told him about the in-house security plan.

KC's large brown eyes blinked once or twice. "How did your buddy, Sam, manage?"

"Well, you remember he had a whole battalion of friendlies surrounding him, so it wasn't quite the same. What we need to do is get those trip flares out and around the building before nightfall. There are a lot of guys in black pajamas walking around this compound, and not all of them have on shoes."

"What? What do *shoes* have to do with it?"

"Never mind. Let's walk the property."

The compound wall ran about thirty feet from the backside of the villa and parallel to it, thus creating a small backyard. Off to the south side of the villa was a covered breezeway, which connected the villa to the kitchen. The backyard was hard-packed dirt with the exception of a very large and very old hardwood tree tucked in the corner of the compound. At the base of the tree was a patch of green plants enclosed by a small brick border that ran in a 90-degree arc from wall to wall. Two windows in addition to the doorway opened out of the villa into the backyard.

The outer compound wall was topped with embedded chunks of glass to deter undesirables from crossing over. At one time a strand of barbed wire was added to improve the deterrence factor, but it could be defeated with the same ease as the glass—a blanket over the top of the wall. We agreed; it wouldn't do.

"Trip flares, you think?" said KC.

"Yeah, string a trip wire across the top and tie it off with a flare. At least we'll get some warning."

We did all four walls. Then we crisscrossed the backyard with four more trip wires about six inches off the ground. By the time we were done the entire back area between the compound walls and the villa was crossed and re-crossed with trip wires tied to as many flares. No human being could walk six feet in any direction between the buildings without setting off at least one flare. Only the front courtyard was clear of trip flares.

"I expect we'd better have two on watch and one asleep tonight just to be on the safe side," I said, walking back into the villa's front room.

Peter joined us. "We got a message through and an acknowledgment."

I nodded. The house was dark now with only the early evening twilight coming through the porch entrance and the two windows on either side of it. They were open-air windows and were narrow—two feet wide maybe, with the sill three feet above the floor and the opening rising to about three feet below the fifteen-foot ceiling. As if by a silent command all three of us began looking for the light switch.

This villa was no different than the ones in Province Town. The electricity was retrofitted to the building and came through the ceiling in the center of the room. The fan turned slowly. The two fluorescent light fixtures were flush-mounted, on line with the ceiling fan, and about one third of the room width from each sidewall. The switches to the fan and the lights were wired across the ceiling and down the wall. In the interest of conserving cable no doubt, the switch boxes were mounted nearly seven feet high on the walls and away from the doorways.

"Here they are." KC turned on the lights. The three of us sat down in the front room.

"Probably should have brought more than one day's rations. We'll take a look at what's on the economy in the morning." I pulled out a meal. The other two took my cue. I laid out what I wanted on the night watch schedule and assigned times. Pete was going to get the short night this time, but no one was going to get a particularly decent night's sleep.

When we were setting up the security, KC had discovered a bathroom of sorts. It was a small room off the kitchen equipped with a conventional toilet and sink. A huge crock of water complete with a gigantic ladle sat in the corner. The runoff water from the sink drained into an open channel in the floor that ran along the wall and disappeared through a hole in the corner. Ladled water flushed the toilet, which was piped out through the same hole in the corner of the room. It worked, and Pete excused himself to prepare for the sack. By now it was fully dark, and the clang of the front tower was matched by a clang from the back. All was well.

"Do you play chess?" KC asked. He reached into his pack.

"As a matter a fact I do, but it's been a while." I flashed back to my days of playing chess with my German friends in the local Gasthaus. In those days it was more an effort to develop my language skills than skill in chess.

KC produced a small set. "How about we get a game up?" He reached back into his duffel again and produced a bottle of brandy. "We can sit playing chess and sipping brandy just like downtown San Francisco."

"Well, I don't know about downtown San Francisco, but I like the program."

I set up the board while KC scouted the left wing room for some kind of glass.

"Can't figure out where the district chief is," I said, almost to myself.

KC returned from the next room with two small juice glasses. "I think we should make that wing room the dining room. It's got that big table in it and a glass-front cupboard." He adjusted his chair to face the chess board. "Is it normal for a district chief to be gone for days on end?"

"Who knows what's normal. Point is, we are here, and he isn't. I have to believe he knew we were coming. Even if he wasn't sure when, why would someone else not know—unless he thought it was safer not to share the information? Very strange." The chessboard was ready for play.

KC passed me a bit of brandy. "It's not a snifter, but it'll do. Here's to our first night in town."

For the first time all day we relaxed—sitting there in the vinyl-covered chairs with the end table between us. We were each playing conservatively, trying to get a feel for each other's style—getting to know each other. We had exchanged pawns, and I was about to run my bishop when it happened.

The explosion was deafening and shook the whole villa. The second explosion followed within seconds, but both of us were already on the floor.

"Get the lights." *Where the hell's my pistol?* "Get the lights!" *Nothing to crawl under.*

KC crawled across the tile floor scrambling for his steel pot. "Where's the damn light switch?"

Peter raced through the doorway with a loaded, unlocked carbine and his helmet on backward. "What the hell's going on?"

"Get your ass down. Turn off the goddamn lights."

"Where's the goddamn light switch?"

Two more explosions in succession. I jumped up and ran to the wall grabbing at the seven-foot-high switch …

Blackness …

Men scurried in the darkness to find their combat gear.

"Clear the building. KC, out the front. Break right: I'll cover. Pete, out the back."

Movement … Silence.

KC and I slowly stood up from our firing positions in the front yard. Pete crept around from the breezeway.

"What in the hell was that?" whispered KC.

"Cover me." I walked carefully to the entrance gate and peered around the pillar into the guard post. All I could see were the white teeth of the guard smiling at me and pointing at the two artillery pieces across the street. The smell of cordite was drifting into the compound. With a sense of total relief, I turned back into the courtyard. *Some professional soldier you are … scared witless by your own outgoing artillery.*

"OK, boys. The battle is won. No need to mention this little incident in the dispatches." I led the way back into the villa. Everyone felt euphoric … and maybe a little chagrined, too.

"Damn, look at that spilled brandy," complained KC, but he didn't really care. He happily refreshed it … maybe even with a little something extra.

★★★

The next day we were in limbo. We pretty much stayed inside the compound. Several Vietnamese in black pajamas and sandals made an effort to learn who we were, but communication was difficult. Peter was making headway with the men in the radio shack. KC and I took a walk around the marketplace during the middle of day two. I recalled my visit of six or so weeks back, but now I saw the town from a different point of view. KC was fascinated with the food products on sale in little ol' Vung Liem. He was positively gleeful when he found canned mushrooms at one of the stalls.

On out third day, a young Vietnamese man presented himself at around 1030 hours. He introduced himself as Ong Hoa Hoang. He wore dark trousers and a white short-sleeved shirt. His sandals were leather—a significant difference from the rubber sandals the average citizen usually wore. He spoke a little English and a little French. He said he was the assistant district chief for administration of Vung Liem. He said that the district chief was expected back tomorrow, maybe, but that no one could really predict when the Chief ever would arrive or depart.

Hoa Hoang explained that he too had been out of town and only returned this morning. He and the district chief used the two sleeping rooms in the other wing opposite the dining room.

"What are the eating arrangements?" I asked.

"We take our meals down the road at a boarding house." Hoa Hoang indicated the building outside the compound wall on the main road leading out of town. "Have you visited the civil guard compound yet?"

"Civil guard compound? Ah, no, I haven't." I was mystified.

"The barracks are on the north side of town on the bank of the canal. *Daui* Sau is the company commander."

"Thank you, Mr. Hoa Hoang. You have been of great assistance. I hope it's all right that we have sort of taken over the villa."

"Oh, yes. All visitors stay there. The district chief and I only need the one wing for sleeping rooms. His wife and children live in My Tho. My parents and sister live in Can Tho to the south. You know Can Tho?"

"Not as well as I would like. I visited one afternoon and was surprised at the size of the city. Had an outstanding Chinese meal in a restaurant I could never find again." I thought about my recon to Tra On District shortly after I first arrived.

After a few more niceties, Mr. Hoa Hoang excused himself. "Welcome to Vung Liem, *Daui* Skeelman."

"Thank you, Ong Hoang. I look forward to working in the district."

I walked back into the villa and joined KC and Peter in the designated dining room. They were munching down on jam and French bread. Two eight-ounce bottles of saussi sat on the table. Saussi was a Vietnamese root beer made in Saigon. It was quite tasty if you liked root beer and an excellent substitute for beer when you were thirsty and just looking for the health protection of a bottled drink. Groundwater could not be trusted.

KC had volunteered to be the team mess officer, which included procurement. His first purchases had been the jam, saussi, and French bread. Maybe Captain Frickey was right. French colonialism was a cultural thing. The French just imposed on the population their language, their cooking—starting with bread, and their wine. The rest was expected to take care of itself.

I sat down at the table. "I have just learned from the district administrator that there is a civil guard barracks on the edge of town. It houses the Regional Force company commanded by a *Daui* Sau."

KC's eyes lit up; he was excited at the adventure. "Let's go see what they're up to."

"You bet. Strap down your pistols, men. Here we go." They collectively cleaned up the six-foot wooden table, then individually secured their sidearms. KC and I carried Colt .45-caliber semiautomatic pistols. Pete was issued the M-2 carbine.

In the center of the district town just north of the marketplace there was a narrow road leading out of town to the east. The road appeared to end at a large double-wide wrought iron gate one hundred or so yards down the road. But the road did not end. Instead it took a sharp left turn and ran along the side of a long one-story adobe-type building. The road continued beyond the building onto the bank of the main canal.

The double gate and fence spanned the thirty feet between two buildings and stood ajar enough for foot traffic to pass but prohibited vehicle entry. We walked through the gate just as an unarmed ARVN soldier came around the inside corner of the building. He nearly jumped out of his skin when he saw Americans.

I gave him my warmest smile. "*Daui* Sau?"

"No … no … um." The soldier disappeared back around the corner. We pushed on through the passage between the buildings into a large quadrangle. Low adobe buildings surrounded a grassy area on three sides. The fourth side of the field was open to the canal. It was a barracks. Banks of apartments made up the three buildings built in the shape of a U. The open area was filled with a variety of activities.

A few men in uniforms lingered around what looked to be a well in the center of the area, but mostly, it was women cooking in woks over small charcoal burners. Each burner was about the size of a three-gallon flower pot, and the clay rim was notched so air flowed when the wok sat over the flame. The women would sit on their heels cooking in the front of their apartments and filling the air with wonderful smells. Today was no exception.

The soldier at the gate was now leading a Vietnamese captain toward us. The age of the captain was difficult to estimate, but he looked seasoned. I saluted as I approached to meet him.

"*Chau, Daui.* I am *Daui* Skillman."

"*Enchanté. Je suis Daui Sau. Comment allez-vous?*" His French had a heavy accent but was recognizable in the standard phrases. He motioned for us to follow. The commander looked older than I had expected, but it was hard to estimate the age of an Asian. The man certainly walked with an air of command.

"*Ça va bien, merci,*" I answered, a little too familiar, but that was the first thing to come out. KC and I followed the *Daui*, but Pete was engaged with the gate guard who was one of the radio operators here in the compound. The *Daui* indicated two chairs in front of the apartment. We sat down. A little Vietnamese woman dressed in black peasant garb brought a third chair out of the apartment, then disappeared back inside. KC introduced himself in English.

The conversation moved from English to French to Vietnamese and eventually wound up with a stick in the dirt. *Daui* Sau outlined the town limits in the dirt and indicated where the night security positions were located. We studied the layout for a few minutes and were feeling a little better about our situation.

The little woman came out again, this time with a pot of tea and four cups. "*C'est ma femme,*" said the *Daui* with a wave. She smiled nervously and poured out three cups of tea, then disappeared again. I could see Pete over my shoulder; he was still walking around the area with the guard. We all sipped a little tea thinking about what to say next. Before the silence became awkward, a high-pitched animal-like scream came from inside the apartment followed by a rapid, angry torrent of Vietnamese. The attention of all snapped to the doorway. A small, maybe twenty pounds, Vietnamese pig shot, as if by guns, through the doorway headed to the far side of the compound. It clipped the tea table and, but for the quick reactions of KC, could have ended the tea party right there.

Daui Sau smiled sheepishly. "Family pet."

Ba (Mrs.) Sau appeared in the doorway with far less decorum than previously shown. She fired a look at the *Daui* that every married man in the world recognizes.

The *Daui* shrugged. "Maybe pet is dinner soon." Everyone laughed except, of course, *Ba* Sau. It seemed like a good time to say good-bye. We had made our introductions and had a feel for what to expect from *Daui* Sau.

I caught Pete's eye as he came out of the building on the far side of the quadrangle. "Peter. Mount 'em up." KC had stepped over to Mrs. Sau and now towered over her by more than two feet. He spoke his most charming English to the lady, and, although she clearly did not understand a word, she allowed him to calm her down.

Daui Sau and I began to walk to the gate. KC and Pete caught up, and we headed back to the villa. The three of us were sitting around the dining table, eating up the last of our issue rations, when Pete casually offered, "You know they got a fifty-foot radio tower in that compound."

I was suddenly focused on Pete. "Is that right? Tell me about that."

"Well, it's a relay tower. Nobody seems to know much about it … but then, it could be I didn't understand what they said. I know the equipment, though. We trained on some of it when I was in communications training at Fort Huachuca."

KC joined the conversation. "Who are they communicating with?"

"I don't think they communicate with anyone on that equipment. It looks to be strictly a relay station … They also got an armory there."

"That's not too surprising. Any idea what kind of weapons they have in supply?" I said.

"Nothing I've ever seen before, but whatever rifles they are, there are maybe a couple hundred. Also a bunch of pistols—revolvers and stuff."

"What do you mean, *stuff*?" KC asked. "And how did you get in the armory?"

"They were showing me their commo gear, and it's right there with the arms room. The stuff was … well, steel packing barrels, for one thing. There may be six or eight of them … about forty inches high and two feet in diameter."

KC looked at me. "What do you suppose that is?"

"I don't know, but there is nothing like being prepared. It's another serious question for the Chief when he gets in." I sat there trying to figure what an arms cache might be doing in this little district, but nothing came.

"Break out the chessboard, boss. Time for the revenge of Godzilla."

CHAPTER EIGHT

Either You Win or You Lose

TIEN VAN QUAN SAT on a low three-legged stool with his legs crossed—not quite in the lotus position. He entertained his visitor in the quiet little garden beside the pagoda. Quan had traveled slowly up from the south of the province observing the activity and talking with the farmers. He seldom spent more than a night in any one village, but sought directions for the next pagoda to the north. As he became familiar with the people and the political activity, particularly the movements of the Vietcong in the region, he lingered a little longer at each of the villages.

It was quite pleasant here in the Japanese garden next to the Japanese-style pagoda. As much as he hated the Japanese, their tributes to Buddha were most esthetically pleasing. The legend was that this pagoda had been built by an imperial Japanese officer who, having acquired financial success after the war, returned to Cang Long to build a physical tribute to the time he lived here.

The structure consisted of four rooms stacked one on top of the other. Each room was smaller than the room below, with the top room barely large enough for one person. A flight of stairs up the outside of each room led to the next level, but each staircase was on a different side of the building. The floor line at each level extended away from the building, creating a narrow roofline that flared along the sides and at the corners and gave the distinctive Japanese appearance. It was stucco white with red tiles and looked like a square lighthouse with Japanese roofs.

Quan reached for the teapot and addressed his guest, "Would you care for more tea?"

The guest nodded yes to the tea. Quan reached over and poured, then returned the pot to the hibachi, "How often do you get explosives?"

When Quan had begun his intelligence gathering he was very careful to whom he spoke, and delicate about the questions he asked. That was part of what kept him traveling—never long enough for the officials to get a line on him. As Quan developed contacts, so his questioning became more direct.

The man sitting on the straw mat in front of him had been referred by an unhappy villager living just south of Tra Vinh. After his first contact with this man, Quan requested and received permission from the resident monk to stay indefinitely. He settled in.

"The comrade commander comes around every month or so, but he brings explosives maybe every third or fourth time." The man sipped his tea and shifted his position.

The afternoon sun shone over the monk's shoulder making it easy to read the man's face. The monk had been in town barely two weeks, and although Quan had spoken with him twice now, he could see that the man was still intimidated by the yellow robes.

"Does the comrade commander select your targets, also?" This was important to Quan. The April operation south of the capitol in Cang Long district had resulted in only a partially disabled bridge, zero government casualties, and a botched opportunity to kill Americans. Precious explosives must not be wasted on low-impact targets. If nothing else, they should interdict lines of communication that impacted on the flow of goods and services from Saigon or My Tho or the like. Quan had come north of Tra Vinh with the intent of influencing that strategy.

The man sipped his tea again before answering. "I have much freedom on target selection, but I am often told the time frame in which something must happen."

That was encouraging. There is room here for Quan to influence the action. The man was clearly uncomfortable with this direct questioning, but perhaps he would try one more. "How do you select a target?"

The man finished his tea, and, clearly, this was the last question he wanted to answer. "It depends a lot on how much explosive I have. It is not always the same amount. And sometimes the target I pick does not need all the explosive I have. The month before last I combined the explosives issued with some that I had held back. I tried to hit an American jeep, but it was not enough explosive for that location ..."

He set down the teacup slowly and with finality. "I must go now. Thank you for the tea and the information. I will tell comrade commander you would like to meet him."

Quan remained seated as the man stood. Both made the sign of peace. The man backed up a few steps and turned into the path away from the pagoda. Quan watched his guest disappear into the edge of town. He allowed himself a smile. This might just be the opportunity he was looking for.

★★★

The villa we now called home was the classic French provincial style with pale yellow stucco walls and the terra-cotta roof. The first and only floor of the villa was three feet above the level of the ground. The porch was an extension of the social room and reached into the courtyard. A four-foot concrete railing surrounded the porch. At the front corners of the railing were pillars that supported a flat roof extension off the eves of the villa. The porch floor was a pattern of colored tiles. The floors throughout the building were red twelve-inch square tiles.

"If we're going to live in this place and not be just squatters, we got to get screens on the doors and windows," KC complained. "The bats and bugs will drive me crazy."

He was right. Just from a defensive posture we needed something that would prevent pitching grenades through the windows. We were playing chess after supper, and I looked up from the game board eyeing the windows.

"'Allo inside." The voice came from out of the dark courtyard. That startled both of us, and I was moving toward my weapon just as a Vietnamese captain came through the doorway from the porch. "*Chau, Capitain* Skeelman. It is a pleasure to see you again."

"Hello, *Daui* Tranh. The pleasure is mine. KC, may I present the district chief of Vung Liem, *Daui* Nguyen Tranh. Daui Tranh this is Captain K. C. Flint, my assistant team leader."

"*Enchanté, mon capitain.*" The Chief didn't speak that much French, but what he spoke was pronounced properly and projected greater knowledge than was there.

"I am pleased to meet you too, *Daui* Tranh." KC waived his hand indicating the Chief take a seat.

Daui Nguyen Tranh was about five foot six—tall for a Vietnamese. He had a square face, slightly pockmarked, clean shaven, and with no signs of baldness in his straight black hair. His mouth was small, and therefore it was all the more surprising when he flashed a broad smile, exposing many straight white teeth. And he smiled often. "How your team like villa?"

"It will work just fine if this is convenient for you," I said.

KC interjected. "Of course, there are a few things that we would like to um ... well, to adjust." He glanced at me.

The Chief was completely unreadable. "What you like adjust?"

I took over. "For security and health reasons, we think that the villa should be equipped with screens on the windows and doors. How much trouble can that be if we pay the cost?"

"I think that good idea for you and for me. I see about it." The Chief went on to make few suggestions of his own. He confirmed that he and Mr. Hoa Hoang took meals at a boardinghouse, and he suggested that he assign a Vietnamese soldier to our team to assist in house chores.

"That will be great. We need to work out details for laundry and local marketing," added KC.

The Chief nodded. "I see about that."

We talked on about the district and how the Chief saw the team helping him. I expressed my concern about the security in the countryside and the training of the regional and popular forces. By the end of the conversation *Daui* Tranh agreed that it was a good idea for the Americans to visit the villages as soon as possible to be seen and to see the local situation.

The Chief stood. "You make this your home here. Mr. Hoa Hoang and I have side entrance to the other wing. We spend little time here. Welcome to Vung Liem." He walked to the back of the room, opened the door to the right, said good night, and closed the door behind him.

"Can you believe that?" said KC. "The guy is AWOL for five days and materializes in here like nothing's new. All he has to say about it is welcome to Vung Liem. A little strange, wouldn't you say?"

It was strange, but what should he have said? *I was at a secret meeting, and you are not to know about it* ... or *I went home to visit my family while the opportunity presented itself.*

I said, "Maybe he just stayed away to see if anything bad was going to happen. Now that he is back, it puts a little better stance on our security. We can go to one man on watch. Why don't you turn in? I'll wake Peter at midnight, and you can take over at three. Get everyone up at six."

"Works for me, boss." KC set the chessboard aside for continuation tomorrow. I pulled out my stationery and sat down at the dining room table. I had an hour and half to get off a few letters.

By midnight I had finished a nice long letter to my wife and daughter and a hasty note to my parents. The question was how were they going to get mailed? ... *Like Scarlett says, I'll worry about that tomorrow.* I went in to wake Peter.

"Wash up quickly, and come in. I need to brief you on the situation."

Pete headed out to the sinks and was back in a flash. "Did I hear strange voices last night?"

"Yes you did. The district chief showed just after you went to bed. He's sleeping in his room right now."

"Did he say where he'd been?"

"No. But we did outline how we can start our mission here." I explained the security plan for the rest of the night. By 1220 hours I was into the soundest sleep I had had since I'd returned from the Philippines. KC, in the cot next to me, was enjoying a similar experience.

At 0436 hours, more or less, the sound of a piercing CRACK snapped everyone in the house to attention in the sitting position. It was like the sound of a board breaking in two. By the next CRACK, only seconds behind the first, everyone in the house was on the floor. Pete did the low crawl into the front room and shut off the lights. I worked into a kneeling position with my charged pistol clutched in both hands aimed out the bedroom window. KC was holding his pistol in the same manner, only from the prone position in the doorway into the backyard. All eyes adjusted to the glare of two flares illuminating the entire backyard. Again, the smell of cordite filled the nostrils. Pete slid to a kneeling position at the other window. White smoke hung in the air.

"DON'T SHOOT! DON'T SHOOT! ... HOLD FIRE!."

In the corner of the backyard, facing the great tree stood *Daui* Tranh—one hand high in the air and the second hand directing, a now intense, urine flow into the greenery at the base of the tree. The flares burned on, the white-hot glare turning night into day. The surreal moment froze in time like a stop-action picture. You could almost hear the man's mind move. *Do I turn around to identify myself? Do I put my hand down and button up? Do I finish?* He turned his head over his shoulder in hope of being identified.

"MY GOD, DON'T SHOOT!"

It is doubtful that *Daui* Tranh saw the incident as humorously as we Americans did, but one thing was certain. Men bond in pain. Being scared to death must qualify as pain because the team and the Chief bonded on our first night together.

★★★

Ong Than had to be the oldest soldier in the entire Regional Force organization. The Chief was as good as his word. The little man showed up at the crack of dawn. He smiled a toothless grin at Peter and promptly began to set up two small charcoal burners in the breezeway between the villa and the kitchen. If his black pajamas were soaking wet, he would not have weighed a hundred pounds. He had black hair, cut about an inch long, and every hair stood straight out of his head. But he was nimble and energetic, and, before Pete knew it, Ong Than had scrambled up a half dozen eggs served with French bread and jam. Hot tea followed.

It probably occurred to Pete that he could eat the entire six eggs by himself, and he, possibly, was weighing the moral decision to call or not to call us to breakfast when we appeared anyway—most likely for the best.

KC was excited. "Ong Than can help me in the marketplace. I've been reluctant to go without a Vietnamese explaining what I'm seeing and negotiating the buy."

With the impetus of command I suggested that we start a house fund to cover the food bill. "You can run that, KC. Once the rest of the team arrives, we'll get a feel for what it costs, and you give us a regular report. Here's ten to get it started."

KC matched the ten, and we officers agreed that Pete needed only add five.

"This works. I'll go now while the marketplace is in full swing." He called to Ong Than and with arm and hand signals indicated that the little man should follow him. It was a bizarre match—KC's tall lanky figure followed closely by the four-foot frame of Ong Than. They looked more like a man walking a large black pet rather than a foraging team for a military operation. Peter and I sat and finished the rest of the tea, and he suggested I visit the communications setup.

We walked across the courtyard to the com shack, which wasn't a shack at all but rather an equipment room internal to one of the apartments. Three little kids peered out the door as we approached. The children scattered with screams of laughter when we walked into the quarters.

I asked Peter if there was a family living there.

"The senior NCO lives here with his wife and three little girls. The signal officer lives in the barracks on the edge of town along with the shift operators." The sergeant smiled hesitantly. Pete nodded. "Good morning."

I shook the sergeant's hand, and we surveyed the equipment. By hasty mental calculation, I could see this was vintage stuff. "Have you ever seen any of these models, Peter?"

"Yeah … Well, I think I got most of it figured out. We put a 'long wire' up yesterday, and that improved our signal clarity with Province by fifty percent."

The Vietnamese operator suddenly snapped to attention, startling everyone in the room.

"*Chau, Daui* Skeelman." The Chief stepped into the room with a broad smile, showing no sign of embarrassment over earlier events of the morning.

"Good morning, *Daui*. And thank you for Ong Than." You had to smile back at the Chief when he did the big smile with the ornery eye.

"I will have people you might want to meet in the conference room this afternoon. Can you come?"

"Name the time."

"We make it 1400."

"Done."

★★★

Ong Than and KC returned from the marketplace before Peter and I had finished in the com shack. KC was as excited as if it were Christmas. "Have you any idea how extraordinary it is to find knives and forks in the middle of the Mekong Delta?" He held up a cheap cafeteria knife and fork as if they were silver plate.

Pete blinked. "Nothing special. That's the same cheap stuff in the campus cafeteria at the University of Colorado." Pete had gone to UC a couple of semesters, but his grades weren't so hot, and the hometown draft was breathing down his neck. He joined up so he could choose his military occupation rather than be drafted and sent anywhere the army wanted. It was how he got into communications school.

"My dear Private First Class de Groot, were it not for this phenomenal find, you would be eating lunch with your fingers or chopsticks."

"Oh."

"And for a pittance, we have ceramic plates and cups." KC waved the plate in the air for all to see.

Pete hesitated. "Did we get food?"

KC turned a hard eye on the lad. "Obviously a rhetorical question, not requiring a response," he sneered.

I changed the direction of the conversation by announcing that the Chief was planning to introduce his staff to us in the conference room at 1400 hours.

KC glanced at his watch. "I'll speed up Ong Than; see if we can't get lunch in fifteen." He sailed out of the dining room into the breezeway.

Pete looked at me in mild wonderment. "Sit down, Peter. Looks like lunch is about to be served. It seems KC takes the mess officer thing pretty seriously."

Lunch consisted of steamed rice served with a chicken and mushroom sort of stroganoff without the sour cream, and a side dish of canned peas. Everyone was pleased including Ong Than.

Promptly, at 1400 hours our team of three showed up in the large suite of rooms at the far end of apartment row. There were two small offices and a third room which was referred to as the conference room or the classroom, depending on the purpose of the assembled group. Mr. Hoa Hoang greeted us at the entrance. Present in the room was a civilian, dressed in black trousers and white short-sleeved shirt like Mr.

Hoang, and two lieutenants. Mr. Hoang had just finished the introductions when the RF commander, *Daui* Sau, and the Chief came in.

"Have you meet everyone?" asked the Chief, "I know you meet *Daui* Sau." The Chief looked at me.

"Yes, we have." I said to Sau, "Good afternoon, sir."

"Bonjour, *mon capitain*," *Daui* Sau responded.

It was difficult to tell the age of the two Vietnamese officers, but it was clear, as they stood side by side, that *Daui* Sau was the older of the two. It was, also, clear that the other staff officers paid as much respect to Sau as they did the Chief.

The Chief continued, "*Daui* Sau plan some of day operations that let you be seen by the population and become familiar with the area of the district. These not be routine or scheduled operations, but I tell you the night before an operation be tomorrow; not predictable."

The Chief turned to the others. "The two lieutenants work direct for *Daui* Sau. Their English not so good, but they told support your needs as best they understand. Lieutenant Vu is the plans and intelligence officer. Lieutenant Van Le is the communications officer."

The Chief went down the line. "Mr. Pham works for me, and he civil affairs officer. He watch over public information, schools, and aid stations. He coordinate the self-help projects, too."

The Chief elaborated on the jobs of each man, but beyond the names and titles, most of what he said we either did not understand or could not relate to. However, it was comforting to know that these functions were manned. I could see that, when we were at full strength, there would be a counterpart for each American.

When he had finished, the Chief turned to my team. I stood and formally introduced myself to the group. I gave a little of my personal background: that I had been in-country three months and had a wife and daughter back in Colorado. Then a little on each of the men. "Captain Flint here is also an infantry officer. He is not married but will be as soon as he returns home, to a lovely and wealthy heiress from Pennsylvania. You are all invited to his wedding … just kidding, KC.

"And Peter de Groot here is a genuine bachelor from Boise, Idaho. He's school trained at Fort Huachuca, Arizona, in military communications. Joining us in a few days or so will be an operations sergeant and an army medic. They will round out the team."

I explained that our job was to observe and advise, and not to direct: "Our biggest contribution to you will be getting American assistance to you until your system can do things for itself."

As the meeting adjourned, KC stopped in the doorway of the building and studied the concrete apron outside the conference room. The apron actually extended from the front edge of the building across the yard to the compound wall. It did not reach into the grassy part of the courtyard in front of the villa. In fact as I looked at the apron and the white lines that were painted on it, it dawned on me. The reason half of the courtyard was a concrete apron was that it was a badminton court.

KC looked up. "Badminton, anyone?"

I turned to catch the Chief going out the gate. "*Daui*, is that a badminton court at the end of the courtyard?"

"Yes, it is," he grinned. "You like play?"

"Absolutely. Is there a set around?"

"I have Lieutenant Vu bring you one tomorrow."

"Terrific. Thank you, *Daui*."

We walked back into the villa. "Now that's a very nice development," said KC. "I used to play varsity tennis at the University of Pennsylvania."

"Swell," said Pete with just a hint of sarcasm.

"Sounds like you have challenged me and Pete to a game," I chided.

"Hope your badminton is better than your chess," said KC.

"What's for dinner?" asked Pete.

We discussed the meeting over a meal, which was a lot like lunch, but no one complained. However, there was no telling what I wouldn't do for a little salt. The main condiment for the Vietnamese was *nuoc mam*. It was similar to soy sauce in color but was an extract of fermented fish and salt.

And just to pump it up a little, it was common to add a slice of jalapeño-like pepper to the saucer in which it was served. It was not something that any of us were willing to try—more than once.

I did not realized they had a public affairs officer. I needed to look into that a little more, and it was clear that *Daui* Sau was more than just a company commander. I said. "I think you, KC, need to keep tabs on what Sau is up to. Make him your counterpart."

"Got it. You notice how he handles himself: like there's nothing he hasn't seen or done? He's going to be an interesting character study."

"Well, I guess if you cut your teeth on fighting the Viet Minh and live to talk about it, you have reason for a little attitude. *Daui* Tranh told me that Sau had a wife and family in the North, and the Viet Minh assassinated them all. He opted to relocate in the South after the French pulled out."

Peter asked, "Who were Viet Minh?"

"They were the insurgents forces that fought and defeated the French, resulting in the division of Vietnam," said KC.

"Guess that pretty well explains intense hate for the Vietcong," concluded Peter.

"Pete, I want you to stay tight with these communications people. I want to know more about what goes on in the barracks, and I want to know what kind of backup communications we have—if any. Keep up the daily situation reports to Province. That's your full-time job."

"Roger that."

I was on a roll. Things were firming up. "I'm going to start meeting the community leaders. I'm not sure who they are, but I intend to begin with the religious types first." The three of us were finishing up the conversation. Pete was having dessert of French bread and jam when *Daui* Tranh walked into the dining room. I offered him a seat and a cup of tea.

"No. No. *Merci*. I come to tell you we go on operation in the morning." He smiled.

"Well, that's good news ... Captain Tranh, would you care for a brandy?" KC offered. The Chief's smile broadened, showing all his teeth. He sat down.

"Ong Than, bring four glasses." KC made arm and hand signals when Ong Than appeared in the breezeway door. "I bought a half dozen of these too today ... not exactly snifters, but if you close your eyes and breathe, it's just like down San Francisco." He started to pour four brandies into three-ounce juice glasses when Pete pulled the fourth glass. "Not for me, Thanks."

"What time we leave in the morning—0500? 0600 hours?" I asked.

"No, no. *Sacré bleu*. We Vietnamese are a civilized people. Beside, this is not a combat mission. We leave around 1000 hours and visit a village." He hoisted his glass, took a deep whiff and said, "Cheers ... that what you say?"

★★★

Sometime the next morning, a kelly green Overland truck appeared in front of the compound. A white square was painted on the top. A similar white square was painted over the back doors. In the middle of each white patch was a painted red cross. The interior of the Overland was not equipped as an ambulance but had seats and a cargo bed as standard equipment. By 1000 hours a beat-up old truck about the size of a pickup came to a hault in front of the compound. It was fully equipped with running boards and a pair of headlamps that stuck out like chrome eyeballs. About a dozen soldiers were draped all over it.

Daui Tranh came out of the com shack and joined me and KC standing at the front gate. He had on a soft-billed olive green cap and was carrying a pistol in his side holster.

"We ride in Overland." The Chief opened the door for us to enter.

"Isn't it against the Geneva Convention to use a Red Cross vehicle for tactical operations?" asked KC.

"Not tactical operation. We *visit* Ap Lin village." The *Daui's* eyes nearly disappeared in his toothy grin.

"Right. And that squad of troops just happens to be going to the same village," acknowledged KC. The *Daui* ignored him and motioned to the driver. The Overland headed out of town along the dirt road past the school and the pagoda. At the gas pump we turned right and headed up Route 8.

Villages, like districts, are areas of land. The village town carries the same name as the land area. Smaller population centers are referred to as hamlets. A few kilometers up the road I sensed a change in the environment. The change was subtle in a way that was not immediately identifiable.

""Is that a Christian church off the right?" KC wondered.

"Yes, that is Catholic church. This is Catholic village. It come here from the North at the end of Viet Minh war," said the Chief.

Then there must be two Catholic churches in the district. I was thinking of the church with the howitzers in the front yard.

"Yes. The one across the road from our villa was established when the French were active in the district," the Chief explained. "This one here came with people when they come from the North. The priest in this village works both churches."

"Is that bamboo growing behind the thatched buildings?" asked KC.

"It is sugarcane."

"No kidding. Son of a gun." Most of the homes had a patch of sugarcane growing alongside the hut one place or another.

"Yes. Every Vietnamese wife grows little sugarcane in backyard. It is for her family cooking."

I silently registered that the road shoulders were neatly maintained and that kilometer markers were freshly painted and lettered. *Indeed the Catholic village from the North had a different public image from the rest of the district.*

The Overland pulled off to the side in front of a high-arched concrete bridge. The driver cut the engine, and the Chief jumped out. "This is the border for the district and the province. Across the bridge is Vinh Long Province. We take a walk now."

"Does this road go near the army airfield at Vinh Long?" I asked.

"Yes, it does ... We go this way." The Chief headed down a dirt road. The truck, aka troop carrier had turned left into a dirt road and pulled to a stop about a hundred yards in. The troops were nearly finished off-loading, and some were spreading out into the village town of Ap Lin. The town boasted several single-story public buildings designed in the French provincial architecture. The marketplace was large and stretched out alongside the canal.

Daui Nguyen Tranh, District Chief of Vung Liem, seemed to know everyone, or at least he waved and smiled at nearly everyone he passed along the way. To some he even reached out to shake hands. We proceeded along the edge of the canal out of the built-up area toward the southwest. We passed among the thatched houses that lined both sides of the road. From time to time the *Daui* would point to one of us Americans, and either I or KC or both would smile and greet the individual in Vietnamese: *Chau, Ong,* Hello, sir ... or *Chau, Ba,* Hello, madam ... or, on occasion, *Chau, Co,* Hello, mademoiselle.

Not quite a kilometer down the road a second canal entered the main canal from the southeast. This canal was obviously a feeder from the interior of the village. It was just wide enough for two sampans to pass. Thatched houses were situated on both sides of the water, and a trail, about the width of an oxcart, also, passed along both sides the canal. From a thousand feet in the air only the straight green line of jungle foliage would have been visible.

With a pair of security troops in front and a pair to the rear, the command party turned down the trail. The *Daui* chatted with the citizenry along the way, introducing us as he went. All the villagers wore black pajamas. The only way to tell a man from a woman was that the woman generally had her hair tied in a bun in the back. I discovered that if I greeted every woman with "*Chau, Co,*" regardless of age, I was an instant hit. KC with his puppy-dog eyes picked up on it. What could be a social blunder between Vietnamese was, from an American; flattering, funny, and forgivable. KC was a quick study.

For the next hour or so the three of us politicked our way to a four-way junction with a northeast canal. The density of thatched houses increased around the canal junction. As we drifted into a turn to the northeast, *Daui* Tranh spied an old woman sitting on her heels at the doorway to her thatched home. At his hello she gave him a toothless smile accented by red betel nut stains down her chin. She answered his greeting and held something out to him. As he walked over to her, he reached into his pocket and pulled out his billfold. Whatever she was selling, he bought ten piaster worth. She cackled, and they exchanged quips.

"What did you buy, *Daui?*" asked KC.

"Raffle tickets."

"No joke? In the middle of water world you find raffle tickets?"

"You can't buy, Captain Flint. I buy all she have."

I asked to see them. KC and I looked at the tickets while Daui was talking to several other villagers. The tickets were in a 1½-inch-by 5-inch book of twenty coupons. The paper was as porous as toilet paper. And the print bled so badly that one could hardly tell the difference between a 3 and an 8. The sequenced numbers were ten digits long.

"Holy cow, *Daui*, do you know the probability of you winning anything from this? It's like one in fifty million—that is, of course, if this is a real raffle and these aren't counterfeit," I said.

Daui Tranh took the tickets back and studied them. He looked back at the old lady who sold them to him and smiled. "No, Captain Skeelman ... No, the probability of me winning something is fifty-fifty."

"You don't believe that, do you?" said KC.

"Oh yes, Captain Flint. The probability *is* fifty-fifty." He glanced again at the old lady and looked straight faced around at the little gathering of villagers. "Fifty-fifty—either I win ... or I lose."

Before either of us could respond, he then spoke to the group in Vietnamese and explained the conversation with the Americans. When he reached the punch line he turned to me and KC as he delivered it. The villagers erupted into laughter. We joined in.

KC gave me an aside. "This guy is one hell of a politician. I'm taking notes in case I ever get the bug."

The command group moved on to the northeast and eventually came out on the hardtop road, along which the vehicles were parked. I became aware that the trail security was growing in number and realized that the troops were closing in behind as the party approached the pickup point. The *Daui* may have billed this as a visit, but it was an operation nonetheless. The question was how much of this was precautionary as opposed to necessary.

As we pulled into the district town, I glanced over at the French Catholic Church across from our villa. I had not given the building too much notice since we had been here. It didn't look like a church ... didn't even have a steeple. Besides, the artillery pieces were the dominant point of interest. *The artillery pieces ... they were gone.* The gun positions were there in the churchyard, but they were vacant. The howitzers were gone.

Privte Peter de Groot greeted us from the villa doorway as we came through the gate. Behind de Groot was another American.

"Boss, this is Sergeant First Class William Kuntz. He came in this afternoon with some great toys."

"Welcome aboard, Sergeant Kuntz. Did you bring that jeep out front?" I asked.

"Thank you, sir. Yes, I did ... Compliments of Major Bass," answered Kuntz.

"Didn't bring a radio, by chance?" I glanced at Peter.

"No such luck. But he did bring a refrigerator," said Pete.

Just what I wanted, a refrigerator. But before I could think of something positive to say, KC jumped in. "Hell, we got a radio of sorts. What we didn't have was a refrigerator. Now, all we need is an electrical outlet put in."

"Actually it's kerosene powered," said Kuntz. "Mr. Ledbetter sent it up to us. The Department of State has called for all dependents to be sent home, so I guess they got some domestic equipment coming available. He says we got a stove coming too." It occurred to me that Letha Ledbetter must be going home to the States. I felt sorry for Jake. In the back of my mind I made the mental note: security, nationwide, was eroding.

"My God, just like downtown San Francisco." KC took the sergeant's hand. "Welcome, Sergeant First Class William Kuntz."

CHAPTER NINE

When Religion Gets Political

"Sᴇᴇ ᴡʜᴏ ɪs ᴄᴏᴍɪɴɢ up the path." Ngoc adjusted his dark glasses with both hands. He sat on the straw mat at the end of the room. The boy was surprised and confused, but he had learned not to doubt the blind old monk.

He went to the window beside the entrance to the pagoda. "I see no one, Master ... Wait ... yes, there are two monks coming through the trees."

"Do you know them?"

"The one I have seen, but the other is a stranger." The boy strained his memory. "I believe the one is the abbot from Cang Long to the south, Master."

The master stood and straightened his robes. He reached out to the boy and moved in his direction. "Let us greet our guests."

They stepped through the passageway onto the small veranda and awaited the approach of the two. The boy spoke quietly, describing the guests: fresh shaved heads, the new face taller than the familiar face; both very old, over forty at least. The master smiled—winced a little—but said nothing until the guests were in range. He spoke first. "Peace and welcome to our sanctuary."

"It is I, Master, Tien Van Quan," said the taller of the visitors.

And at that, the blind man dropped the arm of the boy and stepped off the veranda into the arms of Quan. "My son, how wonderful that you have come." They held the embrace a moment.

The two had renewed their casual friendship in the spring of 1963. Each, without the knowledge of the other, made the pilgrimage back to the Citadels of

Hue for the celebration of Buddha's birthday. Their friendship bonded on May 8 when twenty thousand Buddhists were fired on by government troops who feared the religious celebration was becoming a political demonstration. It became a riot. Quan had led the blind man to safety, but when calm was restored, nine people were dead.

The two spent much time together, discovering they had much in common—most especially, dislike and distrust of all Catholics, the Diem government, and all foreigners who supported them. They became involved in the Buddhist political movement, and the two traveled and proselytized the countryside for the next eight months, winding up in Saigon in January 1964.

Quan turned to introduce the abbot of Cang Long. "This is my friend and mentor, Duc To Ngoc." They bowed their greeting.

"I have heard much of your wisdom," said the abbot with a smile. The blind man acknowledged the compliment, then unhesitatingly turned and stepped up onto the veranda. The boy had returned to the great room as soon as his master had released his arm. By the time the master led his guests into the room the boy had the teapot on the burner and cushions arranged around the mat. The lad unobtrusively tended to the guests, first with drink, then, in time, with nourishment; taking silent cues from his master like a runner on second from the third base coach.

The conversations continued on into the afternoon. Ngoc was surprised to learn that his friend had tried to enroll in the National Liberation Front (NLF). In January after a four-day conference in Saigon between eleven sects of Buddhism, the two monks were uniquely inspired to go their separate ways. Suddenly it seemed imperative to Ngoc that he return to the Delta and fight the creeping Catholicism. He had been away too long. On the other hand, Quan had always been more militant. He hated the landowners who had a lock on wealth and privilege. Ngoc suspected that Quan might join the Vietcong, but that was never expressed.

What was even more surprising was that NLF had encouraged Quan to remain in his position as a monk and suggested he would be of more value in the Delta region watching and reporting. Ngoc suspected that the mission also included sowing political dissention. But whatever the mission, his old friend was welcome to stay in Vung Liem as long as he liked.

"You must stay with us for a while and observe the new activity since the Americans have arrived. There was much movement yesterday; trucks with soldiers and big guns moved out of town." He turned toward Quan. "There is a pagoda at the north edge of town close to the main canal. It is used by traveling brothers, but it is now vacant and should serve you nicely."

Quan brightened. "How perfect for observing our enemies. That is most generous of you, Master. Can we reach the site before darkness?"

"Yes, of course. My student will guide you along the back trails to avoid attention. He shall stay until morning to make sure you are settled and oriented." As Ngoc spoke he projected his voice into the room at large, and the boy made ready to travel.

After lengthy thank-yous and exchanges of blessings, the party of three departed, and Ngoc settled down on his cushion. He disciplined his mind to have no expectations, and he entered into deep meditation.

★★★

In front of the villa there were two wells from which all potable water was drawn for the entire compound. Just in case, mess officer KC instructed Ong Than to boil the water used for drinking and for washing fresh greens bought in the marketplace—not that there was much fresh produce. Canned vegetables were available, which made up most of the variety in the team's diet.

Major Bass, at Province, had Lenny add an extra ration request to the province supply run from Saigon. The guys in Tra Vinh saw to it that a chopper flew in once a week to drop off and pick up mail, and there was always something eatable in the run. The refrigerator greatly expanded KC's ability to plan decent meals, but still we ate a lot of rice—a lot of rice.

I sat Sergeant Bill Kuntz down for orientation the first morning after his arrival. I explained to him that *Daui* Sau was the Regional Force company commander and that KC would introduce Sau to him later. "Normally you wouldn't expect a company commander to have a staff, and Sau doesn't—except that the Chief does, and *Daui* Sau uses them for his support. Lieutenant Vu is the planning and operations officer, and he is your counterpart, as you are the operations sergeant. The lines of responsibility are a little confusing because Lieutenant Vu works for the Chief, but does what the *Daui* Sau says."

KC emphasized, "*Daui* Sau is my charge, so you and I need to keep each other in the loop constantly."

I went on, "Our first priority is to find out what these guys do, how they set up their operations, and where they operate. We had a feel for it yesterday, but that was a walk in the park. We know that VC operate in the district. They use the roads and canals at night and seem to be moving with relative impunity. We want to know the routes they take and the activities they engage in as they move about."

Kuntz looked like he wanted to ask a question, but I pressed on.

"I want to know what kind of training program our local regional forces have, if any, and where it is conducted. Our mission is to monitor what the district leadership is doing and advise them on how to do it better. We must direct military and civilian resources to projects that protect the civilian population and promote a prosperous economy." I paused to let Kuntz digest the information.

He leaned back in the vinyl chair. I would later learn that Pudgy Kuntz, as he was known in high school, was just short of eighteen years in military service. He had seen his share of combat in Korea, but, as he said, this Vietnam thing looked to be a different beast. He even commented that these Vietcong behaved more like juvenile delinquents than soldiers with a cause.

I had to agree, "Most are local bad boys. But, hard-core insurgent cadres, who are seasoned from earlier years of conflict with the French, recruit and train these kids. The recruits then get integrated with VC units. They grow up fast and roam the area disrupting government programs and collecting taxes from the people to support Vietcong political objectives. They may look starved and ill-equipped but they'll kill you without hesitation."

Kuntz sat forward in his chair. "Where do we start?"

"I want you to shadow KC for a couple of days until you're familiar with the town and the Vietnamese don't all look alike to you. We'll all be talking daily, and you and KC will discover soon enough what the next action should be. Right now we just want to know what's going on."

I stood and moved toward the porch. "Peter hangs out over at the com shack. Security of the compound is in your hands, Sergeant. I want at least one American in this compound all the time. You coordinate the movements of the individuals in the team. Pete is most often the man in the rear because that's where the radios are, but if he moves out for some reason, you are his backup, so bone up on the radios."

KC and Kuntz followed me down the steps into the courtyard toward the Chief's office. "I'm going to use the jeep today. I plan to visit the Vietnamese monks. Chief tells me there is another pagoda besides the one across from the soccer field."

KC picked it up: "I'll introduce Sergeant Kuntz to *Daui* Sau, and then we'll catch up to Lieutenant Vu." KC motioned to Kuntz, and the two turned left outside the gate. I headed across the courtyard to the conference room.

After the exchange of greetings, I explained to the Chief what I wanted to do. I offered for him to come with me.

He shook his head. "I do not think so. I think it better you meet these leaders by self. I find you an interpreter to help meetings go."

"That's terrific. Thank you. Will that take a while?"

"Oh, no. Interpreter come this morning. I bring him over when he get here." The Chief grinned, and his eyes disappeared.

This was a pleasant surprise, and I was thinking up new possibilities. As I headed back to the villa to wait for the interpreter, three little kids scattered when I entered the courtyard. I had no idea their gender, but I gave them my "lady killer" line.

"*Chau, Co.*" They screamed and laughed and ran for the doorway. *What a trip.*

My thoughts were interrupted abruptly when I entered the villa living room. Two young boys executed rushed bows and disappeared through the dining room. As I checked the sleeping rooms for anything out of place, Ong Than materialized.

"What's going on, Ong Than?" Ong Than began an unhurried stream of Vietnamese, which more or less boiled down to: he had assigned his sons the daily duty to clean and shine the Americans' boots. He then spoke his one and only English word. "OK?"

You had to smile at this elf. Ong Than continued his one-way conversation as he walked around the sleeping room pointing to the laundry bag at the foot of each man's bunk. The gist of it seemed that he wanted to take the laundry bags and wash the clothes.

Now it was my turn to say, "OK." And Ong Than smiled—big smile.

★★★

Sergeant Kuntz walked along with KC, who had acknowledged to me, he was in awe of the sergeant's Combat Infantryman Badge (CIB). The badge is awarded to infantry soldiers who have experienced hostile fire. The badge is the three dimensional image of a musket mounted on a rectangle. Behind the musket is a field of pale infantry blue enamel. A wreath surrounds the entire device.

The two men were headed over to *Daui Sau's*. Reportedly, Sergeant Kuntz got to talking about his past. He had learned his trade in Germany. At Hoenfelds and Graffenvier he drilled in the small unit tactics and weapons proficiency.

In Germany he met his wife. In Germany he had a son. In Germany he came alive and stayed there as long as he could. But, eventually, after five years, he was transferred to Fort Benning, Georgia. The Korean War broke out, still, he continued at the Infantry School on the mortar committee for a couple of years into the war.

When orders came assigning him to the Third Infantry Division, Korea, he sent his pregnant wife and son back to Wurtzberg, Germany, to be with his mother-in-law.

He told KC, "It was the wife's request, and I honored it."

Six weeks after his arrival in Korea he was awarded the CIB, and six months after his wife arrived in Germany she presented him with a little girl. A year later she filed for divorce, and she and the children never returned to the United States.

"Kids live with their mother. I visit from time to time," he said. "Guess you'd call me a loner." He pressed his lips together. "You have kids, Captain?"

"Planning a big wedding as soon as I get back, and you're invited, Sergeant First Class Kuntz."

They both laughed. "Where is the wedding?"

"Pittsburgh. Her father is a bigwig at Pittsburgh Steel. Our families got to be friends when we all lived in Upper Darby."

Kuntz reflected a few moments, then: "My father was in the steel business—Armco Rolling Mills in Middletown, Ohio."

KC's made a new appraisal of the sergeant. "No kidding? Ever think of following in your dad's footsteps?"

"Nah, Dad was disabled in a plant accident. My mom spent most of her waking hours taking care of him. When a judge gave me the choice between jail for stealing a car or enlisting in the army, the army sounded pretty good. Besides, getting away from home made my dad's workman's compensation check go further."

As the two Americans turned into the civil guard barracks, they were met by a young Vietnamese sergeant, who asked in English if KC was Captain Skillman.

"No, I am not," answered KC. "And who are you?"

"I am to be your interpreter. I am to report to the district chief, *Daui* Tranh."

"Man! Sergeant Kuntz, this is almost better than getting a refrigerator."

Both laughed. The young man looked confused. Kuntz said, "What's your name, soldier?"

"I am Sergeant Khe."

"Well, nice to meet you, Sergeant Khe. This is Captain Flint, and I'm Sergeant Kuntz. You get on over to the villa. You're going to make Captain Skillman's day." KC and Kuntz turned back toward the barracks in search of *Daui* Sau.

The Regional Force commander was stretched out in a hammock in front of his apartment. He did not bother to get up as the two Americans approached, but he grinned. "*Comment ça va?*"

"*Chau, Daui*. Looks like life is good today," said KC. "Want you to meet Sergeant Kuntz, who has just joined our team."

Sergeant Kuntz rendered the reclining *Daui* a semismart salute, which the *Daui* did not bother to return. Instead he offered the two straight chairs in front of the door.

KC sat down and asked him, "I notice the 105 artillery pieces are gone from the churchyard. What happened?"

"*Je ne sais pas*, I don't know why. *C'est la guerre*. That's war."

"Has this hurt your operations?"

"Oui. They send mortar maybe." Sau was clearly ambivalent about the loss of indirect fire support.

The conversation struggled along. They learned that ARVN planned to send the district two heavy mortars, but no time was indicated. *Daui* Sau was cool to the idea because the range of the mortars was so much shorter than the howitzers. He had not pushed it.

Kuntz spoke up. "You know, sir, those tubes could be pre-surveyed for locations around the district. We could shift them around from time to time for harassing and interdictory fire. If H & I fire missions were beyond range, displacement time would be minimized. I used to be on the mortar committee at Fort Benning."

Sau's eyes brightened up. "I have no one trained on mortars now."

"What are we talking about here? I can train on everything … 60s … 81s … My specialty is 4.2 inch."

Sau's eyes positively shot sparks. "We get 4.2. You train?"

"You bet."

"I'm so glad I asked," remarked KC. "How soon do you expect them to arrive?"

"I work on now."

The energy picked up as the conversation progressed, and by the time the two Americans got up to leave, *Daui* Sau was out of his hammock and planning what villages they would survey.

★★★

As promised, the Chief brought Sergeant Khe to me as soon as the man arrived in the compound. We sat down and engaged in chitchat to get a feel for the translation skills of the young sergeant. Sergeant Khe had studied English in a Saigon high school. He was drafted into service to his country and was working in My Tho when *Daui* Tranh contacted him. The Chief immediately arranged his transfer.

After a short while I was satisfied that, if I stayed in simple thoughts, the kid could do a fair job. I dropped in on the Chief to thank him and tell him my plans to meet the Vietnamese monks this morning.

"By the way, Ong Than has taken away our laundry. Is that part of the deal?"

The Chief showed teeth. "Yes and no. Madam Than will wash American laundry, one man every day."

"Got the picture. How about the boys and the boots?"

"Clean boots every day."

"Does Ong Than make more money for that?"

More teeth. "No. Not necessary, but extra service maybe worth extra money—if you like."

"I like. Thanks, *Daui*."

I had started out the door when the Chief said as an afterthought, "Oh, Lieutenant Vu bring badminton game today -- no charge." Grinning, he motioned me away with the back of his hand.

"OK, Sergeant Khe. Let's go visit a Vietnamese monk." I buckled on my web belt and pistol as we walked out of the villa. I asked Khe if he could drive a jeep.

He hesitated and then gave a tentative, "Yes, sir."

The doubt was not lost on me. "Why don't we just do a test run? Do you know the way to the pagoda?"

"Which one?"

"How many are there?"

"Two Vietnamese, one Cao Dia, and one Cambodian."

"Are they all Buddhist?"

"Oh, yes. The Cao Dia is very small sect for wealthy Buddhist I think. The Cambodian is Buddhist, but it is for Cambodian."

"Interesting. All right, let's go to the nearest Vietnamese pagoda. You drive."

We climbed in the jeep. I was pleased to note that Joe Bass had seen to sandbags filled with dirt and placed in the floorboards. *Thank you, Major Joe Bass.* Sergeant Khe started into town, much to my surprise, and then turned left into an alley that I had not realized was there. The alley soon widened and broke out into a dirt road that cut across a huge rice paddy. Before we completely left the natural vegetation, Sergeant Khe turned right, down an extra-wide footpath which barely accommodated the jeep—a little too close for my comfort.

A gray concrete building came into view. It was square with a narrow porch in front and a wide entrance set back in the front wall. A roof extended over the entrance another five or six feet and was supported at the corners by two columns at the edge of the porch. Khe pulled the jeep up to the porch. I stepped out. No one seemed to be around. Khe turned the jeep around while I walked over to the entrance. There was no doorway at the back of the recessed entrance, but rather two doorways inside the entrance opening to either side.

As I hesitantly approached the entrance, a Vietnamese monk appeared from within. He stepped into the open, blocking any further advance by me. His head was shaved billiard-ball close, and he wore a yellow robe wrapped around his body with the tail end draped over his left shoulder.

I gave him a big smile. *"Chau, Ong."*

"*Chau, Ong.*" The monk responded without a smile.

Sergeant Khe had dismounted the jeep and by now stood beside me.

"OK, Sergeant, translate for me. I am new in town, and want to come by and meet the community leaders."

Khe translated, and the monk replied. He did not smile. Khe looked at me. "He is not your friend."

"Is that what he said?"

"No. He said that he was not a leader in the community and that he was just a student of Buddha looking for ways to serve others."

"You're probably right. He is certainly not being friendly, but that's *my* judgment. You are the translator, and I'll be the interpreter." I turned to the monk. "We will be living in the district town and would certainly like to be of assistance to you. If there is ever anything we can do for you, I hope you will give us the opportunity to serve …"

Khe translated. The monk bowed slightly, but did not speak or smile.

"… and I, also, hope that, if we see problems, we can call on you for your assistance."

Khe translated. The monk nodded formally, but, still, did not smile.

"I am pleased to meet you. I hope we can meet again." Khe translated. The monk put his hands together and inclined his head forward. He was gone before I was back in the jeep.

Khe cranked up the jeep, and pulled straight out on to the trail. I looked back over my shoulder. "That went well, don't you think?"

Sergeant Khe glanced sideways at me. "He is not your friend."

"You got that right, Sergeant."

When the jeep pulled up to the compound, the badminton game was already in progress. Peter and KC were going at it hot and heavy. Kuntz was sitting on the sideline with a little girl hanging around his neck. Two other children were sitting on either side of him taking turns poking a finger at his arms and laughing. Pudgy Kuntz was blond with a blonds' complexion. And while there was hair on his head, the graying blond color gave him the look of baldness. He was not in the trimmest shape for an infantry sergeant, and he looked heavier than he actually was. In fact the children saw him as a kind of blond Buddha with yellow hair on his arms.

I stepped out of the jeep and turned back to Khe with instructions to take the jeep back to the barracks for the night. "You and I will head out about ten in the morning." I walked over to Kuntz.

The sergeant had been in-country maybe twelve days, and only the last three or four had he been in the steamy tropical environment of the Mekong Delta. He was sunburned—his face not so badly, since the hat had protected him, but his arms were red. The children had discovered that when you pressed his red skin, it turned white for a moment and then back to red. Red was strange enough, but turning red to white and back again, that was something marvelous—to be repeated over and over. Their giggling stopped immediately when they saw me coming. And, when I kept coming, what had been more affection than Pudgy Kuntz had experienced in many years, ended. The children scrambled down from beside the golden Buddha and ran back to their apartment, laughing and screaming all the way.

"Am I that scary?" I made a face at the kids, which brought more screams and laughter. I sat down next to Kuntz. "You any good at this sport?"

"Not really. 'Bout the only thing I play is the radio. Captain KC looks pretty hot, but Pete is giving him a run for the money."

We watched the two men battle it out, but long tall KC was a bit overwhelming for little Peter. Kuntz and I warmed up a few minutes later, and then KC and Kuntz took on me and Peter. It was a pretty good match. After two long sets, one each between us, KC declared dinnertime, and we all took turns washing up for Ong Than's cooking. Eventually, this evening badminton ritual became the volleyball equivalent for the province team.

The table conversation was animated. Dinner of rice and something took second on the interest scale. It had been a good day. I was pleased to hear about the mortars, and everyone was pleased about Ong Than's family support plan.

I suggested to KC we expand the monthly house bill. I decided one pound a person was good for the laundry and fifty piaster per man per month for the boots. We would pay it lump sum to Ong Than each month.

"A dollar and a half sure doesn't seem like much," said Kuntz.

"Well, it isn't by our standards. But you figure the rice mill owner here in the district probably doesn't make more than twenty or so pounds a month himself. It wouldn't be a healthy *social* structure if the *economic* structure paid the wife of an enlisted soldier more money doing laundry than the rice mill owner earned in the same year."

"I never looked at it that way. Still ... feels like we're cheating them," said Kuntz.

"Stinkin' thinkin'," said KC, excusing himself from the table. "Come on, boss. Time for your nightly chess lesson."

"You wish." I excused myself and went into the living room to set up the chessboard.

KC poured the brandy. "Just like downtown San Francisco," he said not quite to himself.

✯✯✯

Chopper blades whop-whopped over the villa at "07-early" the next morning. I stepped out onto the porch in time to see the tail of the aircraft drop below the tree line toward the soccer field. I headed out the gate to check the jeep and found that, as ordered, Sergeant Khe had delivered the vehicle on time. I thought about going back to get my pistol, but blocked it out of my mind and continued on. The moment I came into view of the Huey sitting on the ground, an American soldier hopped out of the craft with his weapon and duffel bag. By the time I arrived at the entrance to the field, the bird was off the ground, and the soldier was walking to the road. I drove through the gate and up to the master sergeant.

"Good morning, Sergeant." I stepped out of the jeep.

The sergeant dropped his bag and saluted. "Master Sergeant Joe Santana reporting for duty, sir."

I took his salute smartly. "Captain Ed Skillman, Master Sergeant. Welcome to Vung Liem."

"Thank you, sir." He tossed his duffel effortlessly into the back of the jeep. We drove out the gate and turned back to town.

"That a coconut plantation?" asked Santana.

"Yeah, it is. Actually, it was a banana plantation, too, but neither are worked these days … I take it you're our resident medic?"

"That's me."

We pulled up to the compound, and parked the jeep next to the guard post. I led Santana into the courtyard. Pete and KC were standing on the porch supervising a Vietnamese carpenter who was measuring the villa windows.

"Men, meet Master Sergeant Joe Santana. Looks like we got us a doc." Santana shook hands with everyone as they moved into the living room. Sergeant Kuntz joined in from the dining room. My team was now complete and assembled. I looked around the room. They looked strong, and I was proud to be a part of it.

"Sergeant Kuntz, I would like you to take over Doc's orientation. Start with the house. Let him know everyone's job operationally and administratively. Doc, your admin job is the team's health."

Santana smiled. "That's good, 'cause I brought 250 malaria tablets for your weekly living pleasure."

"The guy catches on quick. KC, find that civil affairs man: the one who works for Ong Hoa Hoang. I think he is the start point for Santana. And I'm headed out to meet a Cambodian monk."

KC walked out with me. "The carpenter here is putting up screens on the villa. I'm impressed. The Chief works in wonderful ways."

"He does, doesn't he? See if you can scout up some mosquito nets someplace. Try both Vietnamese and American channels. Screens are good, but nets are even better."

"I'm on it."

Sergeant Khe was standing by the jeep when I walked out the gate. "Good morning, sir."

"Good morning, Sergeant. You know where to find this Cambodian monk?"

"Yes, sir." Khe wasn't really a soldier. He wasn't trained as a soldier, but was awarded the rank for his language skills. Military protocol escaped him. Khe jumped in the jeep, and we headed out of town. As we passed by the coconut plantation, I asked about the type of pagoda way back in the trees.

"It's Vietnamese." The familiarity in Khe's response and manner bristled me a little, but, upon reflection I got over it. If this man was going to speak as me, maybe the familiarity was a good thing.

We pulled up onto the hardtop of Highway 8 and headed southeast. After about half a click, Khe turned into an overgrown road where once vehicles had traveled, but not for a long time. The road was rutted, and progress was slow. After about five minutes the vegetation thinned, and we pulled up in front of a building shaped entirely different from the one we'd visited yesterday. This pagoda was painted and ornate. It seemed to be made of dark wood. I walked up to the porch, but did not step onto it, just knocked on the pillar with three double raps. We waited.

I was about to knock again, when an old man came out onto the porch. His gray hair had been shaved, but not recently. He squinted at us through steel-rimmed glasses. His robe was dark rust-brown. "*Chau, Ong,*" I said.

The old man smiled and said something. I glanced at Khe. The sergeant had a completely blank look on his face. "He is speaking Cambodian. I do not think he understands Vietnamese."

I'm thinking, *now what?* The old man motioned for us to follow him into the pagoda. I was hesitant, but Khe moved right out, so I followed them. We entered a large room with smaller rooms off to the sides like alcoves. There was a skylight at the top of a pitched roof, which gave the room daylight in the center of the building. The old monk directed us into the nearest alcove, and he sat down on a small chair. There was one other chair, which he offered to me. I had no sooner sat down, then a young boy came into the room, also dressed in the robes of a monk. He bowed low to the old monk, and took a place behind his chair.

I spoke. "I am an American, and I have come to live in Vung Liem."

Khe translated. The boy hesitated and then spoke softly to the old man. The old man spoke a few words and the boy translated. Khe spoke back to the boy. They exchanged several times. "He says welcome to Mekong and Vinh Binh. He hopes you will enjoy your stay."

"All that conversation and nothing more than that?"

"I have trouble understanding the boy," said Khe.

"Tell him I am calling on the leaders of the community to show that I am a friend."

Khe translated. The boy asked a question. Khe responded. The boy asked again. I actually couldn't tell if he asked the same question or a different one. The old man continued to smile which was a good sign.

Finally, the boy spoke to the monk. The old man continued with his unreadable smile. He now looked me straight in the eye and held the gaze. I concentrated on not looking away. The old man turned slightly to speak over his shoulder. The boy translated, and the old man watched Khe's face closely. Khe asked the boy something in return. The boy turned to the monk, who responded to the boy, then turned back to me with a smile that said: *Your move.*

"What's going on?"

"He says that if you are his friend, you will pay respects to Buddha in this pagoda."

Now I'm comfortable in my own skin. I know who I am, and I know who is my Peace and my Salvation. I had been active in church youth groups in high school and had taught Sunday school in college. I am secure in my convictions. "How would he like me to do that?"

Without going to the boy, Khe said, "He says you show respect if you place a burning incense stick in the altar before Buddha."

"Show me the way to start." Khe stepped into the center room and took two sticks of incense from a small brass container attached to the wall. He looked around for a light. The boy monk approached and lit the sticks. Khe handed one stick to me, and approached the statue of Buddha slowly with his head down. I did the same moving beside him, although I did not bow so much as just lowered my head. We placed the sticks in a sand-filled urn held by the hands of the sitting Buddha. We slowly backed away.

The old man met us as we turned back into the entrance. He was smiling smugly as he led us out onto the porch. The old monk spoke. I spoke. Khe spoke. No one understood a word, but we all understood mutual respect.

My sergeant and I drove back out onto the highway in silence. As we pulled onto the hardtop, Khe asked, "You are Christian?"

I had to smile. "You're wondering how a real Christian can do that."

"Yes."

"Khe, I do not have to be a Buddhist to respect the religion. Because I respect a religion does not mean I embrace that religion. Buddhism and Christianity have many things in common. Evidence is that Jesus traveled in the plains of India and the Tibetan plateau." Khe looked at me with skepticism.

"Researchers suggest that much of the teachings of Jesus can be found in parallel writings located in Buddhist temples along the Silk Road. If the old monk is as wise as he looked, he knows that too."

Khe drove in silence for a few minutes, then he said, "You did a good thing today, Daui."

"Well, thank you, Sergeant. I guess that really depends on what the monk thinks. He may conclude that he tricked the American into worshiping his deity and that the American is shallow. But that's his business and none of mine."

We turned into the dirt road to town. I was thinking that our next visit would be to the Catholic priest. The jeep pulled up to the gate. "Same arrangement for tomorrow as today, Sergeant."

"Yes, sir." Sergeant Khe headed over to the barracks.

I walked into the courtyard to see a small group of Vietnamese at the side of the villa looking into the breezeway. Ong Than had set up shop in the breezeway from the first day. He had placed three charcoal burners on the edge of the walk, along with a low table and a large crock of water. Clean dishes were stored in the dining room in the one other piece of furniture that came with the house—a china cabinet.

At this moment, KC was clearly agitated with the little barefoot man in black pajamas. Ong Than now stood in front of the captain listening to the giant deliver his wrath. The onlookers were in awe. In a warrior world of the seventeenth century, one would expect the little man's head to roll.

"Afternoon, Captain Flint. What seems to be the trouble?"

Then I saw the gleaming white stove sitting on the edge of the walk next to Ong Than's little table. Clearly the device was not new, but sitting there in contrast to the simple tools of the seventeenth century; it looked like something from the moon.

"This insufferable little man is refusing to get rid of his charcoal burners now that we have a stove."

"When did we get the stove?"

"It came this afternoon with a convoy that brought in three 4.2-inch mortars. Jake Ledbetter sent it."

"The mortars are in too? That's great news," I said.

"Yeah, Kuntz is over helping them set up now. They're going to place them inside the barracks compound for better security." KC had begun to settle down. And Ong Than, taking advantage of the distraction, busied himself in the breezeway.

"What's Ong Than's problem?"

"These people just won't learn anything new. He doesn't want to use the stove since he never did it before."

"I should have brought Sergeant Khe in with me. Maybe he could help convince the man."

"Wouldn't have done any good at this point. The man's as hardheaded as a Dutchman." We were standing away from the breezeway. KC had turned to face me when I arrived so his back was to the kitchen area.

Ong Than approached from KC's rear and reached up to gently pull his shirt. "*Daui.*"

KC turned around to the wrinkled, smiling face of Ong Than. The old soldier pointed at the stove. While we were talking he had lit the three charcoal burners and placed them on top of the stove covering the stove burners. He was now preparing dinner, quite proud of himself and his transition into the modern age.

Long, tall KC looked down on teeny-weeny Ong Than, shrugged, and, with a deep sigh ending in a smile, he winked at the old man.

"Hell, boss. Let's play some badminton. Dinner's not for another half an hour."

CHAPTER TEN

Steel Magnolias

THE VISIT TO THE Catholic priest was postponed. Instead, KC had invited the civil affairs officer, Ong Pham, to come by the villa and brief the team on his activities. I decided that Sergeant Khe would be better utilized getting the details straight from Ong Pham. Besides, I wanted to hear the story firsthand. As it turned out that was a good decision.

Pham revealed that the district plan was to build nine new grade schools—at least one in each of the villages. It was a self-help program. Villages and hamlets throughout the provinces were encouraged to identify projects in which they were willing to invest their own time and skills. The government would provide the materials and special talent where necessary. The villagers would provide the labor and common skills.

Vung Liem already had completed a middle school on the edge of the district town—actually it was more of a renovation. And one of the grade schools was about to open. Two others were under construction. Their biggest problem seemed to be the slow delivery of building supplies.

In addition to the schools, the villagers had voted for a series of first aid stations to be built. Several were in existence, but the problem again was getting medical supplies. The self-help master plan called for a maternity clinic, but no action was scheduled anytime soon to get that going.

The briefing ended, and I looked around the room. There were some fertile possibilities here. "Doc, you got your work cut out for you."

Santana was ahead of me. "I understand now, why I got all the medical supply contacts as I came through the New Arrival Orientation. I couldn't figure out how I would possibly need all those medical supplies for a five-man team. I see that we can help with stocking some of those Vietnamese medical inventories."

I wanted to visit the new schools, and needed KC to clear the security requirements with *Daui* Sau.

"What kind of response do you expect?" KC asked.

"I am interested in the areas in the vicinity of the schools, and whether we can just go in, or whether he thinks we need an armed detail to accompany us," I said. "If we need security to go in, the chances are that those schools are not going be finished very quickly—much less have students. We should focus on the places that are reasonably secure. We will try to precede *development* with *security*."

"You're right, boss," said KC. "Most of the Regional Force actions are about opening the roads keeping the villages connected to the main highway. You know that *visit* we made a couple weeks ago—the one with the Chief riding in his ambulance?"

Ong Than showed up with some hot coffee and, invisibly, freshened the cups.

KC went on, "Kuntz just happened to learn it was a *road opening* operation. VC had scared people off those roads for a couple of months. They cut the hamlets off from the village—kept people from easily going to market."

Kuntz nodded agreement.

"It literally broke down their contact with the outside world. Isolated hamlets are easily manipulated. They think their government doesn't care and can't respond. In fact, there seem to be a number of roads shut down for a long time."

It pleased me that the men were getting the picture. KC even brought up the next point of focus: opening roads. "What about night operations, KC? And how are those mortars coming, Sergeant?"

KC said, "They don't really run patrols or ambushes. They establish roadblocks and checkpoints at intersections of roads and canals."

"As for the mortars," Sergeant Kuntz chimed in, "I think they can cover the district from four village locations that are easily accessible from Highway 8. We surveyed the barracks and Ap Lin Village. We'll survey the parish and one other village to be decided. The gun crews have accuracy problems and need more training."

I turned to the room in general. "Ong Pham, this is very informative, and we thank you. I think we can be of help in expediting your plans. Doc here will be working very closely with you. As soon as we figure out how best to proceed, Doc will come see you."

We were done there for the day, so I sent Sergeant Khe with Doc for the afternoon. Doc took the jeep, and would let Pham show him, firsthand, what he had just revealed. I chose Peter as their driver. "That work for you, Peter?"

"You bet," said Pete, coming alive. Hanging around the com shack could get mighty boring. Peter de Groot was up for a little action. The briefing broke down as Santana led the four out onto the porch.

I looked at Kuntz and KC. "Here's what I think, KC. The security is too static around here. My guess is that the VC wander around on the roads and canals almost at will, and just avoid the roadblocks unless there're looking for trouble."

"Sounds like it. Anyway, for sure, they are not putting out ambushes on any regular basis."

"Well, I want to change that. Suggest to *Daui* Sau that we put ambushes on the road to the Cambodian pagoda tonight. See what happens." I looked at Sergeant Kuntz. "Let's get your mortar crews used to putting rounds in the tube. Have them ready to send illumination rounds over the pagoda."

"I like it," said Kuntz.

✯✯✯

Master Sergeant Jose Santana waited at the jeep while Pete went back to get his pistol. Joe was born in New York City. At 33 years he was a good-looking man—the Latin lover type. He had black hair and brown eyes with a great smile. Women loved him, it seemed, and he endeavored to prove that with every unmarried woman he met. He was well built, five foot ten and around 185 pounds.

When Joe was two years old his mother returned to her parents' home in Puerto Rico. But she went back to New York after a couple of years to get a job and send money home ... which she did. Joe never knew his father. His grandparents raised him in a loving environment, but Joe was determined to leave PR the first chance.

That first chance was the Korean War. He lied about his age, and enlisted. When he took the GED test after Basic, he scored very high—high enough to qualify him for the medical corps. That sounded a lot better than infantry, so he signed up. And he signed up four more times. He loved his job.

Now, here he stood fourteen years later in Vietnam. This was going to be a great opportunity.

Ong Pham said something. Sergeant Khe translated. "Are you married, Sergeant Joe?"

"Oh yes. Got a wife and six kids in Puerto Rico." He spoke with a Hispanic accent which he made little effort to improve.

"Six children?" Sergeant Khe expressed mild amazement.

"That's right."

"Boy, you must miss them." Khe translated for Pham, whose eyes widened noticeably as the two spoke.

"Yeah, I do, but my wife is glad I'm gone. She says every time I get near her, she gets pregnant." He grinned. Sergeant Khe laughed and translated for Pham, who joined the laughter.

Pete came up. "What's so funny?"

"Ah, I was just telling them that my wife sent me out to repopulate Vietnam 'cause I had already done enough damage in Puerto Rico." Santana laughed at his own joke. "Let's go."

Pham and Khe rode in the back. Pete drove. As they headed out to the main road, Pham pointed to a small building near the middle school. Khe translated. "That is our main aid station. We can walk there another time. We will visit the new station in Ech."

They pulled out onto the hardtop and turned right. They drove about ten more minutes past the Catholic village to the place where the Chief had ended the "orientation visit" for me and KC. The hamlet was called Ech. Prompted by Pham, Pete turned left onto a dirt road and then into the front yard of the second permanent building. The village was bigger than the permanent buildings. The other buildings were scattered, thatched structures which lined narrow little trails off both sides of the main dirt road.

To the right of where the jeep parked was the third permanent building. It was much smaller, about twenty-five feet square, made of adobe-type walls on a concrete slab base. It had two rooms, the front room a little larger than the back room. Over the doorway was a sign in Vietnamese and the Red Cross symbol. There were windows in the center of each of the other three walls.

"This aid station finish for some weeks, but aid worker only come twice because he not enough medicine," Pham apologized.

Doc looked around the sparsely furnished room—a few straight chairs, a small table, and a locked wooden medicine cabinet. In the back room were a larger table and two chairs.

"This will work good." Santana cast an appraising eye around the rooms. "We'll need a screen or door or something to provide privacy to the back room. Tell the village chief to announce sick call day after tomorrow."

Santana suddenly turned to Pham. "Can you come with me?"

Ong Pham's mouth worked, but no sound came out. He finally responded. Sergeant Khe translated.

"Yes. I am honored to accompany the doctor." Ong Pham's demeanor noticeably brightened. It seemed to have dawned on him that he must now introduce the Americans to the village chief. Pham would inform him that the American doctor and Ong Pham would conduct a sick call in two days. Pham was a person of importance now.

Sergeant Khe interpreted Pham's excitement. "I will get the village chief right away."

"How you going to run a sick call without medicine?" Pete pointed out.

"Not everything in my duffel bag is clothing, ya know? Besides, most of a sick call is telling people how to take care of themselves and assuring them that whatever they have is treatable. By the end of sick call, I'll have a good idea of what special meds I'll need. Hopefully, the orders I place will be filled by the time I come back for the next sick call. You need to help me open communication channels that get me to my sources."

"All I know is the radio frequency to Province Team," said Pete, dubiously.

"That's a start, but there are others, and we'll find them out."

Pete watched Doc's face suddenly brightened. Ong Pham was returning with the village chief, and in his shadow was a young Vietnamese woman. Master Sergeant Joe Santana drew up two inches in height. Not caring who saw, he flashed the Errol Flynn grin, and melted the girl in her tracks.

Ong Pham made the introductions. Sergeant Khe translated in the background. But, Joe Santana never took his eyes off the young lady as greetings were exchanged.

"And this is Co Mae. She is schoolteacher in this village." Pham indicated for the girl to step forward. She was dressed in the classic female dress of Vietnam, the *ao dai*. The bodice is form-fitted, from the stiff high collar to the waist. The sleeves are long and fitted also. The color is usually a pastel, and in this case it was pale yellow. The skirt amounts to two panels that drop from the waist, front and rear, falling to ankle height. Beneath the split skirt is a pair of billowy trousers either black or white: Co Mae wore white trousers. Hanging down her back from the chinstrap around her slim neck was a conical straw hat that didn't quite cover her straight black hair. She was lovely like a doll.

From lowered eyes she nodded to each of the members of the party as Ong Pham repeated the names.

Pete said, "Um ... 'lo."

Sergeant Khe spoke in Vietnamese, and she smiled demurely. Joe held out his hand palm up. "Hello, young lady."

She hesitated, then quickly passed her hand over his fingers in a way that he could not grip her hand. "Bonjour, Sergeant," with eyes down, and ever so slight a smile…

Pham said, "Co Mae asked can Americans teach English classes if they going to be here a while."

Khe translated, and Santana, with a huge smile, said. "I am sure something can be worked out."

The Vietnamese discussed this for a few moments while Joe and Pete studied Co Mae in every detail. When the discussion concluded, Ong Pham and Sergeant Khe crawled into the back of the jeep. The chief and Co Mae stepped back as Joe swung into the command seat. All waved and the jeep headed back to district town.

It was silent in the vehicle for quite a while. They passed the Catholic parish and were turning into the dirt road at the gas pump when Santana broke the silence. "Don't you just love the delicate beauty of these Vietnamese women?"

"I don't know about all of them, but I do think I'm in love with one of them," Pete sighed with a silly smirk.

"That's the trouble with you, Private. You gotta think bigger if you're going to be noncommissioned officer material. The way I see it, where there's one 'Lovely' in this little ole district, there's got to be more."

Our badminton had already begun when they pulled into the villa courtyard. Ong Pham said his good-bye and disappeared through the gate.

As soon as I saw them, I turned my racket over to Kuntz. "How'd it go?"

"Great. We scheduled a sick call in Ech for the day after tomorrow … and thanks for the use of Sergeant Khe. Could not have gotten started without him."

Santana sat down on the bench against the classroom wall to discuss the events of the day. Pete picked up a racket and joined up with Kuntz to once more try at making the string-bean officer cry *uncle*.

The subject of Co Mae did not come up until suppertime. Then the whole episode was repeated with sound effects and animation. The idea of English lessons struck a harmonic chord when doc had first mentioned it earlier. I had been mulling it around for the last hour.

I liked the way things were shaping up. But looking around the table at four virile young men and their continuing conversation about Co Mae, it was time for a "health and safety" speech.

"Before we go any further, I need to have a little explicit conversation with you all. There are a couple habits which we 'sort of' perform that need to be formalized.

"As of now, I am establishing them as hard, fast rules for the team. Follow these few rules, and you're free to get as creative as you want on your job. Break these rules, and you'll be gone on the first carrier out of here. For these rules, there are no second chances." I was deadly serious, and looked every man in the eye before I continued.

"First, do not leave this compound without your sidearm. If you don't want to carry the weapon issued to you, go over to the armory, and check out the kind that you want to carry—and carry it. Just switch back to your issued weapon when you are reassigned out of Vung Liem." I paused to let that sink in.

"Second, do not leave this town alone. The only place you can go alone in the jeep is to the soccer field when an armed bird is coming in. Otherwise, you travel in pairs, at least. Your counterpart, obviously, counts if you are both armed."

I looked over at Santana, suppressed a smile, and went on. "Third, there will be no messing with any of the women in this district. I mean it—no fraternizing, no public displays of affection, nothing. Anything more intimate than social contact will be deemed unacceptable. To be safe, be in a public place, or at least have more than one other person present in any encounter. If any of you feel your urges are becoming uncontrollable, come see me, and we will find a mission that gets you out of town for a few days."

I looked around the table into every eye again. "There is no quicker way to compromise our mission here, than for one of us to get tangled up with someone's daughter. Any questions?"

After another appropriate pause and no questions, I returned to the proactive. "OK. KC, I want you to go to Saigon tomorrow. Put the Day-Glo orange panel out in the morning, and see what happens. When you get to Saigon, go to MACV and USOM headquarters. See what they have for English as a Second Language courses. Santana, if you have some contacts that will help expedite your supply lines for the aid stations, give them to KC. Let him run them down. Nothing like putting a face on the contact."

The conversation continued as we explored the day's adventures and the possibilities they held. Things were about to break up when the Chief arrived. "Hello, my American friends."

"*Chau, Daui.* Have a seat. What's up?"

As I greeted the Chief, the enlisted men stood, led by Santana. "Excuse us, sir. These guys have got to show me this badminton thing if I'm going to be a card-carrying member of the team."

Daui Tranh waited a moment for the room to clear, then said, "We go on operation tomorrow."

"Outstanding! Care for a cup of tea? Where and when?"

The Chief shook his head, no, to the tea.

KC jumped in. "Want me to stay home tomorrow?"

I deliberately ignored KC, and stayed with the Chief. "How about a cordial of brandy?"

The Chief showed teeth, and his eyes disappeared.

"I have just offered up a nip of your brandy, Captain Flint. Might just as well pick up a new bottle while you're in Saigon."

I looked at KC: he got it.

I turned back to the Chief. "The new bottle will be on me."

KC poured a round of brandy. "Just like downtown San Francisco," he mumbled.

★★★

A mortar round dropping down the tube, striking the firing pin and exploding out the muzzle has a very distinct sound—like *kachunk*. Those who know the sound know also that this is a high-angle weapon, and they have a few seconds to find cover before the round reaches the peak of its trajectory and descends on its target. Experienced combat veterans that they were, both sergeants were already under the bunks and up against the walls before the pop of the flares. The 4.2 illumination round was particularly effective because the height of the flight angle gives the burning flare a little added hang time.

I watched through the window as the horizon lit up to the south. "I think we may have compensated for the loss of those 105s."

KC nodded.

Bill Kuntz crawled out from under his bunk. "I should have known what that was. I set the damn things up myself." He looked a little embarrassed.

Santana thought of the incident as a demonstration of his combat awareness—which it was. Pete recalled his earlier experience with 105s firing and glanced at the two NCOs as they pulled themselves together. He knew he was in seasoned company, and it felt good.

★★★

The next morning came quickly and was unusually busy. Pete drove KC down to the soccer field to lay out the orange panel. I reviewed some operating procedures with Kuntz. "Keep twenty-five yards between us as we travel unless the vegetation is dense. Make certain there's a round in the chamber and the weapon is on safe when we leave the compound."

"Do we know where we are headed?"

I glanced at my watch. "No. Chief said to meet him at the gate at seven, which is in ten minutes. You ready?"

"Let's go." We hooked up our web belts, and Kuntz slung his carbine over his shoulder.

KC watched us from the breakfast table. "Be careful out there."

"You're the one that needs to be careful. Stay too long in that Saigon air-conditioning, and you'll catch pneumonia."

The Chief met them at the gate. Today, he wore a bush hat and looked like Stewart Granger in *Snows of Kilimanjaro*. He carried a carbine on his shoulder. "We travel by boats, today." He strode out toward town and the marketplace. "The village we visit is on the River Ca Chien. It is at the southeast edge of the district."

"Is there no road to the village?" I asked.

"Yes. We walk out on the road. Trucks meet us at highway on way back."

We passed by the Vung Liem Marketplace, and the road began a gentle slope down to the canal. Along the bank of the canal was a landing, parallel to the shore. Perpendicular to the landing was a short pier extending from the center of the landing out into the water. Two sampans, loading eight or nine men each, were tied up to the landing on either side of the pier. As soon as the troops saw the Chief, they hustled up the loading. The Chief hopped in the front boat. I pointed Kuntz to the trail boat and jumped in with the Chief.

The sampans were thirty-some feet long and, maybe, ten or twelve feet wide. They accommodated ten men easily. The pilot was a little Vietnamese man in black pajamas. He wore a conical straw hat, and his trousers were rolled up above his knees. He was barefoot. There was some sort of engine in the stern of the boat that gave torque to a long driveshaft with a propeller at the end. The pilot manned the tiller, as one of the soldiers threw off the bowline and jumped aboard. The sampans moved out into the main stream of the canal.

The Chief and I sat side by side facing the front of the boat. "What was all the sound and light last night?" I said.

"Ambush on road to Cambodian pagoda kill three VC. Maybe two more hit, but they escape." The Chief did not look all that pleased.

"That's terrific."

"Maybe yes, maybe no. VC killed were young boys from this area. People not be happy about this."

"Well, those boys and the people don't need to support the VC."

"Maybe have no choice."

"*Daui*, we always have a choice."

"Maybe people not see that clearly. VC come, take rice, take young men, kill anyone who not agree. Choice is *life or death*, not *support or not support*."

"But, *Daui*, to choose *life* without freedom is no life."

The conversation was abruptly interrupted when a large gunboat pulled into the junction of the canal with the river. It was the same size as a province gunboat, but it looked in a lot better shape and certainly was a lot better armed. An American in fatigue uniform stood on the bow deck. He shouted out something, but the sound of the gunboat engines drowned out any possible exchange as the boats passed. The lieutenant said something more, and then flipped a salute over the sunglasses and big smile. I returned the fellow knight's greeting. There was something vaguely familiar about the man, but the feeling quickly passed.

The sampans picked up speed in the current. At water level, the depth and width of the river were a little surprising. It was wider than the Hudson River at West Point—and this was only one of three, same-size arteries, of the Mekong River. The banks, filled with lush vegetation, slid by rapidly, and in a fast thirty minutes the sampans angled into a small canal entrance. About two hundred yards into the canal, a T-shaped dock reached out into the stream. The sampans avoided the dock and beached on either side of it. Soldiers moved to the front of the boat and jumped onto the beach. A group of five quickly formed and moved over the hill leading up from the beach. I followed the Chief. Kuntz stayed with the trail party.

As we crested the slope, the Chief said, "This is the village of O Lac. The people here are from the North like Ap Chanh, the sugarcane village."

I could see out into a cleared area, which had, as its centerpiece, a large thatch-roofed pavilion. The area was unpaved, and if it was a marketplace, it was not in business at this time. No one was in sight.

"Is this a Catholic parish also?"

"Not really. They came as Catholics, but they do not participate in the church events in the district."

I unsnapped my holster flap. We walked through the market area and down a rutted dirt road that had not been traveled by anything but an oxcart for a long time. A woman holding a child stood in the doorway of their thatched house. They did not smile. The child did not laugh. Fear was palpable. The Chief waved and spoke to another woman. She made no response, whatsoever.

That was spooky. I looked back at Sergeant Kuntz. He was carrying his carbine at the ready. The Chief walked slowly along the road. No one came out, and only a few looked on from the safety of their houses.

A second group of soldiers moved passed the command group and out in front of the column. I could see them fan out into the flanks of the village, and disappear as they moved parallel to the road on both sides. Sometime later, the same soldiers would close in on the back end of the column. Another group would then move out to the front, and repeat the pattern.

I looked over at the Chief. You could just feel the negative vibes.

★★★

Just before noon a chopper flew over the villa, circled once, and headed to the soccer field. KC grabbed his bag and followed Pete, who was already cranking the jeep. He shouted over his shoulder to Santana. "Hold the fort."

"Sí, señor."

The chopper hovered over the rice fields until the jeep came into view. Pete drove onto the field, stopping about ten yards out as the chopper settled down. KC did his bend-over-run trick up to the pilot's door.

The pilot said, "Where you headed, cowboy?" He was handing the mail out the window.

KC took the bundle and waved for Pete to come over. "Going to Saigon. How far can you get me?"

"We're on the way to Vinh Long. Climb in."

Pete took the mail handoff, and returned to the jeep as KC mounted the aircraft. Vinh Long was just a short hop to the North. Before they reached cruising altitude, the pilot had radioed ahead for information on any flights headed to Saigon.

Turned out a flight was just warming up. KC thanked the warrant officer, and as soon as they touched down, he ran to a Caribou sitting on the apron. By 1730 hours KC was in the shower at the Majestic Hotel, and salivating at the prospect of the hotel's French menu.

That evening KC Flint dined. And never, had it seemed more enjoyable than it was that evening. He took his time and ordered a bottle of Beaujolais to extend the pleasure. When he declared himself finished, he wandered into the cabaret.

"Brandy, please." In seconds the waiter returned with a *real* snifter. He sat back to enjoy the little Vietnamese songstress. *My goodness, I do believe she's singing "I Left My Heart in San Francisco."*

★★★

When our column broke out of the tree line into the paddies, what should have been a view of ripening grain, was a scene of fallow mud flats. Acres of paddies were untended on both sides of the road—maybe a few hectares of rice in a puddle here and there. Not until we were about a kilometer from the highway did the fields show any sign of cultivation.

What was going on in this village? To me this was more disturbing than the fighting. This was economic disaster. Famine ranked up there with weapons of mass destruction—indiscriminate with a long lead time to correction.

Daui Tranh slowly surveyed the paddies. "The young men of the village are with the Vietcong. People plant only what they need, because VC take anything more."

Our troops were now spread out along the rutted road between the rice fields. Up ahead, I could see the truck parked at the side of the highway. My jeep was there, as well as the Red Cross vehicle.

"Are the VC really strong enough to shut down this whole village?"

"No, but people think they are. People cut off can't learn the truth. Feel helpless. Afraid."

"What do we do about that?"

"We just did something. We open road. Now we keep open with the flow of services and goods. But if no goods or services are provided, no need to keep road open, much less to fight for. These people live on the river and can survive—barely. But they survive. Security and survival is all that motivates them."

By the time we hit the road, the troops were loaded. The Chief stood at the door of the Red Cross truck. "This a good day, Captain Skeelman. No one hurt." He jumped into the truck -- all teeth. "Chau."

I walked over to the jeep. Kuntz was already in the driver's seat. "Take her home, Sergeant. *Daui* says this was a good day."

And I guess anytime you walk through that kind of environment, and no one shoots at you, it has got to be a good day. I had to agree with the *Daui*.

★★★

KC was up early, a lot of tracking to do that day. He would start at USOM on the trail of English as a Second Language or ESL course material. He would do the commissary last. The first person he talked to at USOM picked up a phone directory, which led to a few calls. The last conversation suggested he visit an outfit called United States Information Agency.

USIA was the source of outstanding documentation on America: its people, its history, its culture, its freedoms. It was classified as propaganda material, and, as such, was not permitted for distribution in the continental United States. But outside the United States, it was dynamite stuff—which also made the agency the target of demonstrations by enemies of America.

USIA was in a separate part of town from USOM, requiring a taxi. As KC requested directions from the information desk, a blond American woman standing behind him spoke up. "I'm on my way over there now. I will show you."

"That's very kind of you. Thank you."

"Let me use this phone a minute, and we'll be on our way." She looked askance at the attendant in front of KC. He nodded. KC watched her. She looked in her mid-thirties. With a little makeup she might have been quite attractive—a little on the voluptuous side, but no sign of flab. She wore a sleeveless frock with a floral print, nothing special. But it was nice to see a round-eyed woman again.

"Ready?" She hung up the phone, and thanked the attendant. "I'm Miranda Meadows."

"My pleasure, Miss. Meadows, I am KC Flint."

"Please, call me Miranda. I am with provincial operations division in USOM. What takes you to USIA?" They walked out of the building. KC waved to a cab. He opened the door for Miranda, and, as she got in, she spoke to the cabby in Vietnamese.

KC was impressed. He climbed in behind her. "I'm looking for some ESL materials for use in our district." KC proceeded to tell the whole story about the teacher who suggested the idea and that Captain Skillman had sent him on this quest.

"USIA will have what you need. I'm headed over to pick up some training materials myself. I teach home economics to village women. USOM has products we distribute to the Vietnamese small towns, but the women need some training before they can get the most benefit out of the products."

"For example?"

"Well, we have a marvelous little pedal-powered sewing machine that can knock out simple clothes. It's not hard to use, but if the user has never seen a sewing machine, she requires a little training. I also give cooking lessons."

KC's eyes widened. "Really?"

"Yes, really." She smiled—a nice, wholesome smile. "The United States distributes tons of bulgur wheat to the Vietnamese, but it requires instruction if it is to be used effectively."

"What's bulgur wheat?"

"It's wheat that has been cooked, dried, and roughly ground. It's how our government stores surplus wheat—makes for a long shelf life. We bag it and distribute it down to the villages, often as partial compensation to the regional force and popular forces."

"So that's how it works."

"That's how it works. I even have a Berkshire boar hog that I bring along to upgrade the pig population. He's getting a little too big for me to do much of that anymore. I'm not ready to call it quits, yet, but he's becoming a pain in the ass. He started out as a pet, would you believe?"

The cab pulled up in front of a walled-in building and announced his fare. Without raising her voice, but with considerable energy, Ms. Miranda proceeded in Vietnamese to coach the driver on the inadvisability of ripping off the Americans who were here to help his country. She then stuffed a few bills in the shrinking driver's hand and thanked him. *Pays to speak the lingo.*

They walked into the building together. Inside Miranda offered her hand. "Nice meeting you, KC Flint. Any time I can be of assistance, look me up."

"The pleasure's mine, Miranda. And thanks for the help."

"Try the first door on the left," and she attacked the stairs.

The first door on the left was a bonanza. The agency had three levels of soft-backed manuals—beginner, intermediate, and advanced. KC requested five copies of each level and ordered thirty more Beginners and ten more intermediates to be shipped ASAP to Tra Vinh. He was feeling very proud of himself as he headed back to the Majestic Hotel. He dropped off the books in the hotel room and returned to the street on the way to dinner.

It was early. About three blocks away was the Rex Hotel, which housed the field grade officers. On the top of the Rex was a U.S. Army field mess run like an officers' club. Tonight he would dine American.

The meal was great, but the problem with Rex was the air-conditioning. Coming from the steamy outdoors into the Rex with air-conditioning really *was* enough to give you pneumonia. Besides, there was no cute little Vietnamese girl to sing "I Left My Heart in San Francisco."

KC went back to the Majestic for a not so quick night cap.

CHAPTER ELEVEN

Merlin the Magician

IN FRONT OF THE modest Catholic church stood the statue of Mother Mary. It was bigger than life and was arranged on a pedestal in the center of a small circular garden—much like countless other Catholic statues the world over—except for one small, but significant, difference. An offhand look at the face of the statue suggested something odd about her. With closer inspection, it was apparent the statue of the Mother of Jesus displayed the almond eye of the Asian world. How extraordinary, and, yet ... Why not?

"Bonjour, *mon capitain*." A small Vietnamese man dressed in the robes of a priest descended the steps of the church.

"Bonjour, *mon père. Je suis Capitain Skillman*." I offered my hand. Sergeant Khe came around from the other side of the jeep, and greeted the priest in Vietnamese. I continued in English. It was important that the first communications be understood correctly. Khe gave him my little speech, which we both had down pat.

The priest responded in halting English: "Welcome to our um ... parish. We are pleased ... no, honored you visit. I am Father Phan." He shook my hand. "Please, you must come in." He continued to smile as he led the way back up the steps into the church. I followed, but Sergeant Khe hung back.

"Come on, Sergeant."

"But I am Buddhist, sir."

"We have already had that conversation. Unless it troubles you, let the father worry about that. You are with me." Khe caught up, and we followed Father Phan down the long center aisle lined with wooden pews on either side. The church was built like a cathedral at one-tenth scale. The walls looked like poured concrete, and the wooden window frames were handmade, with arched tops and no glass. Father Phan walked to the left of the sanctuary and opened a door leading to a suite of rooms in the rear.

"Please, come in. Come in." He indicated a conversation group of two upholstered rattan chairs separated by a small end table. The back wall of the room was constructed in a gentle outward arc toward the backyard of the church. Three paned glass windows side by side in the wall gave the feel of a bay window. Bookcases lined the wall beneath the windows. It was a cheerful room, modestly furnished.

Beside the conversation corner was a wooden table with four wooden chairs around it. The priest pulled one of the chairs over to the conversation area. A large, but simple, desk faced the interior wall. To the left of the desk was a closed door into what must have been sleeping rooms. We continued to stand until Father Phan took a seat in the upholstered chair.

"This is a lovely view." I looked out the windows across the large grass yard that bordered a small field of sugarcane. Beyond the cane was taller jungle vegetation, completing the impression of peace and tranquility.

"Yes, we are grateful …" His face lit up in a smile. "May I serve you glass of wine? Is very nice wine from Algeria."

I hesitated maybe a half second, "That would be very nice."

Father frowned. "Wine be blessed for the sacraments, but that not change taste. Is OK?"

"Works for me. No problem." Father Phan scurried into the back room and returned with a lovely amber bottle of wine. As the priest worked open the cork, Khe and I finished our speech about being here to help.

The little priest produced three small tumblers from somewhere and poured the wine. When he had served it and before he sat down, he raised his glass. "May Lord bless your work."

I sniffed the wine, appraised the color and clarity, and took a sip. "Holy mackerel!" I certainly didn't expect this. This was a *very* nice wine. "Tastes like a Sauterne."

Father Phan beamed. He wasn't sure what a mackerel was, but he knew the American liked the wine. We all sipped again.

"Father Phan," I said, changing the subject, "I see you have a great deal of sugarcane planted in this village." I looked to Khe to translate. "Is there some reason that so much cane grows in this village and only small amounts everywhere else?"

"I don't know about everywhere else," Khe translated. "But yes, I ask villagers to grow sugarcane for church. I cannot ask for money. They have no money. I do not ask for rice crop. VC take so much and only leave enough to eat and plant. So last year I ask all families to plant extra cane for church."

Khe translated for me. "That's a great idea. But, what do you do with it?"

"He say, 'I take it to rice mill in Ap Lin village.'"

"He say, 'Rice mill owner is off-season when they take him the cane, so he has time to press the cane and keeps 10 percent of the molasses, and they sell in Saigon.'"

"Damn. That's great." Khe did not need to translate.

"Oh, yes. So good last year, this year we have much, much more. Very good year."

As our host refilled the wineglasses, the sound of a chopper caught our attention. Suddenly the bird appeared in the widows. It was approaching from the right and setting down on the grass strip directly in front of the cane field. I started to leave the room, but when I recognized KC getting out of the Huey, I sat down again.

"Sergeant Khe, will you bring in KC?" I stepped to the window and watched KC unload a couple of boxes into the jeep.

"That is my assistant. He is returning from Saigon. I'm glad you will have a chance to meet him." The chopper rose, then banked away from the cane field and out over the paddies.

Khe ushered KC in. His energy filled the room.

I said. "Aren't you full of surprises?" Turning to the priest, "I want you to meet this most clever man, Father Phan."

KC wrapped both his hands around the delicate hand of Father Phan. "My very great pleasure, Father."

Father Phan smiled warmly, "You just come in time for last bit of wine. Please sit."

KC complied and turned to me. "I was beginning to think I would have to spend the night in Tra Vinh."

"What happened?"

"Well, we came in over the town and couldn't see the jeep. I remembered rule two about walking out of town alone, so I talked the pilot into a five-minute flight down Highway 8 before we turned on to Tra Vinh. He goes back up to twelve hundred feet, and as we swing back to the south, I see the green Red Cross jeep sitting in Ech."

"Yeah, Doc is running sick call there."

"We were looking for a place to put down when the pilot spotted your jeep *and* the best touchdown spot in the area."

Father Phan pulled up another chair and handed KC a glass of wine. "Welcome to Ap Chanh, *capitain*."

KC's eyes registered surprise at the first sip of wine. "Whoa."

Father Phan, with the assistance of Sergeant Khe, proceeded to tell the group in English about the Algerian wine that had found its way to the altar in Ap Chanh.

We had finished the father's wine. It seemed like a good time to find our way back to our villa before he could break out a second bottle. I looked over at Khe and instructed him to carefully translate my next words and make sure I was understood. I turned to the priest.

"Thank you, Father, for a delightful afternoon. You have been very gracious. Please let us know if we can be of assistance. We are very impressed with what you are accomplishing here in your village. You are setting a great standard." The little priest escorted us out to the jeep. KC gave his farewell along the way. Sergeant Khe finished the conversation in Vietnamese, and we drove out of the churchyard.

★★★

A dozen or so villagers had already gathered at the aid station before the green machine drove up. They were mostly women with children and several old men. Kuntz was riding shotgun, and Ong Pham was the interface with the crowd. Ong Pham could handle a little English, but Sergeant Santana's accent really threw him, so it was up to Kuntz to make the simplest ideas understandable.

Doc set up his gear in the front room of the aid station. The village chief made good on our request for a screen. The back room now provided privacy, when appropriate.

"Bill, will you control the outside, and let no more than two patients in the examining room at one time? A mother with children counts as one patient."

Kuntz nodded.

Doc looked at Pham. "Ong Pham, stay with me always. You understand?"

Ong Pham looked anxious. Kuntz said. "You stay with doctor all the time."

Ong Pham smiled yes.

"And you take this clipboard, write the name of each person I treat, and note what I give them."

Doc held up a couple bottles to show the big numbers on the side. Kuntz translated, taking the clipboard and bottles as training aids.

Ong Pham got it. He was eager.

Doc opened his bag on the table. "OK, it's showtime." He waved the first woman into the chair beside him. Kuntz pointed to the other chair and directed the next patient to it. Ong Pham watched what the Doc did and talked to the patient, almost continuously. None of us was sure what he was saying, but it seemed to relax the patient, and to anticipate Doc's next move.

Outside, Kuntz walked slowly down the line, and then back; talking to the patients, just like they knew what he was saying. Mostly, he entertained the children. Pulling coins out of ears, and *this little piggy*, and a few other Kuntz creations ... All of it worked in any language. Steadily, the line of patients would slim down to three or four, and then another dozen would arrive.

About an hour into the sick call Doc called to Kuntz. "I need some clean water. Think you can help on that?"

"I'll give it a shot."

Kuntz went to the old man waiting patiently near the end of the line. "I need water."

The old man looked blank. Kuntz took out his canteen and poured a drop of water into the old man's hand. "Water. *Nuc da*." Kuntz wasn't sure whether he had said *water* or *ice tea*, but one thing was certain. He had registered. The old man spoke to the woman in line behind him. He turned back to Kuntz, and indicated that the sergeant should wait a bit while the woman did her thing. A few minutes later she returned with a crock of water.

With hand signs, Kuntz asked if the water was drinkable. He dipped his hand in as if to drink and looked at her. She nodded, yes. Kuntz thanked her and took the crock into Santana.

"Lady says this is drinkable." Kuntz placed the crock on the table next to the bag.

"In my bag there is a bottle of iodine. Put three drops into the crock, and swirl them around." Kuntz rummaged through the bag checking labels till he found the right bottle and complied.

"You're all fixed up." Kuntz turned to the door to resume his duties outside. As he stepped into the courtyard, the children clapped and cheered. It startled him, and he choked up, and *that* completely surprised him.

Emotions just did not sneak up on him like that. He acknowledged the attention with a big smile, but he quickly stepped away from the line of patients into the area in front of the permanent buildings—*must not choke up*—anything to change his mind.

He began to examine the area with a professional eye. Yes, it was large enough. Yes, there was sufficient clearance. He turned around a couple times. *Yes, the area is quickly accessible from the hardtop. Yes, this would be a good place to survey in a mortar position.* Sergeant First Class William Kuntz, U.S. Army, was back in control, and now returned to his job at the aid station.

The rate of patient arrivals had dropped off. Kuntz was estimating the time to completion when he heard the sound of the chopper overhead. He caught a glimpse of it headed southeast—a Huey at about a thousand feet. *We got visitors at the Catholic village. Wonder who.*

Thirty minutes later Doc followed the last little boy and his mother out of the aid station. The little fellow had a big white patch on his lower leg. It was covered with the orange signs of antiseptic. The kid made a tiny wave to Kuntz, who returned it with a salute.

Santana stood aside while Pham got into the back of the jeep. "Ong Pham, you did one hell of a job, today." Pham looked blank.

"He says you did good. He is happy." Kuntz interpreted as he fitted himself into the driver's seat. Pham quietly beamed in the backseat.

★★★

The troops were pumped. It had been a rewarding day for everyone on the team -- except maybe, Pete. But there was enough energy to carry him along, too. The badminton was particularly aggressive, with plenty of banter, even in the absence of KC, who was back in the kitchen playing with all the commissary supplies he'd brought back from Saigon.

However, Ong Than was singularly unimpressed as KC unveiled each commissary treasure. There was the powdered milk and powdered ice cream, which had no meaning to the little man. Likewise a box of macaroni was of no concern, and instant mashed potatoes were a completely alien concept. The canned goods were recognizable, but then they could be bought here, so what was the big deal?

Not to be dismayed, KC directed Ong Than to fire up a charcoal burner. KC took up a saucepan and dipped out a couple ladles of water. When the charcoal was burning nicely, KC pointed for Ong Than to put the pan on the burner. KC poured out a cup of instant mashed potatoes and sat the cup on the table. Ong Than looked on with little interest. When the water began to simmer, KC motioned for the cook to begin stirring the water. With complete boredom Ong Than complied. KC added the powder slowly and stepped away. Ong Than, totally blasé, continued to stir with one hand.

Suddenly the potatoes set up, and Ong Than grabbed the panhandle. His eyes widened. "*Daui ... Daui ... Daaauiii.*" He looked up into the face of the tall man whom he began to confuse with God.

For KC it was more emotion than he had ever seen the man display. "Dinner in half an hour, old man." Ong Than watched KC leave with worshiping eyes. For him, KC was clearly, Merlin the Magician.

★★★

Dinner with mashed potatoes was a definite hit. Ong Than proudly made a second batch. The table talk stretched out. KC reported the contacts he'd followed up for Doc.

"Glad you did," said Doc. "I know better, now, what I need, and I must get some requests in right away. I passed out more tetracycline than I normally might, but I saw a lot of festering cuts and sores. Saw what I think are three pregnant women, too. Maybe we want to set up the timing for building that maternity clinic."

"How did Ong Pham work out?" I asked.

"Did a hell of a job, but I need Sergeant Khe when things get complicated—nothing I couldn't handle today. I just gave them guidance, and some aspirin or tetracycline, depending on whether it was pain or infection, then I told them to come back next time. Of course, next time, I will have to question patients more completely."

I conceded, "Yeah, you're right. I needed Khe today to interview Father Phan. But you should get Khe regularly. And think about this. The priest said there were two sisters teaching school in the church across the road here. I have never seen them though."

Pete jumped in. "I've seen them. They bring children out to play during the day. I think they live in buildings on the far side of the church."

Based on the experience with the priest today, we might be able to recruit the sisters into assisting us. I suggested it to Doc.

"How do ya mean?"

"Depends on their language skills, of course, but my guess is, either way, they would be of more assistance than Ong Pham when it comes to female patients."

"Not bad, boss. I'll check it out."

Peter was eager to get in on the action. "How we going to get these English classes started?"

"Good question. Is there anyone who does not want to teach a class?" There was silence around the table. Kuntz looked at Santana. "You sure you want to do that?"

After a long pause Doc volunteered. "May bee no best ting for me, señor." Peels of laughter.

The group was still chuckling when Daui walked in. "Hello, my American friends."

KC went over and picked up the fresh bottle of brandy. Pete offered his seat to the Chief, and excused himself. His sister had sent him four Louis L'Amour Western novels, and he was stuck in a paperback every free minute.

"*Chau, Daui.* Glad you dropped by. We have some good news." I was eager to share the events of the day.

"Have good news, too." The Chief accepted the brandy and took a slow sniff, then swirled it gently. "How was sick call?"

Sergeant Santana retold the sick call story, with praise for Ong Phan. I told the Chief how impressed I was with the entrepreneurial talents of Father Pham. And I asked him about the sisters and the possibility of recruiting them into our health care program.

"I think they already do some help with birth. I not sure about English speaking," the Chief offered.

I assured Santana that the District self-help plan indicated t a maternity clinic was scheduled in the project. Santana looked at the Chief. "Anything we can do to speed up the delivery of building supplies?"

"I think Captain Ed and I speak to Mr. Ledbetter." The Chief looked at me.

"We can do that ... which brings up the next point. KC, tell the Chief what you picked up at USIA."

KC gave the short version of his acquiring the ESL textbooks. "*Daui*, we need to get the word out that English courses will be taught by the Americans. See how many people are interested and what skill level we are talking about."

"I think you talk to Ong Pham. I will tell him to help you." The Chief took the last sip of his brandy.

"Not so fast, *Daui.* What's your good news?" KC reached for the brandy bottle.

"Yes, good news. The ambushes kill more VC near Ap Lin. Also capture many rifles in area. Daui Sau very pleased."

That was outstanding. That would open up those roads for sure ... might even be time for a new self-help school to go in there now.

"Is there a school under construction at Ap Lin, or will this be a start-up?" asked Sergeant Kuntz.

"This be new one—a start-up," the Chief answered.

The discussion then went to the building priority of the new schools. The decisions for the next start-ups were based on the roads cleared and the attitude of the village people toward self-help.

By the time the Chief finished his second brandy, it was decided that, in the next week, Daui Sau would run one more daytime operation in the Ap Lin village area. I would visit the rice mill owner in Ap Lin, and the team, in some combination, would make a show of visiting two or three future school sites.

✯✯✯

Counted among the shops and restaurants surrounding the Vung Liem market was a barbershop. Like most of the shops, it was a three-sided thatched enclosure with a couple of upholstered straight chairs, a large full-length mirror, and two head-and-shoulder mirrors. The first thing I had noticed about KC when he returned from Saigon was his fresh haircut. KC acknowledged the Majestic Hotel was the grooming point.

"Tell you what," I said. "Next time you go into market, stop by the little barbershop. See if one of those guys will come to the villa to do four heads."

"You want him to come here?"

"Yeah. No sense any of us being a sitting duck in the marketplace every time we need a haircut. Too much like something out of *The Godfather*."

"Good thinking."

On this particular morning, KC returned from market with Ong Than trailing behind. The captain was empty-handed. Ong Than carried two large woven straw bags, one over each shoulder, packed with items the captain had carefully selected. Behind Ong Than followed a second little man carrying a small black bag. Unbelievable as it might seem, the man was smaller than Ong Than. The bag he carried looked like a doctor's kit.

I watched the procession from the porch as the Pied Piper led his small band through the courtyard to the breezeway. "You might have distributed the load a little better, Captain."

"The old man wouldn't let me. Said it was bad for *my* image and made *him* look like he couldn't do his job."

"Since when did he get that articulate in English?"

"Don't sell him short. He has his ways, and I got it. Maybe not in those words, but I got it."

"Who's the trail party?"

"Barber. Thought we could set up on the porch."

Time to round up the boys. I stepped back into the villa. Pete was in the front room reading about the Sackett family in his Louis L'Amour paperback. "You're up first for a haircut, soldier. Where are the sergeants?"

"Over in the COM shack. Captain Flint gave Doc some radio frequencies for additional support with drug shipments. Sergeant Kuntz is helping him establish contact." Pete put the book down.

"Place a straight chair on the porch, Peter. That unbelievably small man is a barber." The little man looked scared to death. His face was frozen in a smile that matched the Greek mask of comedy.

"Roger, sir."

I walked over to the COM shack to collect up my NCOs.

Kuntz started to protest. "Me?… Get a haircut? You're kidding… sir."

The sergeant did have a point. I appraise Kuntz's Franciscan fringe. Just the same, he was pretty shaggy down the back. "The barber is on the porch. And I promised him four heads."

Doc wasn't paying attention. "Boss, I think I got a line on a midwife kit from USOM. Maybe we take a look at making a maternity clinic out of an aid station already built?"

"That's up to the Vietnamese, but it shouldn't be a hard sell. Let's go down the road, and look at the aid station near the middle school."

The three walked up onto the porch just as Pete was finishing his haircut. "You got to watch this guy. He's got this little X-Acto kit with all kinds of tiny blades. He thinks it's his job to get every hair on your head, and in your nose and your ears. I think he would have gone for the eyebrows, but I never let him get that far."

The little man with his frozen smile was now trembling. Kuntz gave the barber his just-for-kids smile and sat down. That seemed to settle the barber a little. By the time I sat down, the man seemed composed. When he showed me the X-Acto knife, I indicated to leave the nose alone and just do the neck and ears. Seemed safe enough until the man changed blades. He loaded a very small triangular blade into the knife handle and took hold of my left ear.

Now it's me who was petrified. This was too close to the experiences of several months ago when the doctor started reopening the wounds in my ears.

I stood up. "That's fine, and thank you very much, sir. We don't need to do that again." I immediately paid for all four heads, which brought a genuine smile to the little guy. He policed up his gear, snapped shut his little black bag, and backed off the porch with numerous bows and scurried out the gate.

"Not exactly like downtown San Francisco," I noted.

There was still some time in the day for Doc and me to go down to the aid station next to the intermediate school.

KC suggested, "If you guys are going to do that, why don't Kuntz and I check the school that's finishing up in the next village?"

"It works. You guys take the jeep. Doc and I can walk." With that we split, and Peter found his way back into the Old West.

★★★

The aid station at the intermediate school was bigger than the one at village Ech. It had two small treatment rooms and the one large reception room. Doctor Sergeant Santana had it all laid out in his head. A couple of screens and a couple of cots, and this would do just fine for a maternity clinic. The reception room could be used as a screening area and a waiting area. It seemed a little Spartan to me. We poked around a few more minutes and then headed back to the villa.

"Let's see if we can meet the sisters," I suggested.

As we walked down the path to the road, I saw a monk in his bright yellow robes turn into the footpath leading into the old banana plantation. I waved, but the guy either did not see us or ignored us.

"You get the distinct impression, Doc, that these Vietnamese monks have no love lost for us Americans."

"Yeah. Wasn't it one of those monks that set himself on fire in Hue or some place last year? Gotta figure that for a hostile act," Santana recalled.

"Believe you're right—last June I think—claimed they were fighting for religious freedom, but that's not your typical Buddhist behavior."

We turned up the road to town. Our conversation was casual enough, but we both were experienced soldiers, and were very much aware of our surroundings the potential for trouble.

In 1960, as a young lieutenant, I had walked the streets of Kabul, Afghanistan, with the same heightened sense of awareness. Kabul wasn't a hostile zone at the time. My platoon, representing the United States, had been invited as guests of the Afghan government, which was celebrating its millennial anniversary. Still, we were warned about walking alone in the streets.

For Santana, the first time he had been tuned up like this was patrolling through a little Korean village as the platoon medic on operation.

When we reached the villa, I turned right, toward the church, and we went on the lookout for the likely living quarters of two Catholic nuns. The front yard of the church still showed evidence of the howitzer positions. A very small canal was at the back of the church—actually more like a drainage ditch. It was deep but held very little water, indicating that it might have been a more respectable canal in the rainy season. The church did not seem to have a residence built into the architecture. We walked around to the far side of the building. Across the yard, and in the tree line, was a wooden building.

"Isn't that an icon in front of that building?" asked Santana.

"I believe we have found the sisters." I walked up and knocked on the door. After a second knock and a peek in the window I decided that no one was in and turned back toward the churchyard.

Out of nowhere a sister in full habit was walking toward us.

"*Chau, Co.*"

She grinned at my misuse of her language. "*Chau, Daui.*" *It worked every time.*

"Can we speak in English?"

In English she said, "I can not." We struggled some, and raising the volume did not help. I did learn that she was Sister Lan.

This was a job for Sergeant Khe. "When you take Khe with you on sick call, make time to come visit Sister Lan." We excused ourselves, leaving Sister Lan a little confused, and headed back to the villa.

Meanwhile, Sergeant Kuntz had chauffeured Captain Flint out of town to a nearby about-to-be-completed school. KC had taken directions from one of the men in Ong Pham's office. The office assistant did not speak any English, but seemed to understand what KC wanted and drew a little sketch map.

They were looking at brand-new structure, about seventy-five to a hundred feet long and perhaps thirty feet wide. It was the typical local materials on concrete slab but with a corrugated steel roof, not thatched. There were three rooms, each with a separate entrance to the outside walkway. The roof overhang created a walkway porch. The windows were not completed, but KC reported that the school was a trim-and-paint away from ready.

✯✯✯

Dinner began with an announcement by KC. "Behold, gentlemen, salt and pepper shakers. Found them in the marketplace this morning." They were common glass restaurant shakers with screw-on aluminum tops—the kind found in any diner—in America, that is. Both were filled two-thirds full. KC held them up with pride.

"We have any Tabasco sauce, *patron*?" Chuckles from all but KC. With a flair for the melodramatic, KC enthusiastically, salted his meal, then, with equal enthusiasm, peppered his plate. The man suddenly gasped, his plate was covered with pepper.

"What an idiot! Look what he did! He's got the salt in the pepper shaker and the pepper in the salt shaker." At the top of his voice: "Ong Than." The little man flew up the steps from the breezeway to his master's side.

KC was mad. "Look at this, you insufferable little man. You've got these backward," as if the man understood English. "Now take these back, and put the salt in the cellar with the big holes and the pepper in the one with the small holes."

Ong Than disappeared.

"My God, I cannot believe this man can be so medieval."

Ong Than reappeared.

"What is it that you do not understand?" Ong Than handed the shakers back to KC.

KC looked at the shakers in amazement. "How did he do that? How did he get the salt and pepper switched in those shakers that fast?"

"He unscrewed the tops and switched them, Captain." Private de Groot hung on the word *captain*—not so long as to be declared disrespectful -- but close. At which point, the room went up in laughter and, Ong Than smiled his toothless smile, and retired to the breezeway. Even KC had to laugh at himself.

The day's activities had been chewed over. We were feeling pretty good about the projects and the possibilities. I was about to challenge KC for the grand title of Vung Liem chess championship when the Chief arrived.

"Hello, my American friends." KC reached for the brandy bottle. "I have good news ..." He raised his hand. "No, thank you, Daui KC."

"Have a seat, *Daui*. What's the good news?" As usual Pete stood to let the Chief sit down, but the Chief remained standing this time.

"We have two assassins in town." The room went deadly silent. The Chief paused for dramatic effect. "One for you, *capitain* Skeelman, and one for me." He smiled his sparkly-eyes, no-teeth smile.

"H o l y s m o k e." I said it very slowly and with feeling.

"You call that good news, *Daui*?" snapped KC. "Doesn't sound that good to me."

"Oh, yes. Very good news, *Capitain* KC." The Chief laughed heartily. "You see: we know about it."

CHAPTER TWELVE

Paranoia Is Not All Bad

IN THE TEN DAYS that followed, House Rule Number One, "*Do not leave the compound unarmed,*" was easy to remember. Each team member made a conscious effort to check his weapon before he left the villa—rather like *The Magnificent Seven* minus two. By the end of three weeks Rule One was pure habit. But, the energy of *caution* had worn off, even though there were plenty of signs that the VC still operated in the area. Too frequently, a team member would see a path of trampled rice across a paddy. It was telltale evidence of night travelers who were avoiding roads.

The best evidence of progress was the self-help projects, which were showing clear signs of life. Twenty-three people had turned up to register for English as a Second Language classes.

One particular afternoon, a Huey flew over the villa, circled, and touched down at the soccer field. Before anyone could get there, the aircraft headed back out over the paddies, having left a fair-sized carton in the middle of the field. Pete pulled into the chopper pad, and loaded up ESL manuals. There were more than enough for the one intermediate and three beginner classes.

Kuntz and Peter took two of the beginner classes, as discussed. KC took the intermediate course, and I assigned the third beginner class to myself. I had intended one class to run each evening, Tuesday through Friday. But, student preferences dictated two classes on Thursday: one in the late afternoon and one in the evening. They conflicted with classes for the same time as Wednesday and Friday evenings

Sooner or later, every officer and every noncommissioned officer does a hitch in his career as an instructor. I was comfortable that teaching was nothing new for these men. Peter was the exception. It was too early in his young career for him to have acquired that skill. So, I had Pete sit in on my Wednesday class, and then teach his own class on Thursday.

Peter was game, and everything could have worked out for the young private, if not for Co Mae's attendance as a student in his class. Unfortunately, the kid just couldn't function in her presence. He did fine as assistant instructor in my class. But, left alone in his own little group of five, he couldn't think straight. She was just so cute—all he wanted to do was pet her like a kitten. And if, on rare moments, she looked him in the eye, his heart literally stopped -- as did whatever it was he was saying. He would stutter or blush or both, and he had to look away in order to start the exercise again.

Nor was Co Mae altogether unaware of the power she had over young Peter. She always appeared in the traditional Vietnamese dress, always the fitted bodice, always the flowing skirt, always the soft smile for Private de Groot.

"She's driving me crazy," he confessed to Sergeant Santana. "I've got to get a grip."

"You want me to teach the class?" suggested Santana, tongue in cheek.

"No. Captain Ed would kill us. I just wish I knew what to say to her."

"Say what you would say to your girlfriend back home."

"Don't have a girlfriend back home. My high school steady married my best friend when I joined the Army—ex best friend, I should say."

"That's not what I meant, Private. Talk to her like she was American. She doesn't have to understand the words. It's all in the body language anyway."

"I'm not trying to seduce her, Sarge. I *heard* what the old man said. All I want to do is talk to her a little. You'd think I could do that in an English language class where I'm the instructor."

The Don Juan Sergeant, known father of six, and possibly a significant portion of the children in Puerto Rico, just smiled a knowing smile. "You'll work it out, kid. It's like thumb sucking. No one can do it for you, and everyone outgrows it in time. Good luck on your class tonight."

It turned out that the problem went away. That evening Co Mae arrived at class in the accompaniment of an older man. She led the man up to Peter and said, still holding the old man's hand, "This man ... Father ... to mine." The sentence structure was poor, but the meaning was clear.

Suddenly, the paradigm shifted, and Peter was in control of himself. "How do you do, sir. Welcome to our class."

Remarkable how certain types of family relationships transcend cultural boundaries. It may have been that the old man really wanted to learn English. But, to the father, to the daughter, and to Peter – no, to the whole class-- it was quite clear that Co Mae's father and Captain Ed Skillman were of one mind, with regard to enforcement of House Rule Number Three: fraternizing with local maidens.

★★★

The paranoia of the assassin threat dissolved into routine caution. Besides, a little paranoia isn't all that bad. Sergeant Kuntz and I were soon out visiting the site of another new school. It was coming on line in the vicinity of Ap Lin village. Since Sergeant Khe was with Doc on sick call, I decided it would be a good idea if the operations officer, Lieutenant Vu, and the communications officer, Lieutenant Van Le, accompanied me and Kuntz. The four of us loaded the jeep with Kuntz driving and me in the command seat.

The drive was now routine; that is, if driving along looking out over flourishing green fields of rice could be considered routine. About a kilometer from the village of Ap Lin, a dirt road turned off Highway 8 to the northwest and ran parallel to a small canal. Kuntz turned into the road in response to Lieutenant Vu's directions.

The canal along the left-hand side of the road was little more than a drainage ditch this time of the year. The tree vegetation over the canal was lush. A little water of questionable depth lay stagnant at the bottom of three-foot banks. On our right, fields of rice, now maybe eighteen inches high, spread out from the dirt road and back along Highway 8.

"We go this road one kilometer. See school in trees," Vu directed.

The road was in good condition. Less than five hundred meters ahead, a tree line broke off perpendicular to the road and ran out into the rice field for a couple hundred meters like a border fence.

Kuntz jammed on the brakes. "What the hell is *this?*" It was not apparent until you were right on top of it. But lying across the road were half coconut shells, round side up, about two feet apart. There were six rows of them laid out like a checkerboard.

I looked back at Vu, "What is this? You got any ideas?" Kuntz got out of the jeep and walked up to the first shell.

"No touch," shouted Lieutenant Vu. He jumped out of the jeep. Van Le and I also dismounted.

We stood looking over the field of coconut shells cut in half and laid out like rows of upside down teacups. "VC place hand grenade under coconut shell with pin out … maybe all, maybe none," said Vu. "We walk around." Vu and Van Le proceeded to walk around on the shoulder of the road.

I asked, "How far is the school from here?"

"Only through trees in front," Vu called over his shoulder.

I considered the risk of leaving the jeep unattended and decided that; inasmuch as I could see it from the tree line, it would be all right. Kuntz had begun to follow the two Vietnamese.

I caught up to Kuntz. "Keep an eye over your shoulder on the jeep."

The pair of Vietnamese was about fifty feet ahead of us when I heard the crack of a rifle shot. Both of us Americans were in the bottom of the ditch before we heard the report of the second and third shot.

I shouted, "Did you see where that came from?"

"Right front, I think."

We both crawled up the canal bank to peer out over the road.

Lieutenants Vu and Van Le continued to walk down the road as though on a Sunday outing. They were now nearly one hundred yards ahead.

"You heard the shots, too, didn't you?" Obviously a rhetorical question by me.

"Can't mistake that sound," Kuntz confirmed. "What's the matter with those little guys?"

Van Le and Vu continued up the road, chatting as if they hadn't heard a thing.

"Let's hope they know something more than we do …

My boots were covered with mud that came all the way up to my knees "Look at these damn fatigues. I put them on fresh this morning.".

"Those little munchkins are walking along like nothing happened." Kuntz, somehow, had escaped the mud, but his boots were soaked, and he squished when he walked.

"Come on, let's catch up. Maintaining face is a big deal in this part of the world." I tried to shake off some of the mud. *Damn it. Damn it. Damn it!*

The four of us entered the tree line together and found the school building sitting in the center of a clearing. The building was the same design as the school outside the district town, except that it had only two rooms. As we approached, a man in a white short-sleeved shirt and black trousers came out of the building to greet Lieutenant Vu.

Vu turned to us. "He teacher." We all shook hands around—understanding body language if not words.

"Children no come." said Vu. "Afraid roadblock."

"Roadblock?" Kuntz blurted out. "You call that a roadblock?"

I guess it was, if it kept the children from going to school.

"What's the matter with these people?" Kuntz was on a tear. "Hell, the PTA of Middletown, Ohio, would have sacked these VC singlehandedly if they were keeping kids away from school."

But it wasn't Middletown, Ohio, and there wasn't any PTA. An organization like PTA would have meant these people had committed to some responsibility for their own welfare—not the case here. These folks believed it was government's job to keep them secure. It didn't look like they are going to go against the bad guys as long as they believed that the government couldn't prevent retaliation. I turned to the schoolteacher, "Tell them, Vu, that the road will be opened immediately, and that school should begin as scheduled."

The teacher smiled and bowed politely. Lieutenants Vu and Van Le chatted with him for a few more minutes, and wrapped it up. The four of us started toward the jeep.

As we walked along, I struggled to tell Vu that we would go by the village chief at Ap Lin to report this roadblock, and request that the Popular Force clear the obstacles. I was not the least bit sure I had communicated anything, but when we pulled up in front of the village headquarters, Lieutenant Vu immediately jumped out of the jeep and found the village chief. Vu did most of the talking. Kuntz and I waited at the jeep.

My attention drifted to all the trucks lined up on the side of the road by the bridge to Vinh Long. A half dozen long-haul trucks were parked at the turnoff to market that Daui Tranh had taken me and KC on our first walk in the country. The trucks were unmanned and empty.

"You think there's a whorehouse around here?" said Kuntz, a little too hopefully.

If that was the case, Doc would be running all sick calls out of here. "No, there's something else drawing them in." At that moment two truckers emerged from the market road with crates containing pigs. It dawned on me. "You know what? I bet those truckers are buying pigs to carry back to Saigon so they don't go home empty-handed."

Lieutenant Vu and Lieutenant Van Le returned to the jeep. "Village chief say, OK. Fix road." The two Vietnamese climbed into the jeep. Kuntz turned the vehicle around and headed back down Highway 8 toward the district town and home.

"Vu." I spoke over my shoulder. "Those trucks back there … are they buying pigs to take back to Saigon?"

"Yes. Drivers not want stay Tra Vinh all night. Not want to go back with nothing. Buy in market. But not many pig. Pay much money to farmer."

I was processing that thought as the jeep passed by the road up to the school they had just visited earlier. Lieutenant Vu said something to Lieutenant Van Le, and they both laughed. Vu leaned forward smiling. "Lieutenant Van Le say he glad you come today. We not go to school if you and Sergeant Kuntz not be there. Very dangerous." The little lieutenant smiled broadly. "But VC no mess with *American*. No problem." He and Lieutenant Van Le laughed again.

Suntan not withstanding, Kuntz looked a little pale. I picked at the dried mud on my trousers. Neither of us smiled, much less, laughed.

I'm one lucky son of a bitch; not for the first time.

✯✯✯

Progress over the weeks was steady. Everything the team got into was noticeably better in a matter of days. Peter's reports to Province were positive if not glowing. Visitors were showing up to check on the successes of the new district advisor program. First they came from Province and then from Saigon. The kilometers of road opened, the arms captured, and VC casualty count were getting attention up the military chain. And the schools coming on line, aid stations opened, and sick calls conducted were getting equal billing up the USOM line.

On the first visit from Province, Jake Ledbetter brought along the midwife kit, and Doc behaved like it was Christmas. He ran down the two sisters to show off the prize. The kit was a big black case, a little larger than a footlocker, and contained a whole collection of instruments. None of the men could even recognize the tools, much less have a clue as to how to use them. That probably included Doc, but it never came to the test. The sisters recognized everything and knew what each and every piece was about, even if they weren't all that sure about when to use them. The *when* would have to come with on-the-job training.

It was to the point that I took thirty-five millimeter slides of everything we did, because there was never enough time for guests to visit the sites. I could mail the film to Saigon for development, and have it returned in just days. With the projector Major Bass sent to us, I developed a little dog-and-pony show to brief VIPs on the progress being made in Vung Liem. We had it down to marketing science. As soon as the choppers circled the town, Kuntz would drive to the soccer field to pick up the VIP. KC would signal Ong Than to make tea while he broke out the ice trays from the little freezer compartment in the fridge.

By the time the first visitor entered the social room, I had the couch turned facing the wall and the projector loaded with the first tray of slides. After the introduction to whatever team members were present, Ong Than would serve the iced tea, and the guests settled back for the next twenty or thirty minutes to experience a briefing on the progress of the advisor effort in Vung Ling District. *Produced and Directed by Deux Capitains, Photography by Captain Ed, Casting by Casey.*

Early one morning, the whop-whop overhead indicated there was more than one chopper incoming. Since it was so early, not everyone was fully prepared to assume his role in the VIP scenario. I hopped into the jeep and drove alone to the soccer field.

It was the peak of the dry season, and the dirt road kicked up dust as I raced down past the school. The third chopper was just making its approach over the Vietnamese pagoda and the dirt driveway onto the soccer field. I slowed to give plenty of clearance to the aircraft, but mostly, to avoid the dust being kicked up by the downdraft.

Two things were unusual. First, the aircraft did not approach from over the rice fields as most of the pilots did, but in the opposite direction. It came in over the pagoda. Second, along the side of the road, where the path led to the pagoda, there were, at least, five Vietnamese monks standing side by side waving and smiling to me as I drove by. I thought that, maybe, we were making some inroads into the hearts and minds of the people after all.

I wheeled the jeep through the entrance onto the soccer field, carefully avoiding the dark chuckhole in the center of the driveway. I was waved over to the bird in the center. I could see that the two choppers in the corners of the field were gunships escorting the VIP chopper. Four people hopped out of the aircraft, and did the low run toward me.

I slid out of the jeep and saluted. Whoever was coming was going to have more rank than I had. That was sure. I held the salute.

"Good morning, Captain. I'm Lieutenant Colonel Handy, and this is Colonel Hume. We are in from Fort Bragg." He returned my salute, as did the colonel. "These gentlemen are from USOM."

The two men nodded a greeting.

"Good morning, gentlemen. Welcome to Vung Liem District. I'm having to make two trips, sir, if you don't mind."

"No problem, Captain. The colonel and I will come with you now." He gave a nod to the other two.

I noticed that while the other two wore fatigues, they did not have on military rank. Everyone mounted up, and we headed back to the entrance. I carefully negotiated the chuckhole onto the road, waved again to the monks, and hustled up the road to the villa. KC came out to meet us.

"These gentlemen are from Fort Bragg, KC. There are two more at the soccer field. Make these gents comfortable, and I'll be right back."

KC stepped right up, fired a smart salute, and without waiting for the return said, "Right this way, gentlemen."

I raced back to the soccer field. I noted that the monks were gone as I wheeled into the driveway—once more avoiding the black hole in the road. I drove over to the central chopper, which but was still idling. "Climb aboard, gents."

"Morning, Captain. I am Mr. Dickey, and this is my associate, Mr. Kingwell." I shook hands from the driver's seat. "We're with the Department of Agriculture in DC working with USOM."

"Welcome to Vung Liem, gentlemen." I once more maneuvered the chuckhole and pulled onto the road …

No sign of the monks.

By the time we reached the villa, Ong Than was serving the iced tea. KC manned the slide projector, and I began the show. I took questions as I went, so the briefing was a full thirty minutes, if not more. And inevitably, the briefing came to the one question every visitor asked.

"Well, Captain Skillman, seems that you and your team are winning the war down here?" It was more of a comment than a question, but I chose to treat it as a question.

"Actually, sir, we're not." The faces went blank. "Our self-help programs are doing well so far, but the VC are still moving around here and still intimidating people."

"But you're killing them in your ambushes. They have poor morale. They're poorly equipped and supplied. Surely that's progress."

"You would think so. Yet, as poorly armed as they are, they are still armed. And as frightened as they are, and as miserable as their life is, they are still here fighting and killing. They are armed and dangerous. We can minimize their damage and contain their activity, but, we can't chase them down. There are not enough resources as yet, American or Vietnamese, to overwhelm their disruptive influence."

"Is that what you think is necessary to bring security to the countryside -- the ability to *overwhelm* the insurgents?" asked Colonel Hume.

I hesitated. That question was loaded, and might be above my pay grade here. I answered: "I know this. Back home, in my neighborhood, there are not enough police to prevent a hundred percent of the crime. It's the neighborhood watch groups, and the PTAs, and the citizens who report bad things. They do that with confidence that the police will respond, and take down the bad guys. When the citizenry is safe to report criminal activity, and that activity is promptly acted upon, the criminals, I would say, are *overwhelmed*.

"That is not yet the case in Vung Liem."

"I think you are underestimating the fine work you are accomplishing here, Captain," said Colonel Handy.

One of the agriculture representatives, Mr. Dickey, spoke up. "Don't you think that improved living standards help to motivate the civilian population to support the South Vietnamese government in running down these dissidents?"

"I'm not smart enough to know the answer to that question, sir. But, I do know that the Vietnamese are hardworking, respect education, and are entrepreneurial by nature."

"What brings you to those conclusions?" asked the second civilian, Mr. Kingwell.

I told them about the ESL classes started by popular request. I shared Father Phan's innovative solution to tithing in his parish and the trucker's initiative of buying up pigs for market in Saigon.

"Don't sell your progress short, Captain." said Colonel Hume. "You fellows are doing a fine job down here. Keep up the good work."

Handy leaned over to the colonel, pointing to his watch. Hume nodded. "This has been most informative, Captain Skillman." They all stood. "But it's time to hit the road. Thank you." Colonel Hume took the time to shake every man's hand before he walked out to the jeep. I motioned to Kuntz as they headed out.

"Gentlemen, Sergeant Kuntz will drive you to the aircraft. Thank you for the visit." I stood aside from the jeep and saluted as Kuntz pulled out onto the road—narrowly missing Daui Tranh's green machine as it pulled into the courtyard. Tranh hopped out of the driver's seat, and motioned me to follow him to the rear of the truck. He had an unreadable smile on his face as he swung both back doors open.

Sitting just inside the doors, facing to the rear was a little Vietnamese solder in black pajamas looking like death warmed over. Fear exuded from every pore. In his hands he held a dusty black shoebox-sized package. A small pipelike appendage protruded about two inches out of the top of the box. The little man's eyes were wide with fear.

"What on earth have you got there, *Daui?*" I stepped up for a closer look.

"Package is packed with explosives. Device on top is detonator."

"Shit, oh dear ...," to borrow one of KC's more colorful expressions. I instinctively took a few steps backward. "Where the hell did you get that?"

"It buried in driveway gate to soccer field. Armed and have two-foot pressure bar over the detonator. It covered by tar paper. Dirt on top."

I stared at the black box. A dozen thoughts ran through my head simultaneously. *Those meathead monks weren't waving 'good morning' to me. They were waving 'good-bye' ...*

Choppers approached from an odd direction ...

Must have blown away some of the dirt ...

Tarpaper looked like hole. How many times did I drive around that thing? Is anyone on this team as paranoid about things in the road as I am?

"Son of a bitch ... Now, that *really* pisses me off ...

What are we going to do about it, *Daui?*" I was talking through gritted teeth.

"I have it destroyed, *Daui.*"

"The hell with that. I think we should bury it under the footpath to that pagoda across from the soccer field. Those sorry bastards knew. You *know* they knew." I was steamed. *Sons of bitches even lined up out front to wave me good-bye.*

Daui Tranh laughed. "Good thought, bad plan. You and I both go to jail, *Daui.*"

I stewed a few more minutes, then I finally gave it up: "Although... I sure spoiled their morning for them. Didn't I?"

The little guy in the truck relaxed some, but not much. As far as he was concerned, he was still in the crisis mode. The Chief spoke to him, and then closed both truck doors. He walked back up front, climbed into the Overland, and very, very conservatively, drove the green truck, marked conspicuously with a Red Cross, out of town.

I watched him ease on down the road. *No one will ever believe this ... no one.*

CHAPTER THIRTEEN

Know Your Enemy

ONLY THE BLIND MAN could see how angry his old friend was. The hate resonated deep down in the gut of Tien Van Quan. And worse, not only had they missed the American jeep and its occupants, but they had lost the munitions. It was a total disaster. Ngoc, in his blindness, clearly sensed the hardness in his friend's heart, and knew the degree of change in the spirit of the man. The enemy was Diem's Catholic government and the Americans, who supported it. Ngoc was concerned that his friend might be at the point of attacking anyone: civilian, military, man, woman, or child in order to save face, and make his point for the National Liberation Front.

Quan had brought the "miner" to Tra Vinh expressly to hit an American target. And the bomber had missed—again. If the monks had left the miner alone, he would have, at least, blown up a road or bridge, and they would have that.

No, this was bad. Quan wanted to blame the bomber, and took his frustrations out on the man until Ngoc diverted the one way conversation.

"We plan a bigger and bolder operation for our next move," said the blind man. Quan's ranting stopped in midsentence. All heads turned on Ngoc.

"We must plan an action that sends a real message—an attack that kills both the district chief and the American leader."

In Ngoc's mind, killing Vietnamese, citizens or soldiers, should be avoided. For him the real target was the Catholic district chief. Up to this point he had declined outright support of the Vietcong, but now, he believed the monks needed to involve soldiers.

"What do you have in mind?" asked Quan.

"I think we must arrange a meeting with the Vietcong commander."

★★★

By now, a resupply chopper from Province Headquarters arrived, pretty much, on a weekly basis—usually on Fridays. Mail always came with the supplies. On this Friday morning the troops were hanging around the villa in hopes of an early flight. Doc and Kuntz had walked down to the maternity clinic to see how sick call was going.

Through some mysterious Vietnamese civil affairs process, Ong Pham could come up with a Vietnamese medic as soon as an aid station was opened, or a teacher, when a school started receiving children.

As a result, Doc had a counterpart at every aid station where he ran his periodic sick calls. The Vietnamese medic would run screens during the week and refer the more complicated stuff to Doc.

In effect, Doc had a physician's assistance at each of his aid stations when he showed up. Doc in turn would stock the stations with simple medicines like aspirin and sulfa drugs. The morale of the Vietnamese medics was sky-high. This was so much more than the vitamin K which was the sole drug available to them in the Vietnamese supply channels.

The Vung Liem Maternity Clinic was the *pièce de résistance* for Doc. The Chief had no problem appointing Sister Lan as the senior midwife of the clinic. He actually made a big deal out of opening the station with a ceremony and a photo op—the whole nine yards.

None of the Americans knew the small crowd of a dozen or so people that showed up for the event, but it had all the earmarks of a political maneuver. The Chief made a few remarks, which looked a lot like a campaign speech to KC.

"This guy could give lessons on how to run for office," KC whispered in my ear.

The chopper gods were good this Friday morning. At close to 0930 hours a Huey wound down over the town and headed to the soccer field. With Peter at the wheel, we followed on the ground. The jeep passed Doc and Kuntz on their way to the maternity clinic.

"We'll pick you up on the way back," I called as we passed. The jeep pulled into the field and halted at a respectful distance from the aircraft. The door gunner was struggling with a large carton.

The resupply chopper carried, in addition to the mail, Class I supplies broken out from the rations sent down to Province by the Army quartermaster. From the size of the carton, it looked like the boys at Province had been particularly generous today. I reached out to the pilot's window to receive the mail. "You guys are a welcome sight."

"Got a message for you from your boss," said the pilot.

"You mean Major Bass."

"Yeah. He says there is a CBS news team coming to your district today, and you should be prepared."

"You're kidding?"

"Who would kid about a thing like that?"

"Guess you're right. OK ... Thanks. Be careful out there."

The whine of the engine escalated with the increasing rpms. The Huey lifted and backed away from the jeep, then rose and turned for its run out over the rice paddies.

"Boy, look at all this stuff." Pete was excited. Kuntz and Santana walked up. "Look at this, Sarg, a six-pack of San Miguel beer."

"What they think ... we can't get beer in Vung Liem?" said Santana.

"I 'spec' that's just a nice gesture from Lenny. You ever have a San Miguel, Jose?" said Kuntz.

"With a name like San Miguel, you'd think that I would have, but no, I haven't."

"You're in for a treat. Load up, men." We started back to the villa.

I was thinking about the CBS visit. *What will they expect? Do they want to visit the villa? Have a briefing on our progress?*

The American media was beginning to turn against the Vietnam war effort. I had pointed out an article to KC in the *Newsweek* magazine I'd received in the mail. The article reported the progress of the war. It was extensive with maps and interviews. The gist was that we were losing the effort. The map of Vietnam even colored the Delta region red.

"I guess we don't count" was KC's comment.

It now occurred to me that with the CBS visit, maybe I could set the record straight today.

Back at the villa, I took advantage of the team coming together for mail call. "Listen up, everyone. There will be a CBS news crew coming in sometime today for a segment on who knows what. But we need to be prepared. KC, have Ong Than go get the barber." Groans all around.

"I know it's only been four weeks, but you could wind up on national TV, so just do it. If you are asked questions, talk about stuff you know ... and don't guess or try to speak for anyone else. Don't give numbers or locations. If you talk about schools, talk about 'a school' or 'some schools,' never about 'three schools in Ap Lin village.' Any questions?"

"When do you expect them?" asked KC.

"I don't know if they *will* come, but I got a verbal from Province to be ready."

"If they don't come, can we have a bye on the next haircut?" Kuntz smirked.

"No, smart ass. Next question."

Captain Flint spoke up. "Listen up, everybody. We got powdered orange juice and instant coffee in the food pack today. You got choices, men. In addition to hot or cold tea, you can have Tang or Instant Maxwell House, just like downtown San Francisco." With that, everyone turned to his mail from home.

Lunch, as usual, was a do-it-yourself affair with heavy emphasis on peanut butter and jelly with French bread. Everyone, of course, had to have a glass of orange Tang and a cup of coffee.

The barber arrived, a little less fearful than before. Haircuts began. By early afternoon, Pete was into his latest Louis L'Amour Western, which had arrived today from his sister. Kuntz was now reading Pete's hand-me-down paperbacks, and KC was reading back issues of the *Wall Street Journal*. I was getting mad reading another two-week-old *Newsweek* magazine. I would not, could not, allow myself to believe the American people didn't in their hearts support this effort.

Only Santana was not reading something. He sat at the dining table restocking his medical kit. I sensed him looking at me.

"Captain Ed." I looked up. "I'm running low on some of these meds. Stuff is coming through steady, but not enough of it fast enough. I ought to go up to Saigon and see if I can't speed things along."

I had to laugh. "Sperm count getting a little high, Doc?"

"No, it's not that ... well, yes, that's true, but ... I *am* running low on some of these drugs. My dispensing rate is higher than my supply rate, and to get that changed may require some face-to-face negotiations."

"I get the picture. See if you can catch a chopper out tomorrow."

Then, as if by suggestion, the sound of helicopters brought everyone's head up.

"Santana, come with me." I jumped into the command seat of the jeep, leaving Santana to drive. In minutes we arrived at the soccer field in time to watch a gunship settle at the corner of the field. A second ship hovered closer, and finally, settled into the diagonal corner of the field near the road to town. Two men in khaki, one carrying a large shoulder-mounted camera, jumped out of the plane. I motioned for Santana to drive into the field and approach the two men.

The man without the camera strode toward us. He did not smile. "Hello, I'm Peter Callisher with *CBS Evening News*."

"Good afternoon, sir. I am Captain Skillman, and this is Sergeant Santana. Welcome to Vung Liem."

"Yes, well. Could you move your jeep over there, please and remain with it." He indicated the far area in front of the gunship. It was not a request. Callisher turned and walked back toward his ship without waiting for a reply.

Doc and I moved as requested. All the while the cameraman blocked out his shot. In the background was the green vegetation of the banana plantation with just a corner of the school to the right in the camera frame. In the foreground was the chopper.

Callisher moved to the side door of the chopper showing a frontal of him and a profile of the chopper. Callisher brought the microphone to his mouth and spoke. As he spoke he gestured to the scene to his rear. We onlookers did not hear a word of it.

Then, without a wave or glance our way, the reporter team loaded up and flew away—the gunship tagging along.

Santana's lips barely moved, "I be son of a beech."

"You can say that again," I said.

"I be son of a beech."

I was dumbfounded. "What the hell do you suppose his angle is?"

Santana stomped over to the jeep, and climbed in behind the wheel. "You can be pretty damn sure it won't be about a new maternity clinic in Vung Liem District."

★★★

"Good evening. This is the evening news hour, and we will begin our report tonight with the conflict in Vietnam. U.S. forces suffered another setback today. Three American soldiers were killed when a Vietcong unit hit the small district town of Vinh Chau in the Mekong Delta. Peter Callisher has the story. Peter."

"Thanks, Walter. I am standing here in the middle of the Mekong Delta looking out over the rice paddies. The scene behind me looks serene and peaceful, which it is during the daylight hours. The South Vietnamese district chief and his American advisors are, for the most part, able to maintain this kind of stability during the day.

But, it is at night that the Vietcong exercise their control over the South Vietnamese people, and last night the VC demonstrated just how much power they actually can focus.

These advisor teams are made up of five or so men who live among the Vietnamese people and assist the grass-roots infrastructure on military activities. They are, almost *entirely, dependent on the local population for their security which, in the case of last night, failed to prevent a violent raid on the Americans living here.*

If the United States purpose for being in Vietnam is to stem the tide of Communism, it is very clear that these young Americans did not have enough fingers to stick in the dike.

Back to you, Walter."

"Thanks, Peter. Turning closer to home, the Republican candidate for the November election, Senator Goldwater, said today ..."

★★★

It was early Saturday morning, and Master Sergeant Santana was taking no chances. In a casual moment I had agreed for Santana to go to Saigon, and Doc was leaving before anything changed my mind. Doc spread the Day-Glo panel in the middle of the soccer field and hopped back into the jeep.

When he pulled in at the villa, I was standing in the courtyard with KC. "I can expect you back on Wednesday -- right?" KC replaced him in the driver seat.

"Sí, patrón."

I climbed in next to KC. "Stay out of trouble."

"Sí, patrón. No, patrón." We laughed. Doc sat down on the porch steps, and took up his indefinite wait for the next passing chopper.

KC drove us out of the courtyard and headed over to the barracks. We were going to Ap Lin, and wanted Sergeant Khe to come with us. It was time to check on the school opening that had been held up by the coconut roadblock. Also, I wanted to meet the rice mill owner who had assisted the Catholic village, and for that we definitely needed the help of our translator.

Khe was walking toward us as we pulled up to the barracks entrance. "Good morning, sir." The kid didn't salute. He wasn't rude or disrespectful. He just wasn't a soldier.

"Good morning, Sergeant. Hop in the back." Off we went.

It was a gorgeous day. It was going to be hot. South Vietnam was on the same latitude as Nicaragua and had the same climate. We turned northeast at the old gas pump corner onto Highway 8. The rice fields rolled out on either side of the highway, looking like the great plains of Middle America. The rice was tall now, still green, always reminded me of wheat.

KC ran though the gears of the jeep like it was a sports car—double-clutching into second gear and winding out into third-- a big grin on his face. In another dimension, in another part of the world, we could have been any three young guys racing down a country highway in our hot convertible looking for some action.

We passed through the Catholic village. The stone mileage markers were newly painted, and the roadside grasses were freshly trimmed and policed. The couple of hectares of cane were getting tall, and I wondered when they harvested. I pointed to behind the church.

"Look how tall the cane is getting. You know, Khe, when they harvest cane?"

"No, I city boy," he grinned.

We continued on until we reached the turnoff to the school. I retold the story of the coconut roadblock and the two Vietnamese facing down the Vietcong in the shadow of their "great American" protectors. It gave us a laugh—this time. As we approached the hamlet, people came to the entrances of their thatched homes. Folks smiled, and children waved. This was more like it. We dismounted and walked around the school building.

"Well, looks like it is in use, but it's a pretty bare classroom," said KC.

A Vietnamese man was walking down the footpath from the far side of the hamlet. Sergeant Khe spoke to him for a minute or two, then turned to me. "Here is the teacher of this school. He lives at the other end of the hamlet."

"Good. Ask him how things are going."

The teacher and Khe exchanged a few words. The teacher smiled and said in English, "Thank you."

Khe then repeated his story. "He say after the Americans come, and the village chief clear the road, children come. He teaches two levels. The older level has twelve students and the younger level has seven. He is glad you come. It is good. More books would be better."

"I can believe that," said KC.

"Tell him we are glad that things go well. We will see what can be done about more books. Vietnamese books are not easy for us to get."

Khe finished the conversation, and our little band packed out to the main road. We turned right and drove about another kilometer to the bridge over to Vinh Long. Just before we entered the bridge, we turned right.

As KC made the right turn, I drew everyone's attention to the left side of the road. "You see that truck parked there on the roadside?" KC got a fleeting glance. "That's where we saw all those trucks last time. The truckers stop here to buy pigs to take back to sell in Saigon."

We proceeded down the shaded road along the canal bank and past the village chief's house.

KC spoke. "I told you about Miss Miranda and her boar hog, didn't I? Maybe there's something she could do here to pump up the pig market."

"You might be on to something. Let's give ourselves time to check it out before we go back this afternoon."

The road narrowed down after a few minutes. It took on the appearance of a private driveway, which it turned out to be. The mill and the family quarters were co-located in a large compound overlooking the canal. Solid walls surrounded the complex. From the jeep sitting in front of the wrought iron gates, we could see a green lawn stretching to the veranda of a single-story French villa.

"Not bad," said KC.

I questioned Sergeant Khe on how to announce our presence at this point, but before Khe could answer, a man wearing black pajamas and rubber sandals approached across the lawn. He pointed to the side of the house as he pulled aside the gate. KC followed the drive around to the side and parked. A distinguished-looking Vietnamese gentleman stood at the top of the veranda steps. He wore khaki trousers and leather sandals, with a pale green shirt worn outside his trousers.

"Bonjour, *messieurs.*" He smiled graciously. "*Suivez-moi.*" Without waiting, he motioned us to follow and moved into a large open-aired porch. The two of us with our translator hurried up the steps into the room.

"Bonjour, Messieurs. *Je suis Capitain Ed Skillman et ceci Capitain Flint et Sergeant Khe.*"

"*Je suis Phan Dinh Chi. Comment allez-vous?*" Ong Chi was clearly quite comfortable speaking in French.

Sergeant Khe spoke in Vietnamese. "The Americans have come to meet you. They live in the district town."

"I have heard," replied Phan Dinh Chi in Vietnamese. Then in French, "How may I be of service?" He turned to the room and offered us seats. The furniture was a rattan couch and chair set similar to what was in the team's villa. The conversation group was arranged on a large woven straw mat spread like a rug over a white square-tile floor. It looked very comfortable and cool. We all sat down.

I opened with the story of our visit to the Catholic village on his southern border and how we were told of his entrepreneurial spirit in pressing out the church's sugarcane crop.

Sergeant Khe looked puzzled. "What is 'aunturpeterel'?"

"His business sense for adding value to a product."

Khe's face did not clear up. KC said, "We liked the way he helped out the Catholic Church with the sugarcane."

Khe translated.

"It was nothing," said Ong Chi. "It was not that much cane. And it was off-season from the rice, so I just changed around the machinery a little and, voilà." He smiled broadly.

"Well, this season it will be more than 'nothing.' You're looking at seven, maybe eight trucks of sugarcane this year. Have you been down there lately?"

Ong Chi's smile froze in place. There was no mirth in this smile. "That is too much. The mill is old, and cannot process that much before rice harvest. Cane is hard on machinery."

"Is there another place to press out the cane?" asked Flint, a little surprised.

"Oh yes. Other mills. Maybe, but same problem for others. All Mills old; need new machinery."

The room was quiet. Then Ong Chi said, "Would you like to see the mill?"

I remembered my little hammock episode in Long Toan mill, and nodded with a smile. I doubted we could be of any help, but it would be interesting. We walked to the back of the villa out into a dirt yard. On the other side of the yard was a large shed. It appeared that a water inlet reached in from the canal. Also, a road came from nowhere into the back of the mill shed.

Mr. Chi walked over to the large engine. None of us visitors had any idea what we were looking at. Mr. Chi explained to Khe in Vietnamese what we were seeing. He pointed and talked. He gestured out into the room, and at the large wheels and gears, seldom pausing for breath, let alone for the guests to take it in or the interpreter to translate.

"What's he saying, Khe?"

"I not know. I city boy. Not know English words for this."

We walked around to the backside of the shed, smiling and nodding like we had good sense, but without a clue, beyond general concepts, about how anything worked. The only thing that I could identify was the large engine, which looked like it belonged in a tractor. I acknowledged; it looked old.

Mr. Chi walked us back to the jeep. By now, we were speaking French and Vietnamese and English, but mostly, body language, which was light and cordial. Mr. Chi agreed he would process the same amount of cane as last year, but that would be all he could handle. As we drove out the gate, KC commented. "This is going to put a crimp in Father Phan's economic plan for sure."

It might slow him down, I agreed, but there had to be other mills in the area. What we had here was just a little *failure to communicate*. The jeep pulled up onto the hardtop. "Look at all those trucks, will you. Let's see what's going on."

KC drove across the highway, and into the side road. "As I recall, the market is down here on the right along the canal." His memory was good. The marketplace was jammed, which was even stranger because this was late afternoon. We watched a few minutes. Small spots of order became apparent in the chaos. In the far corner, under the pavilion on the roadside of the market, a group of truckers was talking animatedly. Along the other side were pigpens, which were the object of the group's interest.

"Boy, if anyplace needed an auctioneer, it's this place," said KC. Truckers were walking back to their vehicles carrying anything edible that they thought they could sell in Saigon. But, the big prize seemed to be the pigs. We watched the scene a little longer, until I,, finally, motioned to go. There was economic power here, I was thinking—*not sure how to harness it, but we're going to figure it out.*

KC eased the jeep up onto the hardtop. We turned right, away from the bridge to Vinh Long, and headed out of the village.

"One of these days we ought to drive up to Vinh Long Airfield, and see what's going on," suggested KC. "They got a Class VI store up there, you know."

"What's a Class VI store?" asked Sergeant Khe.

"A liquor store run by the U.S. Army for the morale and welfare of its deserving, long-suffering soldiers." KC smirked.

Sergeant Khe processed the information, but still wasn't sure what it was about. He decided not to ask any further questions. Americans were strange sometimes.

We passed through the Catholic village. I looked again at the amount of sugarcane under cultivation in the side yards of every thatched house I could see from the road. There was probably ten times more cane than we could see from the road. "Father Phan might just be in a pickle when he tries to process his village tithe."

"We can't let that happen. There is too much potential in sugarcane as a cash crop here," said Flint.

"What's a pickle?" asked Khe.

The two officers looked back, laughing at their "number one" man. "And you call yourself a translator?" said KC. "It's a cucumber stored in a spicy or salty solution."

Khe worked over the definition in conjunction with the comment about Father Phan being in a pickle. Americans were certainly strange.

★★★

The badminton matches were already under way when the jeep pulled into the courtyard. Sergeant Santana evidently had caught a flight, since the Americans had recruited their Vietnamese counterparts to the match. Kuntz had his own cheering section composed of three little girls. The laughter turned to screaming as soon as I stepped out of the jeep, and the three little girls ran for the apartment door.

"What is it those kids think of me that makes them run like that?" I was laughing with them as they ran for cover. Three giggling heads peeked back out the door.

"Maybe their mother tells them that she's going to sic the American boss man on them if they don't behave," speculated KC. "Who knows about little kids?"

"I give you three years from your summer wedding, and you'll be your own expert on little kids."

I turned to the badminton players. "I got Winners."

The early evening passed as close to routine as our team ever had in little ol' Vung Liem. Dinner was civilized, but still included a rice dish. Peter got a little extra that night, since Santana was gone. The Chief just *happened* to drop in, and collect his evening brandy. Pete and Kuntz were both into Louis L'Amour novels, and KC and I played chess. It wasn't downtown San Francisco, but things were comfortable, and could have been a whole lot worse, considering that the outside world believed the Mekong Delta was overrun with Vietcong.

I felt like I had just gone to sleep. My night security watch had been midnight to three, and I was in as deep a sleep as I ever got in the villa, when it happened. *Whoom ... not crack or thump or bang ...* but an earthshaking *Whoom.* The villa vibrated. I grabbed under the bed for my pistol, checked for a round in the chamber. Pete and KC were taking the same immediate actions. The lights went out.

Kuntz was on watch. "What in the Sam Hill was that?" He was moving through the dark rooms checking for damage. Nothing there. "House clear," he shouted.

KC and I finished dressing. Pete, in his skivvies and loaded carbine, had joined Kuntz. The gate guards were banging their triangles about every five minutes. Kuntz, covered by Pete from the porch, worked the courtyard. "Courtyard clear."

I turned the lights on. It had sounded like something coming from the north edge of town—an explosion.

KC spoke half to himself. "What's north of town?"

"That pagoda I first visited is that way... And the new school," I said.

"Those bastards hit my school? I'll kill 'em." The normally unflappable Kuntz was clearly upset.

We need to find the Chief. "Peter, get dressed, and get over to the com shack. See if anything is coming through. Kuntz, I presume you didn't see the Chief when you cleared the house?"

"Yes, sir, I did. He went out the side doo, and headed down toward the boardinghouse."

"OK. Kuntz, you come with me, and KC, you stay here and direct traffic."

KC was crestfallen. "Boss ..."

"Your time will come all too soon, KC," I said.

They were about to scramble when the Daui Tranh came into the room.

"Hello, my American friends." His smile was artificial. "We have incident at new school on north edge of town. Vietcong blow hole in wall."

Kuntz was turning red in the face. "I knew it. Those sons of bitches blew up my school."

"Cool it, Sergeant," I said. "How fast can we get up there, *Daui?*"

"Daui Sau is assembling a force now. We leave soon."

"Come on, Chief, we need to be moving now."

"Daui Sau move as soon as possible-- like you Americans say, ASAP." He smiled, but he was deadly serious—end of conversation. It was near 0500 hours, still dark outside.

The Vung Lien advisor team relaxed in the saddle, and we began the most frequently executed activity in the military—waiting. Ong Than appeared on the scene with hot water for coffee. The old man knew the drill; he was remarkable. I sent Pete back over to the com shack. His instructions were not to make a report of this until we had more information, but to let me know if anything about the incident came in.

"Roger that."

KC complained. "What in the hell is taking so long? Some immediate reaction force."

I ignored his gripe. How was it that a couple of VC could get in without tripping an ambush?

KC voiced the same thoughts. "Maybe there were too many VC for the ambush to take on. Maybe the VC slipped around them. Maybe we try some training for our troops. Better question, yet, is how can the VC set up and do damage without anybody knowing or reporting?"

The answer to that was easy—if not satisfying. The villagers did not trust us enough to protect them from retribution if they spilled the beans. I was standing at the window. It was first light, and nothing was happening. "We can forget catching VC today."

KC walked out on the porch. "Looks like some troops are assembling at the gate. They're taking their own sweet time about it though."

"Grab your gear, KC. You might as well come with us." KC snapped to, and was hooked up in seconds. The two of us and our operations sergeant checked our weapons and walked out to the front gate.

The troops were lounging around on both sides of the road. The arrival of Americans made little or no stir. But the Chief was approaching up the road from the boardinghouse. Today he was wearing the military version of a baseball cap. He carried a pistol on his hip. As soon as the soldiers saw the *Daui*, they began to get up, and wrestle into their gear. The *Daui* spoke to one of the soldiers, presumably the platoon leader, who then motioned about six men to move out to the south. What the hell was going on, now? … The explosion was north.

As the Chief walked up, KC asked "Where is Daui Sau?"

"Daui Sau not with this party."

I asked, "Isn't the school the other direction?"

"Yes. School on northeast side of district. We start out this way." The Chief walked back down the road and took a position in the middle of the column that was beginning to form. He was indistinguishable from any other soldier in the column. The tall white Americans joined the column about two-thirds of the way to the rear.

I pulled away from KC and Kuntz. "You two hold this position. I'm going to catch up with the Chief."

I joined up with Daui Tranh about the time the column turned right, down a trail in the direction away from the main river. It made no sense to me, but I kept my mouth shut.

Daui Tranh looked back at me. "That is rice mill ahead. Man who owns is Ong Loc Van Lang."

A middle-aged gentleman stood at the head of the path leading to his villa. It was well maintained, but not as expansive as the mill we had visited yesterday. The *Daui* stopped and talked to Ong Van Lang for a few moments. They smiled and laughed, and the Chief moved on without introductions. I greeted the man, who responded in Vietnamese with a smile.

The column turned right, down another trail. We seemed to be headed toward the canal. The vegetation was low to the ground, with palm trees providing overhead shade from the sun. It was still early in the morning, and, strangely, there were few villagers to be seen.

The *Daui* was quiet, and after about fifteen minutes on this trail, he spoke to the platoon leader. The column stopped. The platoon leader began committing fire teams on line in a flanking movement to the left. The Teams move quietly into a line of skirmishers carefully sweeping through the underbrush.

I could see some sort of building through the vegetation, but, from my position, I could not identify if there were one or two structures. The *Daui* and I kept about thirty yards behind the fire teams on line. I could see KC and Kuntz taking similar positions about fifty yards to my left.

The troops were quiet, but not silent. I heard voices on the right flank. The *Daui* stopped. The advance stopped. All eyes were on the right flank. The platoon leader motioned for the *Daui* to come.

The young officer led the *Daui* Tranh to the wooded side of a tree line. I moved forward with them, and saw there was just one concrete building in a clearing surrounded by low vegetation—maybe a garden. We stood inside the edge of the tree line overlooking a rice field. Beyond the rice field, was a road. The road was high, as if built on top of a dike. Off to the left, at a range of approximately 200 meters, the road emerged from the tree line in which we were standing. It ran at an angle across our front, entering the far tree line about 300 hundred meters to the right.

I decided to step in front of the trees for a better look, and almost fell into a freshly dug hole just on the edge the tree line. I stepped around the hole, and out to the edge of the rice field.

"Perfect field of fire on road," said Daui Tranh. He had moved to my side.

I slowly studied the terrain. He was right.

"Holes are machine-gun positions covering road." We walked along the tree line toward the building. There were five dug-in firing positions beautifully covering the road across the front. Anyone walking that road would be like a duck in a shooting gallery.

"The road goes to the new school that was blown last night." The Chief looked at me. Our eyes locked as we each digested the likelihood that *we* were the *ducks* for this morning's events. I looked over at the building. Two soldiers were escorting the saffron-robed monk into the presence of the district chief. *That sorry little asshole.* But he was not the same monk I had met when I came to town.

KC and Kuntz came up. I showed them the layout of the battlefield, and gave them a moment to deduce the implications.

"Now I recognize this place," said Kuntz. "We go right down that road ourselves when we visit the school."

KC was fired up. "That son of a bitch. Is the Chief going to arrest him?"

"I doubt it. He hides behind the religion," I told them. "You know, these guys have no standards for accreditation. They just put on a yellow robe and shave their head; and you got one each, class A, Vietnamese monk. Ain't *that* a bitch?"

The Chief spoke loudly with authority. He did not raise his voice, but made certain that all around could hear him. He spoke at length, and clearly delivered a tongue-lashing. The monk stood straight, head up, and on the very edge of defiant, if not insubordinate. Finally, the Chief dismissed him.

The platoon continued to sweep the area with negative results. Daui Tranh walked with us Americans out to the school to inspect the damage. For all the noise the explosion made, it did not look that bad. A large hole was blown in the corner of the building, and two of the walls were cracked.

"Fix very fast," said the Chief.

Kuntz laughed. "Hell, those little kids won't even get one day off."

Our command party started back down the road to town. A small security detail picked us up at the pagoda, and tagged along.

"Can you imagine what would have happened if the reaction force had come charging down this road fifteen minutes after the blast?" said KC. "Ambush time."

"Yeah, kinda makes you wonder who's advising who; doesn't it?" The Chief and I exchanged glances--and we bonded… some more.

CHAPTER FOURTEEN

The Squids

IMMEDIATELY AFTER THE SOLDIERS cleared the area, the abbot of Cang Long set out on the road back to his Japanese pagoda. It was just too embarrassing watching and listening to the *Catholic* district chief dress down Tien Van Quan like an errant schoolboy. It was humiliating, and the abbot wanted nothing more to do with this kind of thing. He believed the Chief when he said he would arrest Quan if he saw him again in Vung Liem. The abbot did not need that kind of invitation: he was leaving now.

Ngoc also had listened to the lecture delivered by the Chief. It was true, as the Chief had said: Quan did not fit in around here. He was a foreigner from the north and not motivated to blend into this community. Ngoc knew this in his heart, and because of it, even if the ambush had been successful, Quan would have to leave the district. His presence was too noticeable and without any contribution to the community. He just smelled like trouble. The district chief could probably arrest Quan right now, and very few people would protest. Quan had expended little or no effort at endearing himself to the villagers. By not arresting Quan the district chief demonstrated restraint and mercy and would be viewed favorably in the eyes of the villagers.

Daui Tranh was wise—for a Catholic.

Tien Van Quan was livid, and it took every ounce of self-control not to reach out and choke that little bastard to death. What made it worse was that the Chief had not arrested him. Quan could have protested that, made it an issue of false arrest or something. But the little martinet did not even have the guts to do that. He just stood there with that sanctimonious attitude and loudly lectured the world. How dare he order Quan out of the district? He had no legal right to do that.

But, at the crack of dawn the next morning, Tien Van Quan boarded a northbound sampan to Sa Dec. Tomorrow, maybe the next day, he would report to the National Liberation Front (NLF) headquarters in Saigon. By then he could figure out what to tell them.

★★★

I watched through the window as Private First Class Peter de Groot sailed through the gates into the villa courtyard. He flew up the porch steps and sped through the living room door. I had returned to my letter writing when Peter came around the corner into the dining room. My train of thought had already been broken.

"Hold on there, Tiger. What's going on?"

"… was over at the barracks with Lieutenant Than, and they're packing up the 4.2 mortars."

"You're kidding."

"No, sir. The trucks are there and everything."

"You sure they're not just displacing to a new survey point?"

"I don't think so. The families are packing up, too."

I stood and put my letter writing stuff away—no more of this today. Families packing suggested a permanent relocation. I had no idea what was going on. Peter was clearly exercised, and, therefore, it was important for me to appear calm. In my best casual voice I asked, "You see the Chief around?"

"No, sir. Haven't seen him in a couple of days."

As I thought about it, neither had I. In fact, I hadn't seen him since the school bombing four days ago. "Umm … OK, let's go find out what's happened."

I strapped on my webbing with pistol. We needed Sergeant Khe; except he was with Doc at the maternity clinic. It was important to get the story straight the first time. As I hesitated, I became aware of an aroma coming from the breezeway—smelled delicious. *What could Ong Than be cooking?*

I thought about the hassle at the compound over communication details without a translator. "We'll wait for Santana to get back and then have Sergeant Khe go with us."

Pete seemed surprised at my calm reaction—probably remembering I had been a lot more concerned when the howitzers were pulled.

Pete asked, "Are the 105s coming back?"

"Well, I don't know, Peter. The fact that the 4.2s are moving is a bit of surprise. But I'm sure we'll receive equivalent resources in lieu of the four deuce." I spoke with more confidence than I felt.

When it came down to it, the team's security was a function of the local Regional Force's ability to stand off any VC initiative. Indirect fire support, while its principal mission was to support the district villages, was nonetheless a valuable deterrent to any VC attempt against the American presence in Vung Liem. Three carbines and two .45s were not going to achieve the greatness recorded in the annals of history like *Remember the Alamo*. Without additional firepower available, the tactics of *escape and evade* might be a better choice than *stand and fight*. I needed to rethink our position here—*as soon as I find out what is going on.*

The jeep pulled into the courtyard with KC and Kuntz. KC went straight to the breezeway, and Kuntz came into the living room. "Boy, what a day we've had. I don't know exactly who those guys were from Washington, but since their visit, the supplies are coming through. We got three more new schools started." He caught a whiff of good smells from the breezeway and decided to wash up. Pete sniffed and followed.

With the advent of Engish classes, the badminton matches had taken a backseat. The team was eating earlier in order to accommodate the students. Even at that, it was a little early today for the evening meal, but who was counting? KC came in from the breezeway. "Today we dine, men." He looked around the dining room where everyone had gravitated. "Where's Santana?"

"It's a little early," I said. "Shall we wait a while?"

No one spoke. "Why?" asked Peter. Everyone sat down, and Ong Than came in with the special for the evening entrée.

"What in the name of heaven is that?" Kuntz looked at the two blocks of thinly sliced meat, then at the mess officer. KC frowned deeply. Kuntz amended. "Sure smells good, though."

KC enlightened the table. "Gentlemen, I found two cans of Spam in the marketplace yesterday. Thought we might like the change from chicken and pork." He got no argument.

I cautioned them to leave a couple slices for Doc. And on cue Santana entered.

"Boy, what smells so good? Did I miss mess call?"

"No. But before you sit down, I want you to catch Sergeant Khe and tell him I need him this evening for about an hour. I'll meet him at Daui Sau's."

Santana's eyes scanned the table. "What the ... that looks like Spam." He caught the look on KC's face. "Sure smells good, though. I'll be right back. Save me some."

The meal was topped off with vanilla ice cream from the powdered stuff KC brought down from Saigon. It wasn't farm fresh, but it was cold and sweet, and it went really well topped with strawberry preserves—also in the food pack, along with two giant jars of peanut butter.

Dinner conversation was short lived. I asked Peter to take my class this evening. And I wanted Captain Flint to come with me for the conversation with Daui Sau. As KC and I walked over to the barracks, I related Pete's discovery of the mortar displacement.

"Are they bringing in anything else?" asked Flint.

"That's what we're going to find out." We rounded the corner into the courtyard. The smell of charcoal burners in front of every apartment made us Yanks feel like we were back in suburban America on a summer Sunday evening.

Company Commander Sau and the interpreter, Khe, were sitting in front of the captain's apartment. A smiling Mrs. Sau brought out a pot of hot tea with cups and served us, as the greeting ritual progressed.

"Where have they displaced the mortars?" I asked Sau.

Sergeant Khe translated, but Sau had already begun his response in Vietnamese. "I am not sure." Khe translated the response.

"Are we getting anything in to make up the erosion of resources?" asked Flint.

Daui Sau looked at his hands. Khe spoke: "He does not think so."

From my experience that was a definite no. "How can we organize to offset this reduction in force?" I was probing.

Daui Sau looked away, then went back to inspecting his fingernails. Sergeant Khe spoke. "He said 'no problem.'"

That meant we had a problem. I was sure he had 81mm mortars. I probed further. "Do you have ammunition for your 81s?"

Sau asked Khe a question. They exchanged words, and Khe translated. "He asked me if you Americans had any support. I told him you do not have support, and he say he has three 81mm mortars with plenty of ammunition. But 81s hardly reach the edge of the district town."

Every now and then Khe slipped out of the translator role and into the interpreter role. I reminded the sergeant not to answer for me. I did appreciate his commitments, but I needed him to translate exactly. "Tell him I'll see what resources are possible, but he should not hold out any expectations. Are the 81s set up in firing positions?"

Khe translated. "He said 'absolutely.'"

We talked a little longer, and finished our tea when the situation was understood by all. I moved over to the apartment doorway, and stuck my head in. "*Merci beaucoups*, Ba Sau." The little woman jumped up, placing her hands together, and bowed. She spoke in Vietnamese, but the smile needed no translation. I thanked Khe for the extra time, and, with that, KC and I headed back to the villa.

We walked along in silence for a while, then KC opened up. "First there were two Regional Force companies here in Vung Liem, an ARVN battalion and a section of artillery. One Regional Force company redeploys because the U.S. Special Forces move out to the Cambodian border. We arrive in town, and the ARVN pulls out. We build a working ambush strategy with a preplanned fire support program, and they pull the artillery section. We adjust with the 4.2s by surveying them in all over the district and continue to march. Roads open up. Schools get built. And then they pull the 4.2s. What's wrong with this picture?"

I gave a humorless laugh, but it wasn't funny. "Actually one of Napoleon's Nine Principles of War was *Economy of Force*. You redistribute forces from one place on the battle field in order to concentrate them at another place. You leave just enough to hold the fort at the first position while you pile on at the point of main effort. That was another principle called *Mass*."

KC was upset. "Somehow I have trouble comparing the battlefields of Napoleon, or MacArthur for that matter, with what we got here in little ol' Vung Liem. I sure would like to know where it is we are concentrating *our* Mass."

I thought about that. This certainly wasn't a war of position or place. Maybe it was like Joe Bass said. In this *managed* war, when you need a quarter, they give you twenty cents. If you make do with the twenty, they want a nickel back. I shook it off. *There were still options.*

"Tell me about our options, Ed"

"Well, first off there is a radio relay station in the barracks compound which, if I'm not mistaken, will allow us to pull down any aircraft we might need, from gunship helicopters to fixed-wing fighter planes, and spotter planes in between."

KC visibly brightened up. "That's right."

"And second, we don't know what the Chief knows about all this. Have you seen him lately?"

"No, and his little Peugeot car is gone from the shed."

We came into the villa courtyard about the time the English class let out. The students bowed and passed, and finally Peter came out to join us. We walked into the villa.

Peter was very serious. "You know one of my students said something interesting this evening."

"You mean you could actually understand something they said," joked KC.

"Yes, sir. Remember, boss, that exercise you started a couple sessions ago—the one about making each student prepare a two-minute talk on something that happened to him that day? Well, this evening was pretty good. And one lady told about how happy she was, that her son came home a few days ago. I thought that was interesting."

"*Very* interesting, Peter. It's possible her son is moving around with a VC unit. What village is she from?"

Pete went from chest popped up, to total deflation, in seconds. "I … I don't know."

"Don't beat yourself up, kid. This is going to be a great little source of information, and you're better off just listening and correcting English rather than interrogating." I looked around the room. "Everyone pull up a chair. We need to talk."

I summarized the events of the day, which I wrapped up with some conclusions. Nothing had really changed. We just needed to keep doing our job, and keep our heads up and not get complacent.

"And look for little changes in the daily activities of the locals. Peter, tomorrow I want you to become real familiar with that radio relay station in the barracks. I want you to monitor the channel settings on the transmitter. See who is using it, and how often."

I looked at the others. "All of you; if you have not started having your students speak about their personal activities, start. There is no telling what can come from that. And see if you have a promising student who can work at the maternity clinic. Women sitting around in a waiting room gossiping could be very helpful—but only if we have a receptionist there who speaks a little English."

Santana perked up. "Good idea. Sister Lan is great at taking names and recording history, but I need her more with the pregnancy examinations. Another person would free her up."

"Well, that's good, but the idea is to pick up on people coming and going and on changes in the local habits."

"When we going to get *our* radio?" asked Pete.

"That's a good question. We'll wait around a few days to see what happens. If nothing changes I'll take a trip to Province and see if we can get some answers." I looked around the room for more questions. "OK. No change in the watch schedule." The group then broke up, but I pulled KC aside. "Let's you and I walk the compound tomorrow. I want to check the trip wires, and look around with a new eye to security."

The watch schedule was 2100 to 2400, 2400 to 0300, and 0300 to 0600—three nights on and two nights off. It worked out pretty well. On watch was a chance for the guys to get their letter writing done, and to listen to the big Zenith transistor radio that KC had brought with him from the States. I had the 2400 to 0300 watch this night, and was writing my parents and listening to BBC for news on the progress of world events.

It was a hot summer evening, the second day of August. The front watchtower guard routinely clanged his triangle. I had paused in writing my thoughts, when it dawned on me: *Did I hear the back tower? Maybe I wasn't paying attention. But I was* paying attention, and the back tower did not respond to the front.

I picked up my web gear on the floor next to my chair. I blew out the kerosene lamp KC had bought in town out of house funds. I cut the overheads. I slid quietly down the steps into the breezeway, and paused a moment in the shadows to let my eyes adjust to the dark. The radio was still playing in the background, but the music didn't muffle the metallic sound of the round I chambered in the .45.

The nearly full moon beamed into the villa courtyard, creating weird shadows in all the corners. I stepped around the outside of the old kitchen, carefully avoiding the trip wires. I made it to the compound wall and paused, listening. The wall was continuous without access to the watchtower on the other side. The guard post side was the thickness of the wall away from me.

I stood motionless, scanning the backyard out of the corners of my eyes to maximize my night vision. I looked for movement in dark patches and corners. The front watchtower clanged again …

Nothing on this end… I waited another moment …

Still nothing.

I then sucked up the deepest breath I could hold. And in my loudest parade ground voice shouted as loudly as I could: "WAKE UP OVER THERE, YOU SORRY LITTLE SHIT."

Clang. Clang. Clang-a-dy-clang clang.

Might have to take this up with Daui Sau tomorrow.

I walked back to my letter writing, but did not begin to write. The radio was talking about two North Vietnamese gunboats that attacked a U.S. destroyer in the Gulf of Tonkin. *Where the hell's the Gulf of Tonkin?* The radio announcer interrupted his report with a date and time station break. I checked my watch. It was time to bring KC on watch. I walked back to wake him up. Long, tall KC was stretched out in his skivvies under his mosquito netting.

"Wake up and spit, the world's on fire."

KC was alert in a second. "You think that will do it?"

"No, but it's a start." I went back to the radio, and in a few minutes KC joined me.

We listened to an account of the president of the United States becoming directly involved in the command and control of the USS *Maddox*. The announcer then moved on to a new topic.

KC said, "I can't believe the captain of a warship needs the permission of the president of the United States to return deadly hostile fire."

"Nobody wants history to hold them accountable for starting WW III ... and that's what might happen. Remember, we're still *advising* the South Vietnamese. Kinda brings a new twist to the statement 'the buck stops here,' doesn't it?"...

I went on to bed.

★★★

Ong Than followed Captain Flint dutifully, as KC inspected and selected the produce of the day. Ong Than pointed to the fresh fish, and rattled off recommendations in Vietnamese. KC looked at the fish. "You're right, these look pretty nice. Do you know how to prepare?" Ong Than never spoke English, but he manifested an understanding that was rather remarkable. The old man nodded, OK. KC gave him the sign, and Ong Than opened up on the vender. The exchange was rapid and civil, but haggling nonetheless. When the old man indicated to KC that the price was one pound or dollar per fish, the captain gave him the nod again, and the deal was cut. All three men were happy.

Flint moved on, meandering around the kiosks, and poking into stalls. He was completely comfortable in this logistical role. Ong Than suddenly spoke in the imperative and pointed. Coming up from the docks were two American uniforms. Flint watched the two cautiously walking into the marketplace.

They had not seen KC until he called out, "Hey, sailors. Looking for some action?"

Broad grins broke out. "What you offering, soldier?"

"Well, for openers, how about a cup of coffee at my place? Name's KC Flint."

They shook hands. "I'm Mack Williams, and this is Chief Hanson. Coffee sounds good."

KC turned to Ong Than. "This is good for the day. We'll do fish tonight. Go back to the villa and make a pot of coffee." Ong Than did not wait for introductions but disappeared in an instant.

"What brings you guys ashore?" KC asked. They began walking back to the villa.

"Well, after we passed on the canal a couple of weeks ago, I made a mental note to drop in; see what you John Wayne types are up to. We may be able to help each other."

"Yeah, Captain Skillman told me about you crossing paths. He's the team chief here and the one you passed on the canal."

"I see. How many men you have here?"

KC gave them a quick overview of the team's organization and mission as they walked along. By the time they reached the courtyard it was Lieutenant Williams's turn to show and tell.

Their laughing and loud talking reached into the dining room, and interrupted the completion of the reports I was writing. I could hear KC inviting some people in for a cup of coffee. They moved up the steps and into the villa. I was picking up my papers and organizing a stop point when KC shouted, "Hey, Ed, I found some sailors in the marketplace."

I checked around the room, making sure we were ready for guests. I responded over my shoulder, "Were they on sale?" and then turned back into the living room entrance.

I stopped dead at the sight of the Lieutenant.

Williams ripped off his sunglasses and the two of us stood for a moment trying to reconcile what we were seeing.

I spoke first. "What the hell you doing on dry land?"

"Think you're the only one who gets to have any fun?"

Spontaneously we grabbed each other's hand in our funky kind of handshake, and then smacked each other on the back over and over. We were both talking at the same time. Hansen and Flint looked on in dumb amazement.

The shock was still processing for Mack and me as the introductions were made. KC ushered Hanson into the dining area, and Ong Than did his thing. By this time, Sergeant Kuntz had joined the coffee klatch, and he and Chief Hanson played a little "who do you know and where have you been."

Mack and I had started out in college together before each of us went to the service academies. It had been a long time since we had actually seen each other.

As the coffee flowed and everyone got into his comfort zone, Mack and I began to regale the group with stories of shared adventures. We had pledged the same fraternity at the University of Colorado the year before we went off to West Point and Annapolis, respectively. Mack actually talked me into accepting my appointment by telling me how cool it would be for me to be at West Point and him at Annapolis. We could get together at Army-Navy games, and on exchange weekends, and things like that. It sounded good—that and the fact the fraternity social life might overcome a quality college education. But before we entered the military way of life, we needed to know all that fraternity life had to offer.

"You remember the night the actives took the pledges for a 'ride' into the mountains?" Mack put a special twist on the word *ride*.

"I think that was the night I decided you were going to be my best friend."

Actives were the men who had been accepted into the brotherhood after completing a training period as a pledge. Pledges were on trial: tested and tried under all kinds of conditions from social to physical. The "ride" consisted of piling a couple of pledges under blankets in the backseats of each of a half dozen cars, and driving them into the mountains. The pledges were dropped off individually along back roads and instructed to find their own way out of the mountains back to campus. The roads were patrolled to see that no two pledges teamed up. If they were discovered together, the actives picked them up and redistributed them back into the mountains.

"More coffee?" offered KC. Ong Than had put out some Vietnamese rice cakes that were sweet and sticky. They disappeared -- twice.

Mack took over. "Your leader here was marching down the mountainside when I ran into him. I asked him what he thought he was doing, and he said going back to campus. I informed him that just because he was going downhill didn't mean he was going home. The sneaky actives had dropped us on the reverse side of the valleys so that you had to walk up the mountains before you could walk out of the mountains."

The troops were entertained; It was in their faces. God, it was good to see Mack again.

I picked up. "Thing is, we saw headlights coming off the other side of the valley, and Mack goes off the road on the up side of the mountain, and I go over the down side. When the car passed I find myself hung up in a barbed wire fence that just happened to save me from falling into a ravine."

"That was the good news," Mack continued. "Himself here was so tied up in the barbed wire it took the both of us to get him out."

I rubbed my left thigh. "I still have the scares to prove it."

The genuine laughter all around felt good for a change.

"Good golly, Molly." Mack looked at his watch, and then his chief. "We got to get going. Go tell the boys to crank up. I'll be down in a few minutes … Heading is back upriver."

Kuntz stood. "I'll go with you." The two noncoms walked out jabbering like they had known each other for thirty years.

It was serious time. I told Mack that, if there was any way we could help, all he had to do was ask. We had access to a good supply of small arms ammunition here at the civil guard compound. It was his to tap anytime.

That sounded fine to him. "These suckers are floating in from Cambodia. They drop off supplies and who knows what else. We patrol for them. We chase them up canals, but in the end they scoot back into Cambodia home free. I'd just hate to break off contact and have to go all the way back to base because I'm out of ammo. A little cache at your place would be just the ticket."

"Well, you got it."

By now we were back at the docks. Mack jumped on deck and gave the signal to move out. We rendered each other the ancient sign of warrior respect, and the boat roared away.

The three of us turned back toward the villa, and Kuntz commented, "Those guys are looking for a fight."

I laughed. "I think you're right. Mack may be in the wrong service."

"Nah. It's the whole crew. They're all itching for a fight," said Kuntz.

KC agreed. "You need to tell them, boss. They can be ambushed on a canal just as well as on a road."

★★★

As good as their word, the chopper pilots circled back as soon as they got a visual of the Day-Glo orange panel on the soccer field. This bird came in across the rice field with the downdraft waving the rice like sea spray. I pulled up the panel, handed it off to Peter in the jeep, ran in a crouch to the chopper, and jumped up into the cargo compartment. Even before I was strapped in, the plane was airborne, climbing out to the southeast.

"Welcome aboard, Captain. We'll take you anyplace you want as long as it's to Tra Vinh," said the voice in the headset.

Matching the sarcasm, "How about a lift to Tra Vinh, Chief?" The pilot, a chief warrant officer, gave a thin smile and a thumbs-up over his shoulder.

Less than fifteen minutes later the chief was setting down on the grass strip at the Tra Vinh Province. A loading crew headed to the aircraft, led by Captain Khrol.

I thanked the chief as I pulled off the headset and turned to Khrol. "Good morning, Lenny."

"Same to ya. What brings you to town?"

"Came to see the boss. He around?"

"Joe Bass is ubiquitous." Lenny grabbed a carton off the chopper and headed to the truck. I followed suit.

"You staying for lunch?" asked Lenny.

"Thought I would. Is that a problem?"

"Oh no. But you'll never guess who's coming for dinner."

"You're kidding. Westmoreland is coming again?"

"Nooooh. Raymond Burr," said Lenny with a smirk.

"Well, you're right about that. I would never have guessed that Perry Mason himself would be a guest in Tra Vinh Province. What's the occasion?" We climbed into the truck.

Lenny checked that the crew was secure in the back. "Seems he's doing research for a pilot series about American advisors in Vietnam."

"How long is he going to stay?"

"For lunch ... maybe a couple of hours. Who knows?"

We chatted, and I caught up on changes on the province team, and who'd gone where on R&R. Travel time was just enough to catch up on the local news before we arrived at the MAAG House. It was the early side of 1000 hours. I went looking for Major Bass.

"What's going on that's so important it makes Ed Skillman abandon his post?" The crusty old soldier had that onery in his eye.

"I thought it was time to give a face-to-face accounting of the things going on in Vung Liem. And ... well, I'm looking for some insight on certain developments coming down through the Vietnamese channels. I wanted to talk to Jake, too."

"Let's get some coffee." Before Bass walked into the dining area, he yelled out the back door, "Got any of those cookies left from last night out there?" The room was set up with a help-yourself coffeepot. I poured out two cups of coffee, and we took a seat at the corner of the table. I began discussing the assassins when the Vietnamese cook breathlessly arrived with a plate of cookies.

Joe took two. "Go on."

I continued. I described my first meeting with the monk. Then, in great detail, I told about the mining of the soccer field. And, on the bombing at the new school, my point was this: while their ambush failed, their second objective, blowing up the school, succeeded, and was a hostile action against the villagers. I thought the VC had made a mistake.

"Not necessarily," said Bass. "On your first point, Ngo Dinh Nhu, President Diem's brother, identified the pagodas as actively hostile staging points for resistance against the South Vietnamese government, and he went after them. World public opinion, the Vietnamese people, and, most important, the CIA all vigorously objected to that action. Nhu was forced to resign, taking down his brother with him. The whole exercise resulted in the murder of both men."

"What you're saying, then, is I cannot expect the support of Vietnamese monks, no matter what I do?"

"Bright boy. As to the second point, the attack on the new school is probably not perceived as an assault on the villagers. The school is too new to be viewed by the locals as personal loss, even though it is a self-help project. Their children had not yet attended.

These guys will get away unscathed, and they don't care about public opinion anyway. In fact, since you were most likely the targets, you might check if someone tipped off the Chief and saved your asses."

That was a new thought. I made a mental note of it.

Then I launched into the next subject. I recounted the erosion of resources. I said, "Frankly, we feel like we are being punished for our successes." I asked for a rationale that was explainable to my men.

"Look, Captain, this war is being *managed* before it's being led. Your discussion of the principles of war is out the window on the *political* battlefield. In the managed war it is the principle of *measured response* that has priority application; not Von Clausewitz's principle of mass, or, for that matter, economy of force."

That didn't sit well. It seemed to me I remembered something in my military art courses called *piecemeal* application of resources. Historically, it was the main cause for military failure on the battlefield. *Measured response* sounded suspiciously like *piecemeal*.

Bass filled a dramatic pause with a bite of cookie. "You may be right, son. But you're surfing the wrong wave. Today's army is riding the management wave, and we'll ride that wave until we either wear out or run out—and if you quote me on that, I'll deny it."

I had to think about that. I fussed with another cup of coffee; helped myself to the next to last cookie—left the last for the monster. We sat in silence for a few moments. Both of us pondering the implications of the discussion: me on what to say to my men, and Bass, on what to expect as the eventual outcome of the war.

Joe Bass had fought in Korea and earned his battlefield commission there. Battlefield commissions were not that uncommon, and were awarded to enlisted men who clearly demonstrated leadership capabilities. In many cases the man was already serving in the capacity of a unit leader. Lieutenant Bass was there when President Truman relieved General MacArthur over a disagreement on how the Korean War should be prosecuted.

The North Koreans had completely overrun South Korea in a sweeping act of aggression. MacArthur, with a brilliant envelopment of the Korean peninsula, landed at Inchon and totally cut the lines of supply to the North Koreans. It forced them to withdraw in disarray. The United Nation forces then drove the enemy north all the way to the border of Manchuria at the Yalu River. At that point the Chinese entered the war, swarmed across the border, and pressed the UN forces into an embarrassing retreat.

As Macarthur regained control of the battlefield, he prepared to engage the Chinese. Harry Truman disagreed with the general's plan to destroy the enemy army and summarily relieved him of command. Truman changed the mission too. The UN forces were no longer fighting to defeat the enemy and destroy their will to fight. Instead, they were maneuvering to *negotiate* a peace. It now occurred to Joe Bass that America had not fully mobilized with the intent to unconditionally destroy the enemy since WW II.

I moved on to another topic. I extolled the entrepreneurial spirit I found in the district. I boasted about Father Phan's crop of sugarcane and lamented the status of Ong Van Lang's broken-down rice mill.

Joe must have caught the energy in my voice. "We need to tell Jake about this stuff. Maybe he has some ideas on how to help. Those USOM guys have more money than you can shake a stick at, and all kinds of toys."

The major was right about the toys. That midwife kit was something to behold. There were tools in that kit—well, if a doctor approached me with something like one of those instruments, I'd probably hit him. Our conversation ended when Lenny announced that the VIP was inbound. Bass snatched up the last cookie and stood. "We'll take this up again when Jake is here."

Raymond Burr was a huge man. He filled the backseat of the jeep that chauffeured him up the drive to the MAAG House. He was dressed in fatigues and issue boots. The dark patches of perspiration on his shirt indicated how much the great man suffered in the midday heat of the Delta. He was congenial and asked good questions about the day-to-day life of an American advisor in Vietnam. When asked about his own motives for being here, he outlined the basic premise of a possible TV series. It sounded most interesting.

After nearly two hours, Mr. Burr was rounded up by his escort officer. Burr thanked Bass for the opportunity to chat with the team and for the offer of lunch, which he graciously declined. In retrospect, that was probably a good thing, since it was unlikely that they had prepared enough food for Mr. Burr and his entourage.

However, Mr. Burr's turning down lunch prompted the major to extend an invitation to Jake Ledbetter, who did accept. Jake had dropped over to meet the visitor and add the State Department's story to the research project.

The conversation around the lunch table was light and generally focused on the various episodes of *Perry Mason* shows, and the fact that Raymond Burr, himself, had visited them. It was interesting to me how genuinely pleased the men were that a celebrity had taken the time and, in this case, the enormous effort to visit Vietnam in general, and Tra Vinh in particular.

"Jake," said Bass, "how about sticking around for a few minutes? Ed here has some things to share that you may find of interest."

"You got my attention," said Jake. And with that introduction I retold my story and summarized the discussion with Bass.

The ornery lit up in Bass's eyes. "Ed here, got his feelings hurt 'cause the monks don't like him." Jake smiled. "Bummer about the school, though."

Joe's eyes suddenly sparked. "Point is, kid, there's no fiercer enemy than one motivated by religious fervor. You might want to write them off as crazy; they may well be by our standards, but *crazy* will kill you quicker than *rational*, and *crazy* will damn sure keep hunting you long after *rational* has quit the field." We sat a moment allowing those thoughts to filter into our emotions.

Jake broke the silence. "I might be able to help with the rice mill. Write this name down. Jim Edge is in Saigon with the Agriculture people. I think he should look at your mill. And Miranda Meadows is definitely the one to help with the hog population. I can maybe help there too. What is the state of the market facility in Ap Lin?"

"Well, it's old ... dirt floor, thatched roof ... typical small village marketplace."

"As I suspected. We'll see about building a new one up there with a concrete slab floor and permanent roof. What else?"

I continued my story about the aid station and the midwife clinic. Jake was caught up in the tale of progress being made in Vung Liem. The more I talked, the longer grew the list of names for me to contact.

It didn't take a fortune-teller to predict a trip to Saigon in my near future.

CHAPTER FIFTEEN

Will the Real Advisor Please Stand Up?

THERE IS NO SUCH thing as Vietnamese cuisine in the sense there is a French cuisine or a Japanese cuisine. There is of course *nuoc mam*, which is a sauce, like soy sauce. Nuoc mam is uniquely Vietnamese like *kim chi* is uniquely Korean. But when Vietnamese want to treat a friend to a nice meal, it will generally be either Chinese or French, and the Chinese is more often Cantonese.

Miranda Meadows had selected Chinese, and I was sitting across the table from her enjoying dinner in Saigon. The restaurant was actually in Cholan, the Chinese quarter of Saigon, and had been suggested by Miranda after our late afternoon business meeting had run out of office hours. The meal was superb—especially the spring rolls, which demanded a second order.

In between talking business we exchanged personal histories. Miranda was an Indiana farm girl who just could not stay down on the farm after her bachelor's degree in history from Northwestern University. Foreign Service was a surefire way of getting out of Indiana. Her desire to travel and her sense of history, together with her rural upbringing, made her assignment to the Agricultural Division of USOM a natural. She became the obvious choice for the pilot program directed at Vietnamese women.

We had finished comparing our fortune cookies and were lingering over the tea. I began to wrap up the day's discussions. "So you can get the hog as far as Province, and it's my job to get him down to the village?"

"That's right. I'll come down a day ahead of time to introduce myself to the villagers and let them buy in on what we plan to do," she said.

"Do I need to find a place for you to stay?"

"No. I usually find a place with the village people, and I seldom spend more than two nights. If it takes more, I leave and return at a later date."

"Are you sure I don't need to provide security?"

"Again, I'm safe if I don't stay too long and my movements have no pattern. Remember, I speak Vietnamese, and people take pretty good care of me because they benefit from what I bring."

The waiter appeared with the check. I reached for the bill without a thought, but Miranda's hand slipped under mine and snatched up the paper. "My treat," she said.

No woman, except my old maid Aunt Leila, ever had bought me dinner. I wasn't at all sure how to act. I guess it showed on my face.

"You act like you never had a woman buy you dinner." She smiled coyly. "Don't panic, Captain. This way I don't owe you a thing. And in this environment, my owing you something might just cross your mind."

I was sure I was blushing. "It hadn't crossed my mind." I heard myself stuttering. I had had a delightful time dining and talking with an intelligent woman. It was nice to enjoy the company of a woman again. And maybe somewhere in the back of my mind feelings of attraction were forming, but they had not yet coalesced. It was disturbing that Miranda had stifled such thoughts before they even formed.

"It may not have crossed your mind *yet*, Sir Galahad, but I have lived in this world of de facto bachelors for a long time, and sooner or later it *would* cross your mind … or mine. This way we have had a nice evening. We'll share a cab back to my place, and you will take the cab on to the hotel. Tomorrow we'll both go to work happy with our memories of a nice evening and no associated guilt."

It occurred to me that it would be interesting to know how Miranda got so wise. I smiled to myself. Like my mother used to say, *When someone does something nice for you, accept it graciously, and say thank you.* I shifted the smile to Miranda. "Thank you for a delightful dinner and day. Ready?"

Miranda returned the smile, and I assisted her with the chair. She then led the way out of the restaurant. Cabs were waiting at the curb.

Back in the Majestic Hotel, I entered the elevator and was about to press my floor button when my finger jumped to the button marked Terrace Roof. *Son of a gun.* I walked into the lounge in time to catch the first show of the evening. The bartender surprised me by pulling down a snifter and splashing the bowl with brandy before I had even seated myself. "Brandy, *Daui?*"

I flipped a bill on the bar. "Damn, you're good." I was in fine spirits. It had been a rewarding day. When we started, I couldn't have said how this hog thing would work out, but Miranda had put handles on it. In a hundred and fourteen days, more or less, that Berkshire hog of hers would breed a heavier, healthier pig than those little Vietnamese animals. That adds value to the product, and *that* increases revenues at the hog market. In a little over six months that marketplace should be a booming operation.

Also, Miranda had hooked me up with Jim Edge from Industrial Division. I had an early morning meeting with Mr. Edge, which, if all went well, would allow me to fly back to Province in the afternoon. *Here she goes.* "I left my heart in San Francisco ..." Two months, and I'm on R and R. The little doll sang with all the same emotion ... just like the first time I came in here. She finished the song, and I finished my drink. I left the change on the bar, nodded thanks to the barman, and headed to my room.

★★★

The nervous, wiry man shaking my hand was Jim Edge. He had black eyes and black hair and milk white skin, suggesting he spent most his time in air-conditioned offices of Saigon. He was all business.

"What can I do for you?" It sounded more like an accusation than a question. I gave him the three-minute version of the sugarcane story and the plight of the mill owner.

Without hesitation he asked me when I was headed back. I told him, "The first flight I can catch after I leave here."

Edge grabbed his telephone and punched in three numbers. "Cochran? Edge here. How soon can you get a flight together for a visit to the Delta? ... How about two hours instead? ... No, you'll be back this afternoon." Edge gave an abstract version of the situation in Tra Vinh, and added the mission to inspect the mill.

By the end of the conversation the departure time was 1130 hours. He was now facing me when he hung up the phone. "Bill Cochran is one of the best maintenance men in Indochina. He'll meet you at Military Ops at 1130. He'll fly you down for a look at the problem, see if we can help."

I hardly said thanks and would have gone on, but Edge abruptly stood and opened his office door.

"Nice to meet you, Captain. And thanks for bringing this to our attention. We'll be in touch if there is anything we can do."

Next thing I knew, I was on the street hailing one those kamikaze cabs. This man, Edge, was efficient, but downright abrasive. Evidently, he thought smiling was a waste of time. So much the better: now I had time to go by the tailors for another fitting. Buying that uniform kit at the Fort Carson Quartermaster Store was a good move. It had the right amount of material, the proper padding and patterns, and even the official buttons. This was going to be a five-hundred-dollar, tailor-made uniform for less than a hundred. I was proud of myself.

In less than thirty minutes, I finished with the tailor and was back on Tudo Street. I barely raised my hand when a cab cut across two lanes of traffic and whipped up to the curb. "Tan Son Nhut, si'l vous plait."

The Saigon street scenes never ceased to entertain me. I was almost disappointed when the cab finally dropped me at the airport. I paid the driver and headed to the chopper pads.

"You Ed Skillman?" the man asked. He was in his late forties, heavyset and balding.

"That's right. You must be Mr. Cochran." The man wore pilot's sunglasses that did not fully conceal the deep lines around the corners of his eyes. He had smile wrinkles around the mouth to match.

"Call me 'Cocky.' Everyone else does. Bird's over this way. We're ready to go."

I followed the man. He was average height, wore gray work pants and shirt with the sleeves rolled up over the elbows. He was moving pretty fast for a man who gave the impression of being overweight. We climbed aboard and strapped down. A beat-up black journeyman's tool kit was tied down under Cochran's seat.

The chopper taxied out to the center of the runway. The turbulent air rushing through the interior was welcome relief to us inside. It was late summer. It was hot. It was just plain good to be off the blistering tarmac even if it was only ten feet.

By the time the aircraft reached cruising altitude the door gunners had closed the side doors. Headsets were in place, and the pilot now knew the exact destination. I had suggested that they land in Vung Liem and drive to the village, but Cochran and the pilot seemed to think they could sit down near the mill without a problem. And that was that.

The flight time passed quickly as Cocky and I got acquainted. I gave the long and enhanced version of the sugarcane story, and the project unfolded. Cocky caught the enthusiasm too. We tried out some what-if scenarios, and by the time we were circling the village of Ap Lin, Cochran was a believer.

The pilot selected the mill owner's front yard for a landing site. I could see the old gentleman standing on the veranda, same as he was the day I first met him. His face was unreadable. Not every day an American helicopter landed in his front yard.

It could be good. It could be bad. I was the first out of the Huey and trotted over to Ong Phan Dinh Chi.

"Bonjour, monsieur. Comment allez-vous?"

"C'est bien, mon capitain, et vous?" I struggled along in French and succeeded in introducing Mr. Bill Cochran to the owner of the mill. Cochran, like his boss, went straight to the problem and asked to see the mill operation. Mr. Chi proceeded to guide the party into the mill shed and explain the operation.

Cochran listened and observed the presentation, giving no indication one way or another that he understood. They walked around the tractor engine until Cochran stopped. He set down the journeyman's tool kit he had been carrying since he left the plane. He looked at Mr. Chi. "Can we crank her up?" He moved his closed fist in circles as if to crank open a window.

"Mais oui, monsieur." Dinh Chi clapped his hands twice. A little Vietnamese in black pajamas appeared out of nowhere. He hustled up to the group and exchanged words with Ong Chi. The worker stepped to the end of the engine and fiddled with a couple of levers and buttons. The undulant sound of the engine laboring to start drowned out the sounds of an idling helicopter in the front yard.

It took three attempts before the engine warmed up to its own rhythm. Cochran listened. Like a family in a hospital waiting room, the little party stood around the patient while Dr. Cochran poked and probed the engine with his screwdriver.

Cochran spoke to Mr. Chi, but what he said was for me. "No doubt this engine has been on its last legs for a long time. Someone around here is a damn good mechanic. Couple parts look handmade. I can have a new machine down here in maybe five days. Don't know if you want to make the trade, but the one you got needs to get rebuilt from the ground up."

I wanted to shout for joy, but Mr. Chi looked blank. I asked, "*Comprenez-vous?*"

The gentleman was hesitant. I struggled with my French and slowly it dawned. It wasn't so much the bad French that was hard to understand. It was the idea that someone would give him a new engine that he had trouble understanding. Finally, he smiled broadly and shrugged as if to say, *I'll believe it when I see it.* We walked back to the helicopter chatting lightly in French and English, letting good old body language do the communicating.

When we were back in the air, I gave directions to the district town. The chopper circled the marketplace once before we sat down at the soccer field. I asked Cochran if he really thought he could get an engine down here that quick.

"Probably quicker. All depends on how long it takes to find one in inventory. Then we got to put it in service and make sure it runs. After that, it's just getting it down here."

The Huey settled down on the grass. I hopped out and turned back to Cochran. "Thanks for your help, Cocky. It's been nice meeting you. And please check in when you bring the engine down."

The weathered old mechanic waved as the chopper pulled out, and I waved back. The jeep pulled in behind me. "Welcome home," said Pete.

I sneezed--twice. *Damn Saigon air-conditioning.* "Good to be here, Peter."

Pete was headed up the road to the villa when Doc rushed out of the maternity clinic. "Hey, boss. Hold on. Wait a minute."

Pete stopped. Doc was running down the path toward us. I got out. "What's the problem, Doc?"

Sister Lan was now in the doorway of the clinic. She was holding something. Doc was so excited. "You got to see this, man ... sir."

I started up the path. I could see the newborn snuggled in the sister's black robe. Doc was beside himself. "This is it, man. This is the first baby born in my maternity clinic. Isn't it terrific?" It really was terrific, and I accused him of acting like he was the father, too.

Sergeant Santana stopped in his tracks, and with the straightest face said, "No, *patrón*, this child is not my fault." He broke out in an Errol Flynn grin. "But I would claim him if he were. Isn't he beautiful?" I had to agree.

Conversation was lively at dinner that evening. Each of us had his story and was eager to share. Peter reported on the relay radio tower. Doc, of course, wanted to tell all the details of the birth, but the group unanimously decided that it was not a tale for the dinner table. Kuntz announced that the bombed school was repaired. And I, of course, gave more details on the Saigon trip and the results of the visit to Ap Lin village.

Finally, the conversation turned to KC. "Sergeant Kuntz and I discovered what was in those steel barrels over in the barracks armory." That had my attention.

"Stevens shotguns, fifty of them," said Kuntz.

I asked if they'd broken into them. KC assured me they hadn't. It turned out that Sergeant Kuntz had noticed cases of double-ought shotgun ammunition stacked in a corner. When KC asked Daui Sau about it, Sau said the ammo went with the shotguns ... What shotguns? ... The ones in the steel barrels. QED.

Now, who and why would someone supply these folks with shotguns? The *why* wasn't that hard. It was the *who* that stumped me.

Kuntz asked. "Aren't Stevens shotguns used in a lot of prisons?"

He was right. They were good for close action since the eight pellets have a wider pattern of impact than a single shot, but the pellets, being so few, are heavy enough to cause serious damage. Seems it has a shorter barrel too.

KC began to add it up. "OK. We got short range, scattered strike pattern, and lethal. Sounds like the perfect weapon for ambushes."

Not that it made any difference, but how had they gotten here? These were not the regular army tables of organization and equipment -- at least that I knew.

KC was doing his own self-talk. "My guess is they have been here a long time. But I wonder why we didn't know about the issue before we came here."

"Wonder why they don't use them," said Pete.

Those were all good questions. I indicated to KC and Kuntz that first thing tomorrow they should go back and ask Daui Sau for some answers: see if we could get the ambushes armed with them.

★★★

Seemed like a good idea at the time. Daui Sau had no history of the shotguns. They had always been there. And as far as he was concerned, they weren't any good: range too short, not accurate, and limited magazine. So it was time to enlighten the Regional Force captain. Sixteen soldiers were now assembled at the soccer field for a demonstration and familiarization course in the employment of the Stevens shotgun.

Sergeant Khe stood by and translated as I explained why the shotgun was an ideal weapon for close-in fighting situations like the ambush. The lecture was short. The afternoon sun was hot.

In the meantime KC had policed up a couple of dirt clods about the size of softballs. I had done some trapshooting in my time and was decent at the sport, but not as good as my uncle, who had been a regional champion in his age group for some years. The plan was to demonstrate the accuracy of the weapon at close range. The idea was to build confidence in the gun.

On command KC pitched the clod about twenty feet into the air. I drew a bead and fired. The clod fell harmlessly to earth. KC threw the second clod. I fired and caught a piece of the clod just as it began to fall. There was some mumbling among the troops. KC tossed the third clod in the air, and I nailed it just as it reached the peak of its rise. The troops were all smiles. So was I.

"You want me to get some more?" asked KC. I shook my head. No sense pushing my luck. I walked back to the group of expectant rough puffs—all faces in total deadpan. I called for a volunteer, knowing it was not the Vietnamese way to volunteer for anything, and after an appropriate pause selected my first candidate. I pointed to one of the soldiers sitting on the grass.

Reluctantly the man rose and came forward. I handed him the loaded shotgun and showed him how to shoulder the weapon. I indicated that downrange was the direction of the rice patties. KC had whipped up a cardboard target, two foot by three foot, and had it standing twenty-five feet in front of the group.

The first thing I noticed was that the stock of the weapon was too long for the man's arms. The soldier could just barely reach the trigger with his right hand and his left hand could not firmly grip the stock. Before I could make any adjustments the soldier pulled the trigger. The recoil sent the poor fellow flat on his back.

I dropped to the man's side. The kid was lying there with his eyes open, staring at the sky. Khe was translating everything I was saying to him. Finally, he talks back to Khe.

"Well, what's he say?"

"He asks if he hit the target."

I looked back at the unblemished piece of cardboard. "Tell him the VC have nothing to worry about from Stevens shotguns." We helped the man up. He was rubbing his shoulder and winced a little. KC walked him over to the maternity clinic to have Doc look at him. I turned back to the group. The look on all their faces told the story in an instant. It was crystal clear why Stevens shotguns had not been integrated into the arsenal of Vietnamese rough puffs.

The subject never came up again.

★★★

The following day, about noon, the Chief marched into the villa and announced that the VC had blown up Highway 8 that morning. All traffic was stopped.

"Shit, oh dear" was KC's first reaction.

"What section of the road did they hit?" I asked.

"Southern edge of the district near the border with Cang Long."

"What did they do, dig in from the shoulder of the road?" I was thinking of my own experience in the same area.

"No, *Daui*. He placed explosive in the drain tile under road. It was a drainage point between fields, and whole road collapsed into the culvert." The Chief tapped his temple with his index finger and winked.

That sounded major. *Where will we find drain tile and a couple yards of gravel?* I had seen the materials at the Tra Vinh airfield for converting the field into a hardtop strip. Specifically, I recalled seeing gravel piled up along with barrels of tar. I wasn't sure about drain tile, but it was worth a try.

"*Daui*, we will see if we can bring some gravel and tar up from Tra Vinh ASAP. They're turning the Tra Vinh airfield into a hardtop strip. I'll flag a chopper and …"

"All fixed, Captain Skeelman."

"What? How'd you do *that*?" We advisors stood with our jaws on our chests.

"No problem. Fill culvert with dirt, top off with some gravel, roll with heavy roller, and coat with tar. All fixed." He smiled, and his eyes disappeared.

"Well, I got to see this." KC went for his webbing.

"Me too. Come on, Chief. Show me."

In less than twenty minutes we were at the site. Traffic was moving along smoothly. The black patch was clearly visible, and alongside the road was a huge drum maybe twelve feet across. It had a harness or yoke made of steel and rigged to an axle extending from the ends of the tank so it could be rolled along behind a truck. "I'll be damned," said KC. "How's that work?"

"Fill with water, and pull back and forth till road packed and smooth," answered the Chief.

"I can see that," said KC covering the truth. "But what about drainage?"

"Make drainage, and VC bomber blow up again. Worry about drainage when drainage is problem."

Made me wonder who was advising who. No need to hang around. KC turned the jeep around to the north. We had been driving a few minutes when we passed a dirt road off to the right. I recognized it as the road to O'Lac and asked the Chief if that wasn't the route we cleared from the river inland to this junction.

"Yes, but still not safe. I think the bomber lives in that village," answered the Chief. "Maybe come from Cang Long, but my first think is O Lac."

"Isn't there something we can do about that?" asked KC.

"Maybe," said the Chief.

We drove back in silence. It was the start of September. The rice was hinting yellow. It gleamed in the sun and waved in the wind. It was beautiful; I enjoyed the drive. I was glad to be alive.

★★★

A couple of days after the road mining, my team members were scattered to the winds. Doc and I were on foot and were hanging around the maternity clinic watching Sister Lan run sick call. One of Pete's ESL students was doing the admin work. KC and Kuntz were mobile with the jeep and Sergeant Khe. They were checking progress on the schools in the northern villages. Peter was over at the barracks.

I had left Doc at the maternity clinic and was walking back to the villa. I walked into the living room and dropped my web gear. It was hot, and I was thirsty. But

Ong Than was nowhere to be seen. I walked out into the breezeway; no one there. I went over to dip a cup of water out of the urn when I heard something in the old kitchen. The thought crossed my mind to go back and get my pistol, but curiosity and impatience overcame me. I quietly moved to the side of the kitchen door and peeped around into the kitchen.

In the middle of the empty room was Daui Tranh overseeing two men digging a deep hole in the dirt floor of the kitchen. Sitting to the side of the dig were steel barrels looking suspiciously like the shotgun containers.

I greeted the Chief as I stepped into the room. The Chief nearly jumped out of his skin. When he saw who it was, he flashed his all-teeth no-humor smile. "We bury these weapons here for safekeeping."

He had to be joking. The middle of the Regional Force barracks seemed safe enough after all these years. But he wasn't joking. He had reports that maybe VC were planning an assault on the town tonight. That was definitely not good news. I wondered if the *Daui* would have told me if I had not walked in.

We exchanged a few words; the Chief was evidently embarrassed. I walked back to the breezeway and had that cup of water. By the time the troops began to straggle back to the villa, I had a plan in mind.

As soon as Pete came through the gate, I called him over to the com shack.

"What you doing here, sir?"

"Never mind. Right now, Peter. I want you to set up an AN/PRC-10 radio ... 25 if you can find one... and have it operable from our com shack. Calibrate on the relay station net for observation aircraft. Let me know when you're up, or give me a progress report in sixty minutes."

"How do I know the right frequency?"

"You know what frequencies are being used regularly, and you listened to the kinds of traffic last week. Pick the one or two that sound like observation reports coming from air or ground reconnaissance teams."

"I'm on it." Pete headed back to the barracks. I had no sooner cleared the gate than the jeep pulled in with KC and Kuntz. I motioned for them to follow me.

"What's going on, boss?" asked KC. "You look grim."

I led them down the road in the direction of the soccer field repeating what the Chief had said about the possible VC assault tonight. I decided not to mention the burial of the weapons under the kitchen floor.

As we walked, I outlined my thinking. If there was an assault on the town, the two most likely targets were the barracks and the villa. For us to be in the villa under assault was to be trapped under siege without much firepower. If any firing began, I thought our best chance for survival would be escape and evasion. I stopped walking and looked at the troops. "Any thoughts on the concept?"

Kuntz nervously scratched his head. "Where we going to escape to?"

It was the right question. The first rendezvous point was the cane field behind Father Phan's church. If that was compromised, the second rendezvous point would be under this side of the Highway 8 bridge over to Vinh Long. Everyone acknowledged the checkpoints, and I started them back down the road. I had them looking for possible escape routes between the houses.

We walked down the road about a hundred yards and back. And then we walked around the outside of the compound wall. When we came back in the gate, Santana was standing on the porch. "Where did everybody go?" He looked at the faces of his teammates. "What ... somebody die?"

"Peter back yet?" I brushed by Santana into the living room.

"Nobody here when I came in a few minutes ago. What's going on?"

"A little action," said KC.

"I'll give you the details in a minute," I answered. "Is your aid kit stocked and ready for immediate travel?"

"Well, I haven't repacked it for a couple weeks, but it'll do in an emergency."

My instructions to Santana were to go through his supply shelves and restock now; the rest of the men were to load all their magazines.

"Particularly, *unload* the magazine that you have in your weapon now, and reload it." I said. When the spring in the loaded magazine has been depressed for a long time it may be sluggish chambering the first or second round as it recoils. Unloading and reloading exercises it.

Peter came in as the rest were scattering, and I turned to him. "What you got for me, lad?"

Peter went over the frequencies he had monitored and the ones most likely used for aircraft. "The traffic has been light, but I've calibrated the frequency on which we might best find an airplane."

"Good man. Show Kuntz what you got, and turn it over to him to monitor while you get yourself ready for travel."

"Travel?"

"Just in case. We'll talk about it at dinner." I then set out to follow my own guidance.

As the tasks were completed, the team began to assemble in the dining room. Ong Than was ready to serve dinner and was just waiting for KC to give him the word. I sat down at the table and again explained the events of the afternoon ... still omitting the details on the kitchen burial.

"You want to eat while we talk?" KC interrupted.

I nodded. "And call in Sergeant Kuntz."

After Kuntz joined us and food was served, I reviewed the plan for the evening. "We will monitor the air traffic. Anything we can contact in our vicinity we will request they give us a pass to check for enemy movement in the area. It's a full moon tonight, which makes that workable."

"What happens if they do spot something?" asked Santana.

"Depends on where the target's headed, how many there are, and what time it is. If they're passing by, we let them. And we report it. If they're headed our way, we slide out into the village. If there is any shooting anytime inside the town we evade to the first rally point. We wait at the rally points till dawn, then move to the nearest province town. Do not wait for any missing team members. Sergeant Kuntz is the tactical leader if no officer is present."

Everyone studied his plate for a few moments. Peter spoke first to confirm that the bridge was closer to Vinh Long than Tra Vinh. Then we talked about some what-if drills, and finally, dinner ended with a watch schedule that kept three men awake at all times during the night.

I stood and indicated for everyone to head over to the com shack. I wanted Private de Groot to show the team what he had set up. We filed out through the breezeway and over to the front of the communication apartment.

Private de Groot began. "We have to bring the radio out into the yard a little way because the building interferes with this set's reception. I have us on the relay frequency right now but there is another frequency that seems to be used by reconnaissance aircraft. What call signs you want to use, Captain?"

"You will be *Vung Liem Operator*. I'm *Six*, KC's *Five*, the NCOs are *Four*. We will just monitor until dark. After dark, broadcast for 'Any airborne station' and respond as 'Vung Liem Operator.' If you pick up traffic, report to them that there is possible VC movement in the vicinity of Vung Liem district town. Ask if they are able to fly over the town and check for activity. An air observer in full moonlight is almost as good as daylight. If we don't pick up any traffic in the first hour, try the alternate frequency for an hour ... and so forth. Stay where you get *traffic*. Any questions?"

I peered into the faces of my team. Everyone looked scared—which was OK. I was scared too, and that was good. It meant that we would be careful and alert.

"All right, boys," I said. "The hardest part of this whole thing is right now ... the waiting. Me, I'm going up to catch some Zs."

CHAPTER SIXTEEN

War Without Guns

"Vung Liem Operator, this is Cactus Three Niner." Pete came alive. This was the first response that he pulled all evening. It was 2130 hours. He had put calls out every fifteen minutes since 2030, and he was about to change frequencies if this call failed to turn up anything.

It had occurred to all of us over the last hour that it was unnaturally quiet in the compound. The families living in the apartments were not here tonight. I guessed they were in the barracks or maybe with friends in town; either way it didn't help our feelings of isolation. At least the guards were still here banging their triangles with renewed dedication.

"Cactus Three Niner, This is Vung Liem Operator. We have indications of possible Vietcong activity in the vicinity of Vung Liem district town. Are you in a position to give a flyover for conformation?"

"This is Cactus Three Niner. I'm way north of you, I think ... on the way back to the barn. But, I've enough fuel to make a wide pass your way. Call me in five."

"Roger that. Out." Pete looked over at KC. "That's a start."

I was fully dressed and stretched out on my bunk in a light sleep. The vague flutter of helicopter blades in the distance instantly brought me fully awake. I sat on the edge of the bunk and checked my watch. *Sounds like Peter hooked something.* I got up and walked out onto the porch where I could clearly hear Pete's transmissions in the still night air.

"Cactus Three Niner, this is Vung Liem Operator. I can hear you approaching the town from due north at long range."

"Roger Vung Liem. I see the town lights, I think. You on a canal junction with the River?"

"That's affirmative."

"OK. I have about enough fuel for a slow 360 over town … see if there's anything going on."

"Roger, Cactus." Pete had his eyes peeled to the north as the sound of the chopper came closer.

Kuntz and KC were sitting on the bench next to the badminton court. Santana came out of the villa and sat down on the top step of the porch next to me. "Sounds like we got some friends in high places."

I had to smile. This old sergeant was pretty cool keeping a sense of humor at a time like this. We sat there watching the Huey circle the town at about fifteen hundred feet.

"This is Cactus Three Niner. Town looks quiet … no movement on roads or trails. Any feel for direction of activity?"

I had walked down to Pete's side and took the handset. "This is Vung Liem Six. We are most concerned about the approaches from the south of town … possible trails through the rice fields and the like."

"Roger, Six. I'll take another pass, but after that I got to go."

"Understand, Cactus. We appreciate the visit." I passed the handset to Peter and walked back to the porch. Santana and I listened as the young private finally signed off with Cactus.

The security guards traded signals …

By 0300 hours Kuntz was operating the radio and had pulled in another Huey on the way home to Vinh Long airfield. The exercise was much the same as the first one. The team lingered in the courtyard listening to Kuntz and the pilot exchange information. As before, the chopper completed its reconnaissance and headed for home.

"So far, so good." It was KC's attempt at being casual. But it did not have to be said that the night was entering its most critical period. The moon had set. There was still starlight—and three more hours till dawn. No one was asleep. I sat back down on the top step of the porch. It was deathly quiet—nothing stirring. I thought of all the things I could have done better. Maybe I should have moved the team out of the compound to begin with; waiting this out in a concealed location might have been better. I wondered where the Chief was. Suddenly Santana's voice broke the cotton silence.

"Eagle Seven Five, this is Vung Liem Four." The energy in the sergeant's voice jumped from boredom to excitement. He repeated the request for a flyover.

"This is Eagle Seven Five, I can do that. It's pretty dark, but if there is anything out there, the sound of an aircraft overhead is a strong deterrent. We'll give it a shot."

"Roger, Eagle, we are concerned about routes into town from the south."

Within moments we heard the sound of a single-engine, fixed-wing aircraft approaching from the south. I moved to the side of Santana and took the handset. "Eagle, this is Vung Liem Six. The bad guys only have a few hours to marshal any kind of an assault before dawn. You are correct about overhead aircraft. Even the freshest VC recruit knows that little planes bring big planes and/or artillery. The longer you can stay with us, the less time they have for organized action."

"This is Eagle. I have two hours and fumes. I'll stay as long as I can."

"Thanks, Eagle, we'll be here. Out."

The sound of the L-19 Bird Dog, as the army's light observation aircraft was known, gave a certain amount of confidence to us. It was not that Eagle could really do anything if fighting actually broke out. The fact was: Eagle probably could *not* do anything—not quickly, anyway. The confidence came in knowing that if something *did* happen, someone would know about it and take appropriate action.

And the night dragged on …

"Vung Liem Six, this is Eagle."

"This is Vung Liem Four, Six can hear you."

"This is Eagle. It's 0545, and I'm on gas fumes. Time to go."

"Thank you, Eagle. We greatly appreciate your visit. Vung Liem out." A lonely silence closed in …

At around 0630 hours I stood up to stretch. I walked across the courtyard to the gate and peered out. It was beginning of twilight.

Across the road and down the trail in front of the church I could see a figure walking past the old 105 artillery positions. It was coming straight toward the compound. I drew my pistol. There was no one else on the road. I stepped to the side of the gate and eased the slide on my pistol to check if a round was in the chamber. The figure continued to approach. With arm and hand signals I motioned, to any else watching him, to take cover. The figure looked to be unarmed. The figure looked familiar. The figure looked like it was …

"Good morning, my American friends," said Daui Tranh. It was his 'all teeth' smile as he came through the gate. I was speechless. All I could do was nod my head.

Santana called from the porch, "What's up, Chief?"

"Me," he said. "Up all night. Now sleep." He waved a dismissive hand and moved to his private side entrance into the villa. And that was that.

★★★

In the days following the nonassault, Daui Sau and his troops ran a number of platoon-size operations. For a Regional Force platoon, that was about twenty men, give or take. Rumors had it, and there was some evidence to support it, that a party of Vietcong *had* bypassed the district town on a move to the northeast. The operations that Sau ran were all designed to make the government's presence felt and seen.

Sometimes the company commander, Daui Sau, went along, and sometimes the district chief, Daui Tranh, went. The object was to make a show of strength and unity. There were incidents of searches, and in more than one incident, there were seizures of weapons; nothing huge, but still significant. And there were incidents of shots fired.

I went with those operations led by the Chief. Sergeant Santana would usually accompany me unless he had a sick call scheduled. The Chief liked it when Doc was along. Daui Tranh would identify some villager along the way who needed medical attention. He would call the *American Doctor* forward to take a look at the individual or his family member. Santana, being a showman, too, enjoyed his role as *instrument of good* in the hands of the benevolent district chief. They were a natural political team.

Captain Flint and Sergeant Kuntz would go with the old commander, Daui Sau. As it turned out, the operations under Daui Sau were into the regions less traveled. On the operation down in the vicinity of O Lac and just north of the place where the road was mined, they ran into a little firefight. Three, or perhaps, four VC took the front of the troop column under fire as it approached a hamlet near the Cang Long border. The lead soldiers returned fire.

Sau deployed a couple more riflemen forward to add to the firebase. He then led the remainder of the troops to the left into a tree line so as to maneuver on the flank of the VC position. Flint and Kuntz took cover behind the base of fire. As Kuntz told it, both the Americans were on their stomachs, ten feet apart trying to see where the firing was coming from.

"Does this mean I've qualified for the Combat Infantryman's Badge?" hollered Flint.

"If you see the muzzle flash and hear the crack of the rounds overhead, I think you can claim the CIB."

"Shit, oh dear." yelled Flint. "Not only can I do that, but I can see the rounds hitting in front of me."

"It sounds like hostile fire to me. I'd say that qualifies, for sure," called Kuntz nonchalantly. "Just asking, Captain. But as advisors, do we have any Rules of Engagement here?"

"We are not combatants, but we have the right to defend ourselves," yelled Flint.

But, no sooner had they fired a round, then they were overcome by events. The moment the lead elements of Commander Sau's maneuver column fired into the VC position, the VC pulled up stakes, and faded into the built-up area.

"No runs, no hits, no errors," said KC. Commander Sau gathered up his troops, and proceeded to complete the sweep of the area as planned.

That evening at supper, KC recounted the day's adventure. I promised KC I would write up the recommendation in the morning.

I looked over at Kuntz. "That puts a star on your CIB, doesn't it, Bill?"

"I guess it does." The old sarge's mind flashed back to the Korean countryside. "First one was a daylight reconnaissance patrol that was supposed to be routine—nothing routine about five Chinese roaming the same terrain. Ben what's-his-name was point when he and a Chink surprised each other. Ben got the first shot off; then, all hell broke loose. The patrol leader left me and Ben to hold down a base of fire while he maneuvered with the rest of the patrol. Killed three Chinese that day: ran the others off ..." Kuntz took another huge bite of rice.

★★★

It was mid-September, when the message came through Vietnamese radio channels, that Province had received a hog destined for Vung Liem District. The message went on to say that the hog would be trucked to district for additional directions to its end destination—ETA, early afternoon the same day.

Pete complained that he never got to do anything, so Doc took the young warrior with him on sick call. Just to spice up the trip, Doc decided the two would travel by Lambretta. That freed up the jeep. KC and I were lingering over a cup of coffee, trying to decide where to visit, when Kuntz brought in the message about the hog.

That meant Ms. Miranda was probably in Ap Lin, which reminded me of the engine for the rice mill. I said as much out loud.

"Good question. Maybe we should drop by the mill after we check on Miranda," said KC. "By the way, what's the Chief think about all of this?"

"You know, I have, yet, to give him any details. Let's go find him right now." We geared up and set out for the first checkpoint on the trail of the district chief—the boardinghouse.

The Chief had a personal driver. No one seemed to remember his name, but he was always in the wings. It would be a little much to call him a bodyguard, but he was certainly more personally connected than just being a driver—more like Ong Than was with the Americans. The one obvious thing he did do, was to drive the Chief's little green Peugeot. From time to time he also was seen driving the Willie's Overland truck with its red crosses on the side. This morning he was sitting on the veranda of the boardinghouse when we walked up. I asked if he had seen Daui Tranh.

The young man stood up and pointed down the road in front of the church. He smiled broadly, and I wasn't sure he understood English or just anticipated my needs. I was looking at KC, trying to decide the next move, when the driver said, "Lice mir."

"He must mean the rice mill here in town," said KC. "Maybe we just wait and catch him tonight."

At that moment the assistant district chief, Ong Hoa Hoang, came out of the house. "*Chau, Daui.*"

I explained to Ong Hoang that we were trying to catch up with the Chief.

"He is at the rice mill. He sometimes stays there," said Hoa Hoang.

"Thank you." I glanced at KC who shrugged. "Tell him we were by and we will catch up this evening."

"Of course, no problem." Hoang sat down next to the driver.

As we walked back to the villa, it began to dawn on me. This Chief was pretty damn clever when you looked at his habits over time. He never wore the same headgear twice in a row. It was either the ball cap, the bush hat, or no hat at all whenever he went on operation. And he lived all over town. He's in the villa one night; then he stays over at the boardinghouse. And now we learn he stays with the rice mill owner from time to time. I shared the revelation with KC.

"Come to think of it, that's true." KC was impressed. "You're right. He *is* pretty damn smart. I'll bet he was at the mill on the night of the nonassault."

"I'd make book on it. Too bad a change of hats doesn't help you and me blend in." We both guffawed at the picture of us surrounded by Vietnamese munchkins.

We were turning into the courtyard when a truck horn got our attention. Coming up the road from the soccer field was a half-ton, open-bed truck with a hand waving out the window on the passenger's side. The truck pulled up, and Sergeant Toomey from Province Team jumped out.

"Hear you guys are in the business of pig farming." He was grinning from ear to ear. "Got one horny hog here." We exchanged greetings as we walked to the rear of the truck.

"That's a big porker, all right … with a smell to go with him," said KC. I just stared. Nothing Miranda said had prepared me for the size of this animal.

"Boss said he wouldn't wait for a Huey to move the beast. Said call Skillman and tell him it's coming up. So here we are." Sergeant Toomey obviously thought this was pretty funny.

"OK, Sergeant. Turn your truck around, and follow us." KC and I gathered up our gear at the villa and returned to the scene with our jeep. KC pulled the jeep into the lead. The little convoy moved smartly out onto the highway heading to Ap Lin. I hoped that Miranda would be there. If she wasn't, we could have a real problem.

"What problem?" Said KC. "We just place the hog with the village chief, and he sees to it every farmer gets a shot … excuse the expression."

"If that's what happens, fine. But we have no control over that. What if someone decides to butcher the beast? You going to tell Ms. Miranda her pet pig got butchered, and we didn't even save her a pork chop?"

"You have a point."

We were passing the Catholic village by now. I looked over at the church. Something didn't look right. What was wrong with this picture?

"Will you look at that. The father has harvested his sugarcane."

KC nearly drove off the road trying to look back over his shoulder. "Well, that answers the question about when they harvest sugarcane. All the more reason for us to drop in on the mill while we are up here."

"Got that right."

After another twenty minutes of conversation about my upcoming R & R and KC's wedding plans, he turned the jeep off Highway 8 into the village of Ap Lin and pulled up on the hard stand in front of the aid station. I dismounted and waved the truck alongside. We were all milling around the back of the truck to see if the passenger had arrived in good condition when I saw the village chief coming out of his office.

A villager in black pajamas, wearing a conical straw hat, followed him. The villager was a good seven inches taller than the chief was. The closer they came, the more unnatural the pair looked.

"Holy moley. Would you look at that? It's Miranda." I could not hold back the laugh. "Welcome to Vung Liem."

Miranda put her hands together in front of her ample breasts and gave a short bow. "I am honored." And she too laughed as she knocked back the conical hat so that it hung down her back, as was the custom. Her blond hair was pulled back in a bun.

She could not have looked more plain. But we soldiers were impressed and—believe it or not—charmed.

"You boys have something for me?"

"Yeah, we found this three-hundred-pound dog running through the town … thought it might be your lost puppy."

"Don't go calling my pig a dog, KC. He could get confused about his job."

"Well, we sure can't have that," I said. "Where you want him?"

Miranda walked to the back of the truck. She spoke in Vietnamese. The pig stood up in his cage and the village chief quickly walked back to his office. I glanced over at KC. His look of mild surprise matched what I was feeling.

"See, he knows me," she said.

I asked in my best Clark Gable, "Tell me, Ms. Miranda, do all males jump at just the sound of your sweet voice?"

And Scarlett answered. "Why, Captain, whatever do you mean? I'm just a little ol' country girl."

"In a pig's eye," said KC. It was all too much.

"What you want done with this porker?" asked Sergeant Toomey.

"The village chief has his instructions," she said. "And he is getting his crew together now. We can go down to the market for a cup of tea until the truck is unloaded." Miranda proceeded to lead the way.

I was surprised again when we walked into the market area. Construction was several days under way for a new and improved market pavilion. The concrete slab was laid and curing. Materials were piled at the far end of the site. Jake was making good on his promise.

Miranda had seated herself in the little open-air restaurant overlooking the canal.

Toomey whispered, "I think I'll go back and check on the unloading. I'll come back when we're done." I nodded.

Miranda ordered tea. We men had beer, and for the next thirty minutes the talk was about the potential of the marketplace to become a major trade center.

KC threw out the question: "Does anyone up the line have a clue as to what's coming together here?"

It was a good question which had crossed my mind from time to time.

KC continued. "Well, Ledbetter has a marketplace started, and Miranda is doing her thing here in Tra Vinh Province, and we identified the project. Who in our respective agencies understands what is actually materializing here?"

"I don't know about you guys," said Miranda. "But, in my organization, if I don't jump out in the middle of the circle and say, 'Look at me; see what I have done,' no one would have the foggiest idea what was going on."

In my chain the information started up all right, but I was afraid the progress reports were overcome along the way by battle accounts and body count.

Toomey came up. "This little piggy went to market."

I thanked the sergeant. As we all stood, I put a bill on the table before anyone called for a check. I winked at Miranda. "You going back tomorrow?"

She acknowledged my gesture with a subtle smile. "Yes. I got a lot done yesterday and today. The villagers know how to handle the exercise. I'll catch the afternoon bus back to Saigon tomorrow."

I could only imagine the hassle for an American woman riding a Vietnamese public bus on the long haul back to Saigon. She was one tough cookie.

As we walked back to the truck, KC thanked Sergeant Toomey for today's patriotic sacrifice for God and country. I urged him and his driver to hustle if he wanted to get home before the roadblocks. The sergeant flipped us a salute and mounted up.

I turned back to Miranda and invited her to come with us across the road to see the rice mill owner. But she declined—something about her pet needing some attention and still having things to do before leaving here tomorrow. As she spoke she backed away slowly. "It's been great, guys. Look me up when you're in town."

She suddenly turned, and in a blink, she and her peasant garb blended into the market scene.

"God help the VC who tries to take advantage of that gal," said KC. We laughed and loaded into the jeep. KC drove across the highway and up to the mill.

When the villa came into view, Ong Phan Dinh Chi was standing on his veranda as though he had not left the position since our last visit. But, uncharacteristically, he hurried down the steps and up to us almost before we had dismounted.

"Bonjour, *mes capitains. Comment allez-vous?*" He was excited. "I expect you."

Ong Dinh Chi was talking so fast in French and English and filling the gaps with Vietnamese that we could barely understand a thing he said. Reading the confusion on our faces, he turned and led us around behind the villa to the mill in the back. He marched up to the engine and presented his brand-new diesel power package.

"Holy guacamole. Would you look at that," said KC.

I beamed; it was positively beautiful. Chi reached over to an instrument panel and hit the starter button. We oohed and aahed for a few minutes just listening to the engine. It was a male thing that transcended cultural boundaries. Then Mr. Chi led us back into the mill shed. The little barn was filled with cane. It was apparent that the pressing had just begun, as there were very few jugs of molasses in inventory. It was perfectly clear what Father Phan did with his sugarcane.

"Yes, yes." Mr. Chi smiled. "No problem." The smile grew into chuckles.

We were in business. We walked to the front of the villa and chattered along in three languages, again; relying on body language for translations. We all got it—the pride, the thanks, and the commitment.

Sailing along Highway 8 back to the villa, I broke the silence. We should have been celebrating. But I was unhappy that Cochran had not checked in when he brought that engine down. And there was the new marketplace. People were jumping in and out of the district without our knowledge. It irritated the stew out of me.

KC agreed, "You're right. At best, it's bad manners, and at worst, bad management. I bet the Chief doesn't know any more than we do on this stuff."

It was as though the pyramid was upside down on us. There were a dozen different agencies working their projects at the grass roots, and they should have been coming through the district headquarters for coordination. But, not all of them were. I needed to get a handle on this.

KC pulled into the courtyard. It was late in the afternoon, but there was no badminton match going on. "What the hell? Where is everyone?"

The enlisted men were sitting in the dining room. There was no conversation. They were just sitting there blindly looking at their coffee cups.

"What's going on, men?" asked KC.

"Chief Hanson dropped in this afternoon," said Kuntz.

"And?"

Kuntz took a deep breath. He exhaled as he spoke. "And … well … Lieutenant Williams was killed in an ambush."

"You are shittin' me," burst out of KC.

I asked where it happened, and Kuntz said it was downriver on the Ben Tri Province bank of the river.

Santana picked up the story. Seems they were chasing after a large sampan coming down the river. Hanson said Mack thought it was probably sneaking in from Cambodia like they do with guns or troops or both. He tried to pull them over, but they made a run for it, up one of those little cross-country canals. Williams went after them in hot pursuit. I could guess the result of that move—a boat caught in a defile unable to maneuver freely, taking fire from one or both sides of the canal. Not good.

Santana continued. "They got about two or three hundred yards into the canal and were firing on the sampan when the VC pulled into shore with all hands heading inland. I'm not sure I understand what happened next, but the result was Mack sank the VC sampan. He turned the gunboat around and headed back out to the river. That's when they got ambushed."

"Anybody else get hit?" I was staring out through the breezeway. *Mack* ...

Kuntz answered. "Actually one of the crew got hit first. Lieutenant Williams got really mad and ran forward grabbing the M-60 machine gun. I guess he jumped up topside and started hosing down the canal bank, John Wayne style. Hansen said he took a couple rounds before they brought him down. Guess he was still firing when he hit the deck."

I went over to the sideboard and pulled out the brandy bottle. "Empty your cups, men." I poured a shot into each man's cup. "We're toasting here to a sailor who was one fine warrior."

Mack and I had bonded early in our emerging adulthood. He was one of those guys you can count on one hand that you call friend. Our friendship had grown like snapshots collected in a photo album—a volume of rich emotions—now a closed book. My brother had joined the ranks of heroes, and my emotions were ranging from shock to sorrow to anger. I tossed back the brandy. It burned my throat ... but it seared my heart.

★★★

Daui Tranh came into the dining room as I was washing down my weekly malaria pill with Tang breakfast drink. I offered him a cup of coffee.

"*Merci, non.*" He smiled his toothy smile. "There is an American at the front gate. I think you should meet him."

I downed the Tang and joined the Chief on the way across the courtyard. Leaning against the gate pillar was a young Caucasian about my age. He wore gray work clothes and U.S. military jungle boots. His sleeves were rolled up over his elbows. Around his waist was a military web belt with a pistol holster on the right hip.

I introduced myself and invited him in for a cup of coffee.

The man pulled away from the pillar. "Thank you, but I will stay with my people here. We've come to ask for your support."

I surveyed the six men sitting on the other side of the road. They all wore black pajamas and black tennis shoes. They had no headgear and they were unarmed. What made them unusual was that they had long hair and wispy facial hair. Generally, Vietnamese men, as an ethnic group, have very little facial hair. These men looked shaggy.

"We'll do what we can. What's on your mind?"

The American stepped closer to the Chief and me and lowered his voice. "These guys are part of a sanctioned counterterror squad. We have been training for about a week outside of Tra Vinh, and now we are ready to go on a mission. What we need to do is borrow some weapons. We will return them at the completion of the job."

The Chief studied the tops of his boots. I asked them what kind of targets they were talking about.

"They are across the river in Ben Tre Province. But if you have a target, we will hit that too."

The mention of Ben Tri refreshed my emotions surrounding the death of Mack Williams. I thought about *counter terror* and what that meant. I needed to get clear here. "Are we talking about assassinations?"

The man nodded. I looked at the Chief. Did we have any 'targets'?

Daui Tranh said, unhesitatingly, "Yes. Southwest of here on border Cang Long, there is miner who keeps blowing up Highway 8. We think he lives in one of those hamlets."

"We'll try to take care of that for you. Anything else?"

The Chief looked at me. Nothing came up. So, I said we should take these guys over to the armory and sign out some weapons to them. The Chief nodded agreement.

The American turned to his men and spoke in Vietnamese. They slowly stood up. They were a motley crew indeed.

"Thanks, Captain. We'll see you in about ten days." He and his men followed the Chief, who was already headed toward the barracks.

I turned back into the courtyard. Something to ponder: *Targets, he calls them. Let's hope his "targets" include the guys who got Mack. And let's not forget our bomber ... Interesting how we dehumanize our intentions to ease our conscience.*

CHAPTER SEVENTEEN

The Rum Runners

I WAS COUNTING THE days until my R & R leave. Each soldier was allowed two weeks of rest and recuperation leave during his one-year tour of duty, but he could only take one week every six months, duties permitting. I had requested my first week at the end of the first six months and my second week at the beginning of the second six months, making my R & R two weeks back-to-back in the middle of my tour—duties permitting.

And duties permitted. With two weeks of leave I could fly all the way back to Denver Colorado and have nearly ten days with my wife and family. The cost of the flight was less than trying to meet the family someplace in between. Reunion was down to six weeks away and closing -- oh, so slowly.

Life in the district was slipping into routine. The step-up in operations in the last few weeks had seemed to make a difference in VC activity. The enemy was still out there, but keeping a lower profile, fewer violent incidents. They were avoiding roads and moving, exclusively, at night and by water. The counter terror squad had pulled into the district late one afternoon two weeks after their launch. The young CIA man was unemotional as he described the success of his outfit. He claimed to have hit five targets plus the one the Chief offered.

The assassins had dropped the body of the dead bomber at the front gate of the villa. While the motley crew dragged themselves over to the armory to turn in their weapons, the CIA agent recounted his story to me and the Chief. But the Chief made a closer inspection of the body of the alleged bomber after the unit with its leader was out of town. Daui Tranh was skeptical. He sent for his own intelligence officer.

"We not know who or what the targets were. So how we know they are hit?" He was thinking out loud. "This may or may not be our bomber here."

The intelligence officer seemed to think it was, but the Chief was reluctant to confirm the kill. "We see if the attacks on road stop. Then maybe we say we get our man."

It was now early evening three days after the counter terror squad had made their drop. KC and I were playing chess over the usual brandy. Peter, who had last watch, had gone to bed, and the sergeants were each into one of Pete's hand-me-down Louis L'Amour novels. The Zenith transistor radio was tuned to BBC music and news. It was altogether a disgustingly wholesome scene -- deceptively so. The guards' banging on the triangles was the only reminder that danger was ever present.

I watched KC ponder his next chess move. I asked if anyone seen the Chief lately.

KC castled—a move which tucked the king into the corner of the board, shielded by the rook. It was the only move in chess involving two pieces at once.

Satisfied, KC sat back. "Come to think of it, I haven't seen him since the counter terror boys blew through. Not like him to miss his nightcap that often."

I looked over at the NCOs and repeated the question.

Both answered without looking up. "Uh-uh." "Nope."

I took that as a collective "no, sir," and a resounding testimony in support of Louis L'Amour.

KC squeezed the last drop out of the brandy bottle. "Your move, boss." I studied the chessboard as KC wondered out loud, "Where do you suppose that guy goes when he disappears like this? Seems like every time he comes back, something big happens."

I attacked with my knight. "What do you mean something big?"

"I don't know; something political. He was gone when we arrived. Expanding advisors down to district level, in essence, becomes a significant increase in American support to Vietnam. He disappeared again right after the Gulf of Tonkin affair. He comes back and we start bombing Hanoi. Now, Prime Minister Khanh is getting heavy flak from the Vietnamese people, and the Chief disappears. What do you suppose will happen when he gets back?" KC looked back at the board.

"It might not be that complicated. Remember, his wife lives in My Tho, which is not all that far away by car, bus, or sampan. Maybe he just needs to get home every now and then. Did you notice how quick he was to finger the hit on the bomber?"

"Yeah, and he wasn't too pleased with the execution of the deed or the results; so much for due process of law. More like vigilantes."

I knew that this kind of thing was a tough call. Terror incidents were most of the violence we got, and they were not just a matter for police action. Flint's attention was still on the chessboard; I was lecturing, and I knew it. But, I went on with the thought I had been wrestling with ever since the CIA man came to town.

Police action was attendant to civil rights and enforced by a *civil* district chief. Appropriate rules of evidence only applied to an attack *after* the incident occurred. However, when the terrorists were classified as insurgents in a guerrilla war, it became the job of the *military* district chief. In this case, his job was to *prevent* the incident and to *destroy* the enemy *before* it became an event. No rules of evidence, no civil rights, just destruction of the enemy force. It's another one of Napoleon's nine principles of war, the principle of the Objective."

Flint:"Check."

"What?"

Flint:"Checkmate in two moves."

"You haven't heard a word I said."

"That's 'cause I'm playing a game I can see 'clearly.' You're talking a game I can only 'see through a glass darkly.'"

I finished my brandy. I studied the board. The hell with it; I went to bed.

★★★

"Chopper coming," Pete shouted. His ears could pick up the sounds seconds before anyone else. The rest of us had been in the army long enough to have suffered the standard occupational hearing loss, but not Peter.

Kuntz headed the jeep down to the soccer field, and returned with two civilian visitors. Flint had quickly set up the briefing area, and Ong Than had the tea going. I was putting the latest pictures in the slide tray when the visitors came into the courtyard.

KC went out to greet them."Good morning, gentlemen." He introduced himself and led them into the villa. Neither man smiled during the introductions. They were vague about the agency they came from—identifying themselves as simply USOM workers.

Nor did they elaborate further when they met me. It was embarrassingly silent as Ong Than poured the tea.

KC made the effort at conversation."You fellows been in-country long?"

Both men nodded, but focused on sugaring their tea. I asked them if there was a particular area of interest. The older man said they wanted to hear about the school projects in particular, but the overall progress would be of interest, too.

I shuffled around a few slides in the trays. I decided to go through a quick overview, and wind up with a focus on the self-help projects. After about ten minutes and five slides on general progress, which included some statistics, I got down to the schools.

"We have eight schools in all stages of development. Three are completed, four are in progress, and one more is on the waiting list."

Again, the older man spoke, "What is holding up the waiting list?"

"Materials, mostly," I said. "We could possibly stretch the labor pool beyond the availability of skilled workers, but that hasn't happened. The lead time for cement deliveries is the main constraint. As you know, these are self-help projects, so the labor comes from the village or hamlet."

"Do you know how much cement has been shipped into the district?"

"In what period of time? We have only been here five and a butt months," I said.

The younger man spoke for the first time. "Since the first of the year, this District has received enough cement for all of your schools to have been completed."

I took a moment to digest that information. KC spoke. "How can you determine the number of schools built based on the cement shipped? Not all the schools are the same size."

The younger man spoke again. "We know the size of each planned school and the amount of concrete in each school of a particular size. We know that there are actually nine schools planned. This district has received enough cement for all nine of these schools to have been completed as planned."

It was KC's turn to be stumped. I picked it up. Something was going on here, and these guys weren't Vung Liem to find out how well the projects were progressing. They looked to be checking on the allocation of resources.

"What seems to be your concern?" A little edge crept into my voice.

The older man spoke. "We are concerned about the concrete that is being shipped here for school projects. It would appear that someone is shaving the shipments, with the likely intent to sell a little cement for personal gain."

There was dead silence in the room. KC was turning red with anger, and about to burst, but I spoke first. I told KC to put out an all points bulletin for the Chief, and then see if Ong Hoa Hoang was in the office.

I turned to the visitors. "Ong Hoang is the assistant district chief, and is, perhaps, best able to respond to your concerns."

There was awkwardness in the room. I took a sip of tea, and moved to the next slide. "This is the school in Ap Chan. It is the latest school to be started under this plan. We just got these pictures back in the mail yesterday. They were taken last week. There hasn't been much progress since then. We will be out of cement before we complete the project."

Ong Hoang eased into the room—looking fearful. "Ah, good. Thank you for coming, Mr. Hoang. These gentlemen are from USOM in Saigon, and we've been discussing the village school construction plan. Perhaps you can enlighten us. They were under the impression that there were to be nine new schools instead of the eight we are building. Can you shed any light on the issue?"

Mr. Hoang struggled with his English. "We start with nine school. We plan for a bridge, too."

A bridge? What did he mean a bridge? That was news to me.

"The bridge go over canal to school." Hoang was increasingly nervous.

The older American spoke. "Those appropriations were for schools. We would not have approved cement for a bridge."

"Yes," said Hoang. "Bridge not OK by America in Saigon. Daui Tranh say build anyway, and we build eight schools."

"That clearly is misappropriation of materials," said the young visitor.

I ignored the comment. I asked Mr. Hoang why he thought the Daui would do that.

"Because children can no go school without bridge."

I exchanged glances with KC. KC asked, "Is this the school the Vietcong hit on the edge of the district town, near the pagoda?"

"Yes, *Daui*."

I squared off with the visitors. "This school is in a fairly populated area with children living on both sides of a small canal. When the school is built, it is likely that the bridge is necessary for children to cross the canal in order to attend."

The two men looked disappointed.

"That bridge was not authorized use of the resources allocated, and the district chief can be held liable for the misappropriation of the cement."

Captain Flint jumped in. "Maybe you two don't get it. If there is no bridge, half the children will be unable to attend, no matter which side of the canal the school is built. Would you like to visit the site?"

The older man cleared his throat. "I do not believe we have time for that. I *do* think that the district chief will have to answer for altering the school building plan without authorization."

Before KC could open up, I said, "Gentlemen, I think *you* should know that we do support the decision of the district chief. Further, this advisor team will *not* support any allegations that come this way suggesting inappropriate behavior on the part of the Chief." I turned to KC. "Have Sergeant Kuntz bring up the jeep?"

KC spun out of the room. I stood up. "Gentlemen, thank you for visiting us here. I would suggest that in the future when you have issues about a USOM project, you pass it by the USOM representative at Province level. Mr. Jake Ledbetter is very much on top of these things. We keep him informed in detail. We will, of course, relay to him the results of your visit today. I hope that seems reasonable to you."

The two visitors rose. The older man said, "Yes, of course. And thank you for your hospitality." I walked them to the jeep. The visitors initiated no further conversation, and neither did I. Kuntz drove them back to the soccer field.

Walking back to the villa, KC said, "Man, who are those jerks?"

"Just a couple foreign service officers trying to justify their positions. I can't believe they would come straight here without coordinating with Jake. I wonder whose toes we stepped on today." When we reentered the villa, there was Mr. Hoang, still standing in the living room.

I thanked him for coming and told him he did very well. I asked him to take Sergeant Kuntz and Sergeant Santana out to see the bridge in question as soon as the sergeant came back with the jeep. Mr. Hoang smiled for the first time since he arrived, and was, clearly, glad to be excused from the room.

KC rearranged the furniture out of the "briefing" mode back into "living room" mode. We both flopped down in a chair.

"And where the hell is the Chief?" I was thinking out loud again.

"Beats me how that man can appear and disappear like Merlin the Magician," said KC. "We ought to go down and see if his driver is here." KC glanced at me to see how the idea went over.

We did have a lot of stuff to talk over with him. And it was a good idea to find him or at least learn where he was; so we headed out to the boardinghouse.

Between our compound wall and the boardinghouse wall was a narrow space that had been covered over with a shed-like roof. Narrow as the space was, it, nonetheless, was wide enough to park the Chief's little green Peugeot. Add a couple of wooden doors to the front edge of the roof and a wall to the back edge of the roof, and you had a very satisfactory parking garage.

At the moment the two of us came out the compound gates, the car was parked in front of the shed. The driver was wiping it down. I asked him if he had seen the Chief.

The driver stopped wiping. "No see."

"Nice little car," observed KC.

"You rike? I take you lide." The driver grinned. He was obviously proud of the car.

"You want to take us a ride?" I asked.

"Is OK. Daui Tranh say, OK. Where want go?"

"Vinh Long." The words popped right out of KC.

I was astonished. "What are you talking about?"

"OK," said the driver.

"I'm talking about the Chief is gone, the jeep is off with the sergeants, and we are out of brandy. That's what I'm talking about."

I thought about it. But the fact that it was a dumb idea seemed to get pushed right out of my mind. "It's almost too late in the afternoon in order to get back before dark."

"Not if we get started now," was KC's comeback.

The driver asked, "OK?"

"OK," said KC. "Turn that thing around, and I'll be right back." He headed into the villa.

I yelled after him, "Tell Peter where we're going."

KC was back by the time the driver had turned the car around. KC had on a Hawaiian shirt over his fatigues, and was carrying a carbine. The absurdity of it stuck me as comical, and I couldn't help laughing out loud. "Have you lost your mind?"

KC was laughing, too. "The shirt is my low profile disguise, and the carbine is in case it doesn't work."

Maybe it's me who's lost his mind.

We piled into the car and tore down the road to Highway 8. It didn't take long to know why the Chief had this guy as a driver. He was clearly the Vietnamese version of the desert cuckoo bird indigenous to New Mexico and known affectionately as the Road Runner.

We had arrived at the canal bridge into Vinh Long Province in barely half the time it took to get there by jeep. In less than an hour we were entering the capital town of Vinh Long. The driver was looking for instructions.

"You know where the airfield is?" KC asked over his shoulder. He was sitting in the front passenger's seat.

Vinh Long Air Base was an army airfield and, as such, an American installation. It was home for mostly helicopter units that supported the advisor effort in the Delta region. It was not, generally, a destination for anyone but pilots coming home to roost.

But as an American installation, it had some American facilities—in this case a post exchange. I gave out instructions.

KC was taking off his Hawaiian shirt as we pulled up to the compound gate. He directed the driver to a parking place and indicated for him to wait. We walked up to the MP at the gate. He checked our ID and waved us through. I asked directions to the post exchange. The guard gave us clear simple directions, and then added, "But the Class VI is over off the flight line, that way."

Class VI is the universal military code word for liquor store. Since the days of Napoleon there were five classes of supply ranging from food, ammunition, and petroleum products to animal forage and building supplies. Alcohol did not fit into any of those classes, so the modern soldier created a special class for alcoholic beverages to meet his soldierly needs—the army equivalent of the navy rum ration, only designated Class VI supply.

"Do we look like a couple of alcoholics or something?" asked KC.

"Is that a rhetorical question?" I chuckled. "Truth is, let's check the post exchange first. There are a couple of items I could use."

The PX was tiny, but the fact that there *was* a PX was big. We picked up two or three items each, and could have browsed longer, but time was slipping away. We headed over to the Class VI. Shopping there didn't take long either, when you knew what you wanted.

It was the latter part of October then, and the days were noticeably short. At this latitude, and at this time of year, the twilight period was shorter than either I or KC was used to. About a half hour down the road it became apparent that arriving back in Vung Liem before dusk was going to be close. Each of us made poor attempts at nonchalance—that is until we were about five kilometers from the canal bridge.

The road ahead was empty at that time of the day, so the soldiers in black uniforms standing beside the road could easily be seen two hundred yards ahead. What were they doing?

The driver, without being prompted, began to accelerate—*beep, beep*. The road was straight as an arrow with rice fields on both sides and a tree line in the distance. *Beep, beep*. The Road Runner leaned into the steering wheel. *Beep, beep*. KC went white-knuckled on the door grip as the car accelerated. I was torn between throwing myself on the floor and just hunkering down enough to see what was going to happen next.

The black uniforms marked the soldiers as rough puffs—who knew what they would do? They held what looked like a portable barrier that they intended to place across the road.

But the Road Runner was not to be intimidated—*beep, beep*. Too late, it dawned upon the popular force soldiers that the approaching car was flying low. They threw down the barrier and scrambled aside, as "green" streaked by their position. I could see through the back window that several soldiers were trying to get their rifles off their shoulders in time for a shot at the speeding car.

The driver did not slow down to any kind of reasonable pace until the bridge into Vung Liem was in sight. Rough puffs there were also preparing to place roadblocks, but they jumped aside as the Peugeot raced cleanly across the bridge. I began to breathe. Clearly our man here had done this sort of thing before.

KC didn't ... no... couldn't speak. Roadblocks were going up behind us every step of the way as we headed down the highway, past the Catholic village, to our turnoff at the gas pump, and finally left into town.

The driver pulled up in front of the shed. It was still light, barely. KC policed up all the packages and, hurriedly, went into the compound. I stayed to help the driver push the car into its cubbyhole. The space was too narrow to drive in the car and still be able to open the car door.

When we finally closed up the shed, I spoke. "Thank you, soldier, for the ride. You are *very* good."

The young man smiled from ear to ear. "No ploblem."

I walked slowly back to the villa, trying to regain my composure. *I ought to have my head examined-- misappropriating the Chief's car, endangering the life of his driver, traveling with a soldier disguised as a civilian—however poorly.*

Had anyone been hurt, we'd have been court-martialed before we ever got to a Purple Heart?

KC had already poured out two drinks, and was sipping his. When I entered the living room. I walked straight to the second glass and took a healthy quaff. I paused to absorb the burn, and looked KC dead in the eye. I made it crystal clear that we didn't need to ever do that again.

KC answered with a nod of agreement, and hoisted his glass. Together, without any pretense of sniffing, swirling, or sipping, we shot the brandy, thus sealing an unspoken pact never to repeat such foolishness.

CHAPTER EIGHTEEN

Red Is for Luck

I RETURNED FROM R & R unsettled. Six months ago I had arrived in Saigon feeling anxious—maybe fearful—but certainly eager to do the job and confident that I could. I felt that I was part of something big and good. This time the flight back to Vietnam was an entirely different feeling. But the anxious feelings had yet to formulate into conscious thoughts.

Of course there were all the fresh memories of my wife and three-year-old daughter. And yes, it had been a bit early in the season to have celebrated Thanksgiving and Christmas all in one week in November.

But the retail world had helped the illusion with their earlier-than-ever marketing displays. In some respects, this year was a cozy and more natural Christmas than the year before. Last year the family had done Thanksgiving and Christmas on the fly—traveling between Fort Bragg and the Presidio of Monterey—trying to set up temporary quarters, find Santa Claus, trim a tree, try to be normal in an abnormal situation.

This year it was different. I even had watched the Army-Navy game, a game Army won. I thought about Mack Williams and our annual tradition of getting in touch each Army-Navy game.

When I was a cadet, I won every wager on the game. I won Mack's bathrobe and his cufflinks and his warm-up jacket—never bought a drink after the game. Those were the days; but Army's luck had changed, and a year out of the academies, I got a collect phone call in Germany from Pensacola, Florida. It was Mack calling to give me the score on the big game with Navy on top.

And almost every year since, I received collect calls from all over the world letting me know the score of the great tradition. I missed the idea of my making a collect call this year, almost as much as I missed knowing that my old friend was out there.

Yes, this Christmas definitely had been better, even if it did come in November.

But the backdrop to it all was the changing attitudes of the American public toward the war. People didn't really know what was going on. I tried to ignore the public by not watching TV. But family and neighbors, who were sympathetic to me, were *too* sympathetic. They treated me like a victim … a victim of an inept government and managed by a bumbling military.

I leaned back in my cabin class seat. I thought about the asshole CBS reporter who came to Vung Liem with his own agenda. *No wonder the American people have a morale problem. They have an incomplete idea of what is going well. All they know is that the big American airfield at Ben Hoa was viciously attacked on the last day of October. They don't know that in October, kids in Vung Liem District had four new schools with new teachers, which they could attend safely. Maybe that's just not a big enough deal.*

I squirmed in the seat, and tried to get comfortable enough for sleep. I only knew that I could cope with the ugliness of this war if I felt I was a part of something important. My background and training were all about duty. Duty demanded sacrifice if it was to be worthy of respect from a grateful nation. But what if no one cared? Was duty then just a matter of the discipline of a professional soldier who had chosen the martial life? I could cope with killing people and destroying property, if I felt that the purpose of those acts was meaningful, if it advanced a just cause.

But what if the nation didn't appreciate the sacrifice? I began to realize the source of my angst. My coping mechanism was out of kilter. I was angry and frustrated, and self-doubt was creeping in. Eventually, I dozed off, but sleep did not produce rest.

It was early afternoon by the time I had checked into the Majestic Hotel. There was time enough for me to drop by the tailors before jet lag caught up. That uniform was going to look great. I watched in the mirror while the little tailor fussed about the shoulders and then the trousers. In less than twenty minutes I was back on Tudo Street walking to the hotel. Fatigue was suddenly beginning to hit me. I needed a bed.

★★★

Eighteen hours later I woke and was ravenous. I dressed quickly with idea of a fast lunch. I would take a taxi to Flight Ops, hook up on a flight south, and be in the province by evening.

The top of the Majestic open-air dining room was quiet, and I had no trouble being served quickly. I felt like I could eat breakfast and dinner back to back. Near the end of the meal I noticed several officers gathering on the edge of the restaurant veranda. They were peering intently over the balustrade.

Curiosity got the best of me. I had intended to return to the room for my bags, but, instead, I walked out onto the veranda and looked over the railing.

Holy horse hockey!

The military tanks looked like toys from the top of the Majestic. There were two of them slowly moving down Tudo Street toward the river. They were in trail and moved twenty or so yards then stopped. They sat there traversing their turrets from side to side ... one to the left, one to the right, then reverse. I could see troops on the sidewalk getting people off the street and into whatever building was closest.

I asked the little crowd what was going on. No one turned away from the scene below, but an anonymous voice responded that he wasn't sure, but there seemed to be a riot someplace in town. Someone else added that all Americans were confined to the hotel until further notice.

The tanks moved down the street another ten yards. I went back to my table, which the waiter was clearing. I waved the man off, and ordered a pot of coffee along with the dessert menu. Might as well finish my meal properly; I sat down again.

"Looks like you got the right idea. Mind if I join you?" I looked up at the uniform in front of me. The name tag read Fletcher. I nodded to the chair.

Jim Fletcher was an older-than-most captain with a balding head—the kind with a salt-and-pepper fringe over the ears and around the back of his head. He wore round wire-rimmed glasses that gave him a professorial look. And he had a quick, engaging smile with the accompanying crow's feet around the eyes.

"Where did you go on R & R?" He pointed to the cup of coffee that the waiter had just brought and indicated the same for himself. I went on to tell about my leave adventure, which seemed to entertain him until the mention of the public's attitude toward the war.

"It makes me mad as hell." Fletcher's eyes lit up. "I just can't understand the press. When I was growing up during World War II, I remember my dad listening to H. V. Kaltenborn on the radio. I didn't understand much then, but I never felt fear, and I always felt proud of our soldiers. And Ernie Pyle in the papers—he always gave you hope and made you proud of the men who were fighting for America."

I nodded with my own recollections of the same people, but the details of the reports were not of interest to a kid at age seven.

"So where were you headed when your world stopped?" I asked.

"Home. My year is up—flight heads out tomorrow unless this current situation holds me up. Wouldn't that be a bitch?"

"Let's hope that doesn't happen, for all our sakes," I said.

The conversation moved along as we shared information about each other. I learned that James Fletcher had been working on his doctorate in business management at Columbia but ran out of funds. Since he was a reservist, he volunteered to go active duty before his draft deferment ran out too. He planned to finish his obligation, and get back to school on the GI Bill as soon as possible.

I asked him if he'd learned anything about management and leadership on his tour this year.

"Well, I don't know if I learned anything, but I have made some serious observations."

"What do you mean, serious observations? Give me an example?"

"OK. For example, management and leadership are similar but different functions. They have a lot of overlapping skills, but managers are about bringing order out of chaos. They organize for the mission, assign tasks, set priorities, and allocate resources. It's nice if the leader can do these things—at least some of them. But, if he can't, he surrounds himself with people who can.

The leader's main function is to give vision to the mission and motivate the organization to accomplish said mission.

"We have a war here, being run by a Secretary of Defense, who is allegedly one of the smartest managers that American industry has ever produced, but, to tell you the truth, I don't think he has any vision, whatsoever, as to how to really *win* this war. I don't even think he sees winning, as his job. He is about making peace the cheapest way we can."

"Does that mean you think our leadership at the top is failing us?" I asked.

"I didn't say that. But ask yourself this: How do we know when our job here is done?"

I thought about my efforts in Vung Liem. Military success was measured in VC killed and weapons captured. Success on the civil ledger was measured in kilometers of road secured, schools and aid-stations built, and local commerce developed.

I thought we would have done our job when the community could educate its children without fear for their safety, and local business could be freely transacted without fear of extortion by elements outside the law.

Fletcher lifted one eyebrow. "Ever been to the garment district or Chinatown in New York City? If that's our criteria, we haven't pacified Manhattan yet." Fletcher studied his coffee cup, then swallowed the dregs. "No, from where I was on my province team, I never had a clear idea of what my long-term strategic objective was. The short-term tactical objective was to prevent the Vietcong from disturbing the peace by any means possible. Rather open ended, wouldn't you say? Not like 'Take that hill.'"

He pushed back from the table. "Let's go down to the lobby and see what we can learn about the current developments."

We paid our checks, and the conversation lightened up as we walked to the elevator. At the ground floor, the elevator doors opened into a very congested lobby. There was a crowd around the reservation desk. A lot of civilians were milling around, obviously shunted into the building under duress. I followed Fletcher over to the military liaison desk. The master sergeant behind the desk was explaining the situation to several others gathered around.

"There has been a riot by Vietnamese citizens against Prime Minister Khanh and his handling of the war. The city was placed under martial law, and a curfew is in effect until 0600 tomorrow morning. Assuming there is no continued disruption, the city will return to normal traffic."

Fletcher turned around. "Did you get all that?"

"What I got is that we are here until tomorrow morning."

"That's about it … Why don't we meet later for dinner on the top and a nightcap in the lounge? You can bid me bon voyage, and I'll toast to your good luck." It was a deal.

★★★

I sneezed again; that damn Saigon air-conditioning. The Huey was at cruising altitude, and the door gunners had closed the doors, but I was still chilled. I rolled down my sleeves and settled back into the canvas seat. I thought about Jim Fletcher returning home: seemed like Jim appreciated someone seeing him off last night, even a total stranger.

Then I started thinking about getting back to Vung Liem. Thinking about the projects and the men, I felt myself getting a little excited to get back. R & R was perfect, but I was a soldier, and it was time to get back to work.

I glanced out the window. The rice fields were golden now. They stretched to the horizon, interrupted by thin green tree lines. Again, it reminded me of wheat. Harvesting had started.

My headset startled me out of the sleep induced by lingering jet lag. "Vung Liem at the canal junction with the Co Chien?"

"Roger that. There's a soccer field on the south end of town."

"Coming up. You're almost home, Captain." The Huey did the once-over-the-town bit and headed out across the fields on the downwind leg. The pilot made a nice sensible final approach and touched down just as the jeep pulled through the gate. I was surprised at what I was feeling—it was excitement. I pulled my gear off the aircraft and mouthed, "Thank you," to the pilot.

When I turned back, Peter was already picking up the duffel bag. "Welcome home, Captain." It didn't strike ether of us as odd that Peter used the word *home*.

"Thank you, Peter. Good to be back."

I was OK now. I was with my team. It was from the team that I drew my strength. It was for them I did my duty. Not letting them down was the thing that motivated me. And that *demanded* my best. My self-doubt faded into the background—for now. The folks at home would eventually get it, I was sure.

KC was standing on the porch when I walked into the courtyard. The young captain drew up to his full height, and delivered a proper hand salute to the returning officer. "You're three days AWOL, sir."

I returned the salute and the smile. "I had to put down a coup d'état before I left Saigon." I came up on the porch and could see that KC was not laughing.

"What coup d'état? Are you kidding?" KC's brown eyes went wide. To four Americans, alone in a district, with a chief who could out do a Houdini disappearing act, a government rollover was not a joking matter.

I confessed to kidding, but reported that there'd been a riot against Khanh that shut the city down for a day and a half and held me up till the curfew lifted. Martial law was still in effect.

We went into the living room. Ong Than met me with a cup of coffee in his hand and a big toothless smile on his face. The old man gave a slight bow and offered me the cup. "Thank you, Ong Than." I sat down and asked for the news.

KC sat. "It's like déjà vu talking about a riot in Saigon. We heard about it on BBC, but we couldn't tell how big a deal it might be. It doesn't surprise me, though. The Chief's been gone for about five days; hasn't returned yet."

Things looked back to normal when I left Saigon that morning. If there was any validity to KC's theory on the Chief's disappearances, the *Daui* should be back tomorrow or late this evening.

"What else is going on?"

"You want the good news first or the bad news?"

"Oh boy. Give me the bad news first."

"OK. The ARVN have pulled the radio relay station and relocated it God knows where."

I thought about the night of the nonassault. *Could be someone got upset about our use of the service.* "Have we been issued our own radio yet?"

"No."

"Well ... What's the good news?"

"The good news is that the violent incident rate is down, and we've had none since you were gone. Doc has delivered two more babies, and nobody has come down looking to arrest the Chief for embezzlement."

I was pleased. "Sounds like all is well in Camelot."

"Don't know about Camelot, but things are moving along in little ol' Vung Liem. School construction is still a little slow. We need to build a fire there. How was the leave?"

I told my story, without comment on public attitudes. Maybe that was all my imagination.

★★★

Anytime people gather in the fruit of their labor, it is a time of joy. And no place is the exhilaration more directly connected to the action than at harvest time in farming communities the world over. Reaping the rice is a happy time, and, even in the throes of violence, people struggle to capture the joys of tradition and ritual, if just for the children.

The beginning of harvest signaled the beginning of the holiday season. There was Christmas and New Year's, then Memorial Day and Labor Day equivalents, woven in and around Tet—the Chinese New Year, which symbolized the start of a new planting season—according to the lunar calendar.

Christmas was coming.

As far as our American advisor team in Vung Liem District was concerned, pine trees in South Vietnam were nonexistent. For Sergeant First Class William Kuntz, that was an unacceptable excuse for not having a Holiday Tree. It was true that Sergeant Kuntz was now known among the children of the Town as *Uncle*. As such, it was his self-appointed duty to provide the children of the compound with a Christmas tree—American style, or as close to it as possible.

He had begun working on a plan in early December, and by midmonth he had identified four fir-like trees of the proper size and fullness at various places around the district. Whether they were fir trees or not, wasn't important. They had thin, evergreen needle-like leaves, and they were coniferous—although the foliage was wispy at best.

In the second week of December, Kuntz requested that Pete join him on a progress inspection of school buildings. Together they piled into the jeep. Had anyone watched them closely, they would have detected a conspiratorial air about the two. But as it was, no one noticed.

At 1500 hours KC and I were with the Chief and Daui Sau, revising the district security plan. We were exploring new ambush patterns to respond to the changing travel routes by the VC. Only Santana was present at the villa when the jeep returned with four fir trees hanging out the rear.

"Now what in the name of Saint Christopher are you guys going to do with those trees?" Doc chided.

"Hold your horses, you quack. Give us an hour, and you will see something never before observed in this region of the world." Kuntz was pulling the trees off the jeep.

Pete went into the com shack, and returned with a spool of communications wire and a pair of wire cutters. Santana stood on the porch watching the two soldiers lay the trees on their side, one directly on top of the other. Kuntz lined up the tops of the trees so that any difference in length became apparent at the bottoms of the trees.

Kuntz instructed Pete. "Start the wiring at the bottom." Pete began to wire the tree trunks together with about six inches of communications wire. Every three feet or so, up the length of the trees he wired the trunks together until he reached the tops. Kuntz picked up a hand ax out of the jeep. He chopped the base of the trees down so that they were approximately even.

By now, three little girls were watching the whole process with wide-eyed fascination. Uncle and Mr. Pete were strange.

"OK, let's stand her up," said Kuntz. The two of them struggled to get the bundled trees into a vertical position. "Get your Don Juan ass down off that porch and help us here."

As soon as Santana was in a position of support, Kuntz said to Pete, "Cut us three, twelve-foot lengths of wire, and get those tent stakes out of the jeep."

When Pete had cut the lengths of wire, he handed the ends to Kuntz. Kuntz released the tree to Santana and intended to wrap one end of the wire around the bundled trees about halfway up from the base. However, when Kuntz released his support of the tree, it threw Santana off balance, and the tree began to tip out of the vertical. He and the tree would have fallen over had not the children screamed with laugher. That alerted Pete to the impending disaster, and he grabbed the tree before it toppled Santana to the ground.

"Don't say nothing," warned Kuntz, preempting Santana's would-be remark. "OK, Pete, tie one of those guide wires to a stake, and pound it into the ground when

I tell you. Santana, hold the tree in the vertical as best you see it. I'm going to step back so I can align the tree."

Using the three guide wires, they were able to fix the bundled tree in a vertical position. When Kuntz was satisfied, he and the others backed away to admire their handiwork. The children clapped and laughed.

"That is one sorry looking tree," said Santana.

Kuntz said, "It'll look a lot better when we straighten out the branches so they don't all stick out the same side."

Pete smiled. "Makes Charlie Brown's Christmas tree look like the tree at Rockefeller Center."

They began twisting the tree trunks around so as to distribute the branches around a full 360 degrees. In the end, after more time and effort than expected, they were reasonably successful. The children and a couple of adults were now staring at the facsimile tree erected in front of the villa porch. It was over fifteen feet high. The Vietnamese looked at the tree as though they had never seen anything like it—which they probably hadn't. And that might have included the Americans.

The Christmas tree was the main topic of conversation at dinner that night. It also opened up a conversation about a Christmas party for the Chief and his staff. I asked KC what he had in mind.

"My fiancée has already started sending the home-baked cookies. We can hold back all our homegrown CARE packages for a buffet—add some local sweets if it's not enough. We can make powdered eggnog and put plenty of hooch in it so nobody will be concerned about the quality of the *powdered* stuff -- your basic open house."

KC had given this thing some thought. "Have we got powdered eggnog?"

"Yeah, we got some in the food pack for Thanksgiving while you were gone. I saved it back."

The discussion was brief; the decision, swift. Everyone agreed to contribute his edible Christmas packages to the party. All that was needed was to coordinate a date with the Chief.

On cue the *Daui* entered. "You have Christmas tree. Need decoration."

KC didn't ask. He poured the Chief a brandy and handed it to him. He accepted the drink and said, "I think I have some things you can use." He took a deep sniff and then a slight sip. "I see what Ong Hoa Hoang can find."

The Chief was chatty, and we discussed the recent riots in Saigon. KC and I were particularly interested in his analysis of what was behind the unrest. One by one the NCOs excused themselves to go about other business.

"People not happy with way Prime Minister Khanh running government. Your ambassador urge Khanh leave Vietnam."

"How do you know that?" asked KC.

The Chief smiled and stood. "One minute, please." He set his brandy down and walked back to his apartment door and unlocked it. In a moment he was back with a framed picture in his hand.

"This my class picture from Vietnamese Military Academy at Dalat." The Chief laid on the table a typical eight-by-ten group photo of men in uniforms without hats. He smiled his all-teeth smile and pointed. "That me ... there." He began to name the men in his class who were now general officers. He pointed out General Khanh. "And this general in air force is Nguyen Cao Ky. Very important."

We talked on awhile longer. The conversation led into the plans for a Christmas party, and a date was settled. When KC reached to refresh the Chief's drink, he set the empty glass down. "Thank you, but I sleep now." His smile was genuine as he picked up the picture and excused himself to his apartment.

"I told you he was wired," said KC.

"Well, he certainly knows some powerful people. That's for sure."

"I'm saying he's in closer contact than just what he reads in the paper."

"You may be right, but whether he is or not, it makes no difference to us. Want to play some chess?"

"I think I'll write some Christmas letters, actually."

That was fine with me. I had wanted to start one of Peter's Louis L'Amour novels.

★★★

The Chief came through again. Midmorning, Ong Hoang, the assistant chief, came into the villa with a large box of colored pennants. They were eight inches from base to point and strung together in chains twenty-five feet long. Peter found a ladder some place and began to string the pennants around the tree like laurels of cranberry.

Suddenly, it was Christmas time. Kuntz was cutting up paper into strips and showing the children how to make paper chains to add to the decorations. Kids' mothers were making four-inch round popcorn balls. Dads were wrapping them in red tissue paper. The kids would run each red ball out to Uncle Kuntz, who would tie it to a branch or hand it up to Pete on the ladder for a higher place on the tree.

By late afternoon the tree was fully loaded. But Peter still had pennants left over. That would never do. Uncle Kuntz made the command decision.

He climbed up the ladder behind Pete and held him steady, while Pete tied off the last four strands of pennants to the very top of the tree. Santana was already on the porch roof. Kuntz handed him ends of two pennant strands, which Santana tied to the corners of the porch roof. A third strand stretched out to the gatepost. The fourth strand had to be extended with communication wire before it could be tied off on the com shack radio antenna.

The *elves* stood back to admire their work. Uncle Kuntz declared the tree "magnificent" and the project "complete." The children sang an unidentifiable song. The adults—Americans and Vietnamese—went inside and took a nap.

As KC and I approached up the road to the villa, I noticed a small crowd of civilians in front of the compound gate. We each had a spasm of anxiety. KC slowed the jeep. I undid the flap on my holster and hand-signaled KC to stop.

We both scanned the group of maybe six adults and as many children. "I don't see any weapons," said KC.

"You stay here." I got out of the jeep and walked slowly up to the gate. Whatever was happening, was happening inside the compound. At least, that's where everyone's attention was focused. Someone noticed me approaching, and, like a school of fish, the crowd turned. Children and adults, alike, were smiling, and they parted, making a path into the compound. I saw the tree as soon as the path cleared.

I shouted for KC to come on in. *He wasn't going to believe this.*

We gazed around the courtyard in dumb amazement. "Looks like a used car lot," said KC.

I suggested he strike that image from his mind. Better he see the most beautiful Christmas tree in the whole world.

"Got it, boss."

★★★

The open house for the district chief and his staff was on the twenty-fourth of December, and was deemed a great success. KC sent Pete and Ong Than out to appropriate the largest banana tree leaf they could find—which they did. The leaf they brought back was easily six feet long and two feet at its widest. KC cut out the silhouette of a pine tree from the waxy deep green leaf. After Ong Than spread a bedsheet over the dining table, KC laid the pine tree cutout, like an appliqué, on top of the tablecloth.

The care packages from wives, mothers, and sweethearts were offered up to the pleasure of all guests. And, if there was any doubt about the eggnog, it was put to rest with a quart of bourbon.

The Chief let it be known he had a Christmas surprise for the team, and that all should come by and see it at a little celebration in the Regional Force barracks the day after Christmas. He also mentioned that there would be a midnight mass celebrated at the Catholic Church across the street from the villa.

None of the team members were Catholic, but KC and I decided it would be a good gesture to attend the Mass, anyway. In fact, we broke out fresh khakis just for the occasion, which was a big deal, as khakis could only be starched and ironed in Saigon.

Christmas Mass was celebrated in the French tradition. A few minutes prior to midnight the congregation makes a candle light procession around the outside of the church. The procession is led by four altar boys bearing a miniature manger sitting on a wooden stretcher. The manger is from the Nativity scene that sits in the front of the church sanctuary. The Nativity scene is on display from the beginning of the season, but the manger is always empty until midnight Christmas Eve. Each year the challenge for the altar boys is to get the figure of baby Jesus into the manger just before midnight without the Congregation seeing the act.

KC and I arrived at quarter to twelve, and stood in the rear of the packed church. The Congregation stood as it sang the traditional Christmas Carols in Vietnamese. We sang along in English, or in some cases, just hummed. The altar boys moved to the Nativity scene and secured the manger. The priest came down the center aisle and was followed by the boys. The congregation fell in behind. The Priest led the procession around the Church. Each parishioner carried a candle wrapped in a white paper collar, and lit it, as he exited the church and joined the procession.

The two of us followed along at the rear without candles. It was haunting and lovely. The candlelit faces sang and strolled around the church three times—in the name of the Father, the Son, and the Holy Ghost.

With perfect timing the procession reentered the church and moved up the aisle. At the stroke of midnight the manger was replaced in the Nativity scene, complete with the Baby Jesus.

I recognized the melody of "Silent Night." We joined in the song, but before we could voice the words "All is calm, all is bright …," we heard the unmistakable sound of mortars.

CHUNK … CHUNK … CHUNK.

We were both out the back doors in a flash. I jumped the three steps to the yard. KC with his long legs just took one long step to the yard. We flew across the twenty feet of grass, into the canal ditch. The canal was nearly waterless, but it had plenty of mud. I vaulted clear of the bank and landed smack in the middle of the mud. KC made a dive and roll move, that got him over the edge and kept him tumbling right down to the bottom.

POP ... POP ... POP ...
Three bright lights burst into the cloudless sky ... *flares!*

"Shit, oh dear. Who's firing mortars?" KC yelled.

"Why illumination? What's going on here?" I was beginning to sit up.

"My American friends." It was Daui Tranh. "You OK?"

"What in the Sam Hill is going on, *Daui?*" I looked up at the silhouette of a man pointing up into the sky. Behind the figure were three orbs of bright light gently falling from the heavens.

"Father, the Son, and Holy Ghost. Pretty good, yes?"

CHAPTER NINETEEN

The Face of the Enemy

It was the second day of Christmas. I broke out my last pair of starched khakis for the soirée at the barracks. Ong Than's wife took charge of the khakis trousers I had dunked in river mud. The chances that they would ever be clean again were slim to none. Daui Tranh was something else. I was to the point where I understood what the man did, after the fact, but, I doubted if I would ever be able to predict what the man would do in advance. It was just a different thought pattern.

I walked out to the men waiting in the courtyard; everyone ready. We planned to arrive as a group, be tolerably tardy, partake of the strange foods, have the refreshment of the day, and leave as a group after an hour or so.

"All present and accounted for, sir." KC smiled at his simulated parade ground report.

I walked around the Christmas tree on the way out the gate. In passing, I noticed that all the popcorn balls around the bottom three feet of the tree were missing. Edible ornaments ... wonder if you could market that at home. If the kids in our compound were any kind of sample market, it would be a winner. Santa Claus meets Easter Bunny.

"Any idea what the Chief wants to show us?" asked KC.

"No idea. But he seemed pretty pleased with himself Christmas Eve."

The inner yard of the barracks compound was decked out for the season. Two long rows of tables were arranged in parallel under a tented pavilion. The pavilion was just a roof, and pennants were draped around the perimeter.

"Dammed if we don't have another used car lot," said KC under his breath.

"Think beer garden," said Kuntz.

Daui Sau spotted us first, and approached with a big smile. "Bonjour, *mes amis*."

The Regional Force soldiers sat helter skelter at the tables, and, wherever they were grouped, there were large, half-liter glasses of beer.

"Now beer's a pleasant surprise," observed Santana.

Doc and Kuntz hooked up with a couple of civic action employees they recognized, and the communications sergeant brought Pete a beer by way of invitation to join his group.

"Merry Christmas, Daui Sau." KC shook the extended hand of Daui Sau, who was now grinning like the proverbial Cheshire cat.

"Daui Tranh have surprise." He looked across the yard. The Chief was headed our way.

As he approached, I announced loudly that I wanted no mortar rounds today. Daui Sau choked on his beer.

"No mortars, my American friends. Have something better. Look over at second table. See man in black sit between two soldiers with other soldiers around?"

The chief tilted his head, and our eyes swung that direction. A little guy was sitting there very still. In front of him was a glass of beer, which he did not appear to be drinking. He wore a pasted smile. "Yeah. Got him," I said. KC nodded.

"He is captured VC," announced the Chief with pride.

KC's and my mouths fell open. The Chief was looking very pleased with himself. But the VC looked like he was barely drinking age (as if that counted for anything), and here he was a prisoner of war at a Christmas party.

"OK. How did you capture him? And why is he here, and what has he told you?" I was trying to get oriented.

"He walked into our security position three nights ago."

"All by himself?" asked KC.

"Yes. He want to give information."

"And what information did he give?" I asked.

"He say VC soldiers moving north soon, for long stay. He no want to go away."

"So why is he here now?"

"He is under arrest."

"You call this party, arrest?" KC's sarcasm was not very well hidden.

"He is in barracks jail most time, but guards want to come party, too."

"You take the cake, *Daui*," KC threw up his hands.

"He no get cake. He just get one beer."

KC blinked and sighed. "Never mind."

"Are you going to release him?" I asked.

"Maybe tomorrow … after he tell all he know."

That last sounded a little ominous. I decided to let it go. "Nice party, Daui Tranh. Thanks for inviting us."

"You like my surprise?"

"Yes indeed, *Daui*. Any idea why the VC are moving north?"

"Maybe have better idea tomorrow."

This definitely did not sound good. But my questioning was interrupted when Peter came up.

"Excuse me, sir. The com shack just got a message from their guys at Province. The province team chief wants you to report to Tra Vinh ASAP." I waited for additional information.

"Is that it? No reason or explanation?"

"No, sir. But it's not really a secure net. If the Vietnamese authenticate their messages, I don't know how to do it. Simple sentences are about all I dare to exchange on this net. When you get down there, sir, could you check on when we can expect our own radio?"

"Yes, I will; thanks, Peter." Now my mind was racing.

KC was in an extended conversation with the Chief and Daui Sau. I checked my watch. It was late afternoon—not a particularly good time to hitchhike south. I eased over to the ongoing conversation between the captains. After I topped off my beer, I tried to catch up to the topic. But my mind was on other things. Listening to English, French, and Vietnamese against a body language backdrop required more concentration than I was able to put to it. Other things were suddenly on my mind.

I faked paying attention to the conversation, and drank frequent, large swallows of beer, trying not to look like I was chugalugging. Finally, at the risk of displaying very bad manners, I excused myself and thanked the Chief again for the invitation.

"Stay as long as you like, KC. I need to get back and put some things together before I answer a call to visit Province tomorrow."

KC recognized a cover story when he heard it. "I'll catch up to you at supper, boss."

✯✯✯

It was not until the following morning that the Day-Glo panel flagged down a Huey heading south. I had not slept well last night, and it was now nearly 10 a.m. Peter whisked me down to the soccer field and waited in the jeep while I checked to see if this was a good hookup.

The copilot slid open the chopper's side window. "Need a lift to Tra Vinh," I shouted.

"We're headed to Soc Trang; stand by." The copilot turned to the pilot beside him. I could see the helmet move up and down, yes. I waved Peter off, and threw my overnight bag on the chopper. The door gunner helped me up, handing me a helmet at the same time. The aircraft was in flight before I had my seat belt on. These guys weren't fooling around.

The chopper lit out low over the freshly cut rice fields, then swooped up to some twelve hundred feet. Tra Vinh was a little out of the way for a flight to Soc Trang, which was further to the south. These guys were definitely doing me a favor and were flying like they had a schedule to keep.

Tra Vinh was up ahead before I hardly had time to worry about why I was being summoned to town. The Huey zoomed over the MAAG House, and was on the ground even before transportation had departed the house. I hopped down and walked around to the pilot side of the aircraft to thank the man for his special effort. He grinned with a thumbs-up acknowledgment, then looked around the field for signs of a jeep.

"You OK?"

I backed away from the bird and returned the thumbs-up.

As the pilot revved and swooped away, it occurred to me that I was, in fact, quite alone, and without any assurance that transportation was on its way. I had to smile, remembering my feelings the first landing at this field. Now, I looked at it. Piles of construction materials were all around—just waiting for an engineer team to come and convert the grass into asphalt.

I noticed a strange pile of materials. It didn't look like construction material. I was walking over for a closer look when the sound of the jeep redirected my attention. As it drew alongside, I swung into the passenger seat. "Lenny, how they hanging, buddy?"

"Pretty good, stranger." Lenny made a one-eighty turn back to the entrance.

"I'm surprised to see you. You have got to be short."

"Leaving next week on the freedom bird; me and the major got the same flight out."

I shared Lenny's enthusiasm about going home, but the thought that Joe Bass was leaving, too, was startling. Joe had welcomed me aboard, and winked at my paranoia when I first came to town. Joe was my boss. He had given me a loose rein in doing the job, and good counsel on how to do it. It was sad that somehow the integrity of the unit was breaking up.

"So what brings you to town?"

"I've been summoned." I tried to make light of it, but inside I was nervous.

"Must be about that CIA plane that flew in yesterday morning. Well, they say it was CIA. All I saw was a twin-engine, fixed-wing aircraft painted dull gray with black tail numbers about six inches high. It looked like a resupply plane to Stillwell in the China–Burma–India campaign of 1944."

"You're a romantic, Lenny."

"I'm not kidding. It looked like a C-47, and it just taxied down to the end of the runway, opened its side door, and began dumping stuff out on the apron. When the plane was empty, they pulled in the hatch and flew away."

That *was* weird. But no more so than an agriculture guy hitchhiking on a gunboat or a counter terror advisor borrowing weapons to arm his death squad. I wondered out loud what it had to do with me.

"You're about to find out." Lenny wheeled the jeep into the driveway and up to the back veranda. I hopped out of the vehicle and skipped up the four steps. The first thing to strike me when I walked through the door was Joe Bass coming out of the dining room—fresh coffee in one hand and a cookie in the other.

"Well, merry Christmas, young man." The old soldier did not look upset. "Santa bring you any surprises?"

I relaxed a little. "As a matter of fact he did. You wanted to see me, sir?"

"Come on in, and have a cup of coffee. I'll tell you what old Saint Nick left for you under our tree by mistake."

I was smiling then. Joe poured a cup of coffee for me and helped himself to another cookie. "Better eat that last cookie before I do." I obliged. "How's that sugarcane project going these days?"

We sat down at the dining table. Since the USOM boys put the new engine in the rice mill, there was nothing but happy campers. The priest put the cash right back into village maintenance. The place looked camera-ready for postcards.

Bass was pleased.

"Could the system use more cane at harvest time?"

I couldn't imagine a limit to growing cane, but there must be one from a practical point of view. The priest was taking some overflow to a second mill on the edge of the district town. It was a small mill, but I didn't think the work challenged its capacity.

"That's good to hear, because you are about to go into the sugarcane business, big time. You got a shipment of hybrid cane developed in the Philippines. It's stacked out on the end of the runway. They flew in a planeload from Manila yesterday."

"Son of a gun. Guess I better talk to Ramsey about some trucks and a loading crew."

"Hartmann has rotated home just before Thanksgiving; got assigned as an ROTC instructor at the University of Maryland. But, a new guy is in, and he's already lining something up for you."

I went over to the coffeepot and poured myself a refill, picked up the pot, and moved toward the major. Joe lifted his cup to accept the warm-up. We both looked at the empty cookie plate.

"Probably could have trucked the cane up to you without needing you to come to town, but I wanted to see you before I left. This was as good an excuse as any. Stay for lunch. Plenty of time to get the cane loaded and back to Vung Liem. You guys are doing some great stuff up there, but I want to give you a few thoughts before I leave town."

That suited me just fine. I asked about Jake.

"Yeah, he extended another six months last fall. USOM will leave him here till March. Let's go sit in my office. We're less likely to be interrupted." We walked to the other wing of the house.

Bass asked, "Tell me, Ed, how do you think it's going in Vung Liem?"

That surprised me a little, since no one in my own chain of command had ever asked me what I thought. The question always came from outside visitors, and they never liked my answer. I sipped the coffee. The self-help projects were doing just great, and with this new hybrid cane we'd get another boost in local support.

But as for military activities, I told him my concerns. "The ARVN has pulled out the radio relay station from our district town and left us without direct communications with any American forces under any circumstances."

The major gave no indication that he was surprised. He put his cup down. "But your incident rate is down, isn't it?"

"Yes, for now. But all we've done is interrupt their violent assaults. VC own the same hamlets that they owned when I arrived. They still move around and proselytize the population at night, and we still need armed escort to go into the same hostile areas in the daytime."

Joe sat forward in his chair. "You put your finger on the problem right there. Villagers want three things: first, to live in peace and security for themselves and their families; second, to have a fair and competent local government attentive to their common needs; and third, have the opportunity for improving their lot in life. That's not much different than anyone else in the world."

Joe spoke with passion. "These villagers don't care whether it is the government or the Vietcong who run things. Whoever that peasant thinks can meet those three needs is the organization he will support. But, there is no enduring progress if you cannot fulfill number one—security."

I nodded in agreement. "So what do we do to improve security?"

"That's the sixty-four-dollar question. Up to now, the State Department has been driving this train, no matter what anyone says. The president won't let the military chase the enemy back into Cambodia. The State Department thinks we can win this war without guns—simply pump the Vietnamese with money. The political attitude seems to be, if we develop enough commerce, everyone will be so busy making money, they won't want to fight."

I thought about that. It might not be a bad idea.

"Wrong. If you can't meet the villagers' need to feel safe against a committed enemy, bound and determined to disrupt the order of things, you never can get the second and third concerns accomplished with any degree of permanence. The enemy just sabotages the progress."

"Why can't we negotiate a cease-fire till the South Vietnamese stabilize their government, and then they all can negotiate a new treaty?"

Major Bass looked at me in mock disdain. "I thought you were smarter than that, kid. First, you can negotiate only with someone who believes and respects you. Otherwise, if there is no respect or credibility, they agree to anything, and they hold to nothing. If someone doesn't believe you, or at least fear what you can do to them, they won't compromise a single point."

I could agree in theory, but how did that apply in the real world?

"Think about the Cuban Missile Crisis. The Russians backed down because they believed Kennedy was willing to throw everything we had at them if they continued placing missiles in Cuba—we could negotiate. Does that monk up in your district have any respect for you?"

Joe had made his point.

"You and I have already had this conversation, son. You win wars by overwhelming the enemy. Remember the Bay of Pigs? We lost that one when Kennedy wouldn't commit the needed air support to do the job. But, take the Dominican Republic incident. We so overwhelmed the island that hardly a shot was fired. We established order and sorted out the bad guys almost before the faint of heart knew what had happened."

The wizened major sighed, and sat back in his chair. "If America cannot or will not do what is necessary to overwhelm the enemy, then there is no conversation about winning the war, only about negotiating the peace. And it's hard to negotiate with someone who does not believe you can or will hurt them."

Major Bass took a long draw on his coffee. "The only reason China negotiated the end of the Korean War was that they believed President Eisenhower. In a behind-the-scenes meeting he threatened to use nukes on China if they continued their aggression. They believed him as the former commander of the European forces that defeated Nazis Germany."

I stared at the bottom of my coffee cup. The major's history lesson was more incisive than I'd ever had in a classroom.

"Here in Vietnam we just keep adding onto the war effort in an incremental way, referred to as *measured response*, so as not to offend anyone. The United States hasn't decided, yet, what it means or takes to win this war. If you want to kill an octopus you don't chop off tentacles one at a time to see how many it takes before it dies. You go after the head.

We can't chase bad guys into Cambodia, and we aren't allowed to enter North Vietnam. We just cripple them in one aspect, and they go back to Hanoi and figure out how to come at us a different way."

"I thought we *were* bombing North Vietnam."

"Very limited. But do you really think this enemy is going to be bombed into defeat? You're an infantryman. You know it is *boots* on the ground that take the day—the last nine yards so to speak. And so far, our leaders aren't ready to do that. Besides, Ho Chi Minh and General Vo Nguyen Giap are more interested in being right, and in control, than they are in being prosperous, and letting the individual make his own destiny. Adam Smith's *Wealth of Nations* is not on Uncle Ho's reading list."

I was really disturbed. "So what do we do out here?"

"You do what every professional does. You go back to your mission statement, and you execute. For us, it's stop the advance of Communism, and guide the application of U.S. capital into the economy."

"OK. But every mission is broken down into objectives. What is our objective?"

"Here is the tricky part. You can influence priorities with the 'carrot and stick' application of aid. You can do extensive strategic, and some tactical, planning as an advisor. But, it is the Vietnamese who must choose and commit to the objectives *they* establish. You're an advisor. That's it. You advise on how to implement *their* plan."

"The only semblance of a plan that I have seen is the self-help civic action plans."

Bass drained his coffee cup. "There is the New Life Hamlet Program developed by the Saigon government. Under Diem, it was a program that *forced* relocation of civilians into defensible hamlets. But, it was revised into a *volunteer* program when Diem was assassinated. Unfortunately, there have been four province chiefs here in Tra Vinh from July 1963 to present. That's less than five months apiece. Each one had his own ideas on how to implement the program. The district chiefs have gotten damn little guidance in setting objectives beyond the basic concept statement. Coordination and implementation of the program has come largely from the American advisory side."

I finished my coffee, too. "I don't know. Sometimes I wonder about who's advising who."

"Advising isn't telling your counterpart what to do. You might like to, and we maybe ought to, but that's not the game. The game is showing him how to accomplish what *he* wants to accomplish. It's setting the example by your blending into the environment and delivering on your commitments. It's making the district chief look good to his people. You are up there coordinating the self-help projects and promoting economic growth.

"The fact that there is no erosion in the security of Vung Liem District is testimony to the success of these self-help and economic development projects. Everywhere else in the Delta, security is slipping, but not in your district. The farmers of Vung Liem evidently are taking 'ownership' of those self-help projects, and they are resisting VC pressures to join the movement." He stood. "Let's go eat lunch."

We moved back to the dining room. The table was set family style, as usual, with all the do-it-yourself sandwich fixings. A young captain about my age was already at the table.

"Ed, meet Ramsey Hartmann's replacement," said Bass.

"Sam Tillman. Good to meet you." The captain stood and offered his hand. "Got you a truck and crew out at the airstrip. They are loading up the cane as we speak."

"Appreciate that, Sam." I shook the extended hand then seated myself.

Bass passed the lunch-meat platter. "I told Jake that you were coming in this morning. He said he would drop by after lunch."

The conversation then focused on the new captain. We old hands began to spin tales of the good old days, like when I drove over a land mine and the day when Joe took sniper fire, and anything else that was sure to scare the bejesus out of the new guy.

At about the same time the cookies were served, Jake Ledbetter showed up as planned. He poured himself a cup of coffee, and helped himself to a cookie as he sat down. "Hear you're going into the sugar business."

I guessed I was. And asked how on earth these things happen.

"Well, it's not that big a mystery. Most every in-country agency wants the Vietnamese people to succeed. Vietnamese are kind, friendly, and hardworking. They have great respect for education and will soak up knowledge anywhere they recognize it. The country is rich in agricultural potential. The French knew that, and concentrated on rubber plantations, mostly in the North." Jake dunked his cookie into his coffee.

"But, there is much more than that in the South. Coconuts and bananas are commercial crops, and rice still has the greatest potential as a cash crop. Also there has been a strengthening school of thought that sugarcane could be a significant cash crop in the South. So, when you stumbled on the Catholic father and his tithing program, everyone up the line jumped in to make it work. It culminated when the last player in the chain arrived in Tra Vinh in an unmarked aircraft from Manila filled with hybrid cane. And now, you really are in business."

Jake swished the rest of his cookie in his coffee and popped it in his mouth, then continued. "We have all kinds of toys just waiting for an opportunity. We have a handheld brick-making machine and a rope-making machine that makes rope out of coconut hair. Which brings …"

I had to stop him. "Wait a minute. What's coconut hair?"

"You know the husk that is left over after you strip out the coconut-- like a walnut husk?"

I nodded.

"Well, that husk is about 90 percent fiber, and the fiber can be spun into a coarse rope. Think you could put that to work?"

"Not immediately, but I'm sure I can find a place to start, given a little research."

"It's worth thinking about, as is the brick machine. Right now everything is built out of concrete, which makes a huge demand on the imported cement.

But that's not what interests us right now. How do you think the rice farmer would like to get two rice crops a year rather than one?"

"How can you do that?"

"The Department of Agriculture has developed a hybrid rice that grows much faster than what the Vietnamese are using. This new rice allows two growing seasons, much the way you can grow summer and winter wheat."

I had to think that over a few moments. At first blush one would say, "Great." But, as I thought about it, the whole life pattern of the rice farmer and his community was built around the annual rice season. "Maybe a farmer wouldn't see this as such a great idea. The family might see it as a disruption of family traditions and religious holidays. Right now it might look like a greater benefit to government taxes and VC assessments, both of which barely leave him enough for his family. I'm not sure that's such a good idea."

Jake was a little surprised at my response. He studied me for a long moment.

Bass said. "I think Ed means if you can't secure the ownership of the crop to the farmer, there is no incentive for him to overproduce. And, right now, the government cannot give that assurance."

We batted the point around some more, but in the end, we decided that a two-crop season was something of great potential; but now was not the time.

What it *was*, was time for me to get on the road, and move the load of sugarcane up to Vung Liem. In the interest of time, I took the truck straight to the Catholic village. We drove around to the back of the church and dumped the new cane on the patch where last season's crop had grown. Father Phan was shocked at the size of the stalks. The caliper was easily three times the thickness of the cane his village was growing. The father was ecstatic, and could not thank me enough.

The loading crew mounted up, and raced back down the road to Tra Vinh in order to arrive before dark. I showed up in time for dinner and found an audience eager to hear my tale. I repeated all that had been discussed with both Bass and Ledbetter.

KC summarized. "So basically, in the province point of view, security is steadily eroding, and any successes we experience with our self-help projects can, and probably will, be undone if we don't strengthen the protection of our citizens in the long run."

"That's kind of depressing," said Kuntz

"How do we explain why the VC are moving north?" asked Santana.

I shifted gears. "Explain what you mean."

Flint answered. "The Chief said that's what the VC prisoner gave up. He said that other Vietcong were being moved to the north, and that's why he turned himself in. He doesn't want to leave."

"I have been hearing that rumor in the aid stations myself," said Santana.

"Do we know anything else?" I asked.

Flint said, "I think the Chief got some other intelligence. They beat up the kid pretty good."

I was concerned. *This is not like the Chief. I'll have to look into this.*

Flint continued, "Chief plans to run an operation back into the hamlet that the prisoner came from."

That much was encouraging.

✯✯✯

Two days later the rough puff company commander, Daui Sau, with a reinforced platoon, moved out along the northern border of Vung Liem District--the border canal connecting the fingers of the Mekong River. The operation jumped off at the hog pens established after Miranda's visit to Ap Lin. The command and control party trailed the operation and consisted of the district chief, a small security team, a radio operator, and two civic action officers. Doc and I traveled with the Chief. KC and Kuntz were with Commander Sau.

The objective was to visit a small hamlet on the border of Tra On District adjacent to Vung Liem. This hamlet was midway between district towns, and the canal was its main means of communication—profile of a VC target hamlet. I asked the Chief what he expected to find there.

"Not sure, but prisoner come from there. Time to have look."

"Was it really necessary to beat up the kid to get this information?"

"Not beat up for information. Boy tell us everything we asked. But he wanted to go home. If we visit hamlet, VC know he talked to us. They forgive him if they believe he was tortured, but they kill him if he comes home unhurt. We save his life."

That was going to take some thought before I could accept the premise, but for now there was nothing to be done about it-- if in fact; something should be done about it. My thoughts were immediately brought back to the present. The sound of gunfire pumped everyone's adrenaline.

The command group took cover, and the security took up firing positions. The rifle fire continued intermittently. Then we heard the *chunk* of the small 60mm mortars. I couldn't stand it.

I looked over at the Chief and nodded toward the firefight. The Chief flashed his all-teeth, no-humor grin and moved the command party forward.

We stopped in sight of Daui Sau's operations group. I could see KC up ahead. He was motioning for me to join them. The mortars burped another salvo.

"What's the situation?" I asked.

"They ran into four or five riflemen on the edge of the hamlet. Daui Sau built up a base of fire to the front and took a maneuver force around to the south so as to come at the hamlet from the inland side—pin these little shits against the canal. The mortars are sealing off the backside of town."

The sporadic rifle fire had suddenly picked up. The sound was now continuously building from two directions, then from one direction, and then abruptly it stopped.

"Where's Kuntz?" I asked.

"He went with the maneuver element," said Flint. Santana brushed past us in a big hurry. We looked after him and saw two soldiers carrying a third over their shoulders. Doc to the rescue.

The Chief and Daui Sau were walking toward the hamlet. KC and I followed along behind. The hamlet was a cluster of thatched homes that ran alongside the canal. A small channel of water the width of a sampan ran perpendicular to the canal and reached into the underbrush. The trail on which we were walking crossed over the channel bridge, passed thatched homes on either side, and led into a kind of town square. No one was in sight. Soldiers were clearing the houses. Two barefoot bodies in black pajamas had been dragged into the square.

Daui Sau was talking to several of his men. The Chief motioned for me and KC to follow him. We walked out the other side of the hamlet and continued down the trail. The vegetation was so thick, the main canal could not be seen. The security detail surrounded the captains. Daui Tranh moved slowly, allowing his security to scout around to the front and flanks as we moved forward.

Before I realized it, we were in before of very high, very old iron gates chained together with a relatively new chain. The walls were covered with all kinds of vegetation, and the stucco was green with algae. It could have been the set for a 1939 Hollywood horror flick. An old man in short khaki trousers and a denim shirt worn outside his trousers came to the gate. He had on sandals without socks. His face showed no emotion as he unlocked the chain. Daui Tranh spoke to the old man sharply in rapid Vietnamese. The old man answered mildly, but in two words. He swung open the gate.

Inside the walls was a large courtyard—larger than the courtyard back at the villa. In the center was a fountain, now in sad disarray. Stacks of empty crates stood against the side walls, in no apparent order. The back wall was actually, the front of, what might once have been, a lovely French villa-- also in disarray. It suffered from the same lack of paint as the compound walls. The tiled floor of the porch was so grimy that the colored mosaic was barely identifiable.

The courtyard was overgrown with weeds that were laced with paths to and from the house, and other points in the compound. Along the gate wall were hutches, like rabbit hutches. The cages stood on legs four feet high, and were covered with simple thatched roof. The hutches ran the length of the front wall on both sides of the gate.

I think I spoke for everyone. "Well, I'll be a dingdong daddy; would you look at all those baby chicks?"

I walked along the cages filled with chicks barely out of the egg. At the end of the row, were more than a dozen bags of bulgur wheat. The sacks were clearly identifiable as products of America. I wondered if Miranda knew about this.

The Chief was still talking to the old man. They did not smile, and it did not appear cordial. The old man showed the Chief around the compound but did not bring him into the house. He only answered questions and volunteered nothing.

"No doubt this is a chicken farm," said Flint, deadpan.

It was clearly a commercial venture. It looked to me that the operation had as much potential as the pig auctions, maybe more.

The two Vietnamese completed their circuit and returned to the gate where KC and I were standing. They ended their conversation, and Daui Tranh led our little party out the gate.

I asked what was going on here, and *Daui* said that this old man was a servant in this villa during the old days under the French. "The man has always cared for this property, and now want to claim it for self, but under current law he cannot. He stayed alive by raising chickens."

"I'd say he raises a lot of chickens," said Flint.

Since there was a presence of American bulgur wheat, there might be ways to take advantage of the man's need for chicken feed.

"Maybe," said Daui Tranh. "But very hard." He walked on in thought for a few moments. "Old man and man's family have worked land for maybe generations. He believe land should belong to government, not to wealthy absentee family. And he think he should be chief man to run plantation for government."

The Chief walked along a little further. Then, with a deep sigh, he said, "I think you have just met the face of the Vietcong."

CHAPTER TWENTY

A Grateful Nation

IT WAS THE FIRST day of the Chinese New Year, a major festival of the Vietnamese culture. It consisted of a three-day celebration in February depending on the lunar calendar. The first day is for family visits and thanksgiving. The home is cleaned, and three days of meals are cooked ahead of time so that no one enters the New Year working.

For me, it also marked my official status as *short timer*. In thirty days I would be on my way home. All I had to do now was to stay out of trouble—not a small order but a pleasant thought.

The families in the compound dressed their children in new clothes. The adults were less inclined to follow the Easter-like tradition—perhaps a matter of income. But it was everybody's birthday, so gifts were also appropriate—always wrapped in red paper, the wish of good luck. In the Vietnamese culture the individual day of birth is not celebrated, only the year. Everyone celebrates his birthday on the first day of Tet.

In keeping with the *new beginning* theme, the district chief had seen to it that the villa and compound walls were all whitewashed. That was a bit of a misnomer, since the color was really cream-coffee, common to the area. KC joined me on the porch.

We watched our three enlisted soldiers standing in the courtyard entrance on the edge of a crowd. The crowd's attention was directed across the road. Each soldier had a child on his shoulders. Spectators had gathered to watch the minstrel who set up shop on the roadside.

Beside him was a refreshment stand—despite looks to the contrary. It was a pushcart whose bed was lined with a large metal pan. It had two wagon wheels with large spokes that carried the bed of the cart nearly three feet above the ground. The pan was filled with shaved ice and also a large solid ice block at the ready. A wooden box sat on top of the pan at the cart end with the fold-a-way legs. The crank on the side of this box chopped chunks of ice into shavings that dropped into the pan. At the front of the cart was a contraption that looked like the wringers out of an old washer.

This fake popcorn machine was manned by a very serious individual. He stood beside the wringers and, without humor, inserted a six-inch stick of sugarcane just far enough between the rollers to hold the cane. He then scooped up some shaved ice into a paper cone. With one hand he turned the crank, squeezing the nectar into a trough. With the other hand at the end of the trough, he caught the syrup in the cup of ice.

What child, of any age, could resist such a treat? Certainly no one I or KC knew. We looked on at three soldiers, three children on their shoulders, and six dripping cups of sugar ice.

But the main attraction consisted of an aging, seriously out of shape, "has been" muscle man juggling some knives. He was dressed in the style of old Siam, with pantaloons, a sash at the waist, and no shirt. He wore funky slippers that turned up at the toes. His attire on the whole, however, looked faded if not downright shabby.

I came off the porch with KC beside me, and we walked over to the gate. "They are probably VC spies," said KC wryly.

"If they are not, they certainly will be questioned by VC. Wonder if the Chief has had a talk with them?"

The muscle man finished his knife juggling bit, set his scimitars aside, and approached a meter-square wooden box with breathing holes in the sides. He slowly opened the box from the top. With an effort that briefly revealed where muscles had once been, he hoisted a huge twelve-foot, black and yellow python over his head and brought it to rest around his neck.

And yes, it *was* the Year of the Snake.

The crowd gave a collective *ahh*. The children screamed with joyful fright. And the little one dumped her ice cone on Sergeant Kuntz's head—all in keeping with the astrological demands associated with the sign of the snake.

As the viewing crowd was breaking up, the assistant district chief, Hoa Hoang, caught up to me. "Daui Skeelm?"

It took Hoa Hoang several attempts to get the message across, but eventually I understood that I, including KC, was invited to the home of the rice mill owner the day after tomorrow.

On the third day of Tet, special guests are invited into the home. Usually, these are business associates or special friends, other than relatives or family members. I was surprised and delighted to have been invited and acknowledged the invitation to Hoang.

When Hoang was out of earshot, KC said, "It's about time we made a visit to the Chief's home away from home … away from home."

"It will be interesting to see what this is about." I had no doubt this was more than a seasonal social call. I turned back to the crowd and watched our team members deliver the children back to their mothers. Uncle Kuntz made a detour to the washroom.

★★★

The days of Tet passed slowly for the Americans. The entire community was taken up with the holidays, and there wasn't much for the troops to do but entertain themselves. Badminton became the activity of choice.

The sides were pretty standard by now. It was KC and Kuntz against me and Peter, with Santana switch-hitting whenever one of the others was absent. Competition was keen, and the sides were evenly matched. The only combination of players that did not work was Kuntz and Santana against KC and Pete. The ol' NCOs had to be spotted points just to avoid total humiliation.

What Kuntz lacked in agility and speed, KC made up in skill and just plain height. Peter was the agile one on my team and made up for being short with good eye-hand coordination. I on the other hand was athletic, but eye-hand coordination was not my long suit. Track and swimming were my events. Activities requiring me to hit or catch a ball were not the sports that got me through the academy.

The spirited matches kept everyone engaged in a physical activity on a regular basis. However, as it turned out, when the NCOs played as a team, they drew the most attention from the Vietnamese spectators inside the compound. That was the situation one day when I had received notification that my next duty assignment was to graduate school at Georgia Tech. I was excited and wanted to write some letters home in preparation for my return and to alert the family for a move.

Out on the court the Doc and the Uncle entertained the entire group of Vietnamese residents. KC and Pete made a fatal error in negotiating a spread and gave the shrewd old noncommissioned officers too many points. Add a peewee cheering section, and the "stripers" took down the favorite sons, three matches out of five. It was good that the sergeants won the fifth game because, had they lost, pride would demand they challenge for four out of seven. And had *that* happened, it is likely that badminton would have killed the old-timers, succeeding where the VC had thus far failed.

I had sent a message to Sergeant Khe late in the afternoon of the day before our visit to the rice mill. I asked Khe to meet us at the villa around 1330 hours. Khe wasn't an invited guest, but to my way of thinking, this meeting with the mill owner should be understood clearly.

KC came into the living room carrying his web belt and pistol in his hand. "Do you think we need to carry arms on this visit?"

I thought about it. It was Tet. It has been very quiet these past weeks. The house, a private home, was just a block away. I asked KC what he thought.

"I think it's a hard fast rule that the boss laid down, and anyone who violates will be fired … unless the rule changes."

"Rule stands. Hook up." Not what KC expected. We wrapped into our webbing and went out to meet Sergeant Khe.

Normally, Khe spent most of his time with Sergeant Santana on sick calls and at the maternity clinic. He liked working with Doc, but, when he worked with me, it became a matter of a social standing not otherwise attainable by a Vietnamese sergeant. He was proud of that standing. Today was no exception and perhaps even an enhancement since he also would be a guest in the home of the mill owner—a prominent local citizen.

We arrived at the villa of Ong Van Lang promptly at 1400 hours. A houseman met us at the front gate and escorted us into the front room. Lang welcomed us to his home, Sergeant Khe helping with the introductions. Mr. Van Lang then led us into a patio area enclosed by extensions of the single-story villa. The building was larger than it looked from the road. The wings were added rooms, which formed a U-shaped footprint. The patio was set up for afternoon tea.

It did not take long for me to learn from the conversation that Mr. Van Lang was fully informed about the activities at the rice mill at Ap Lin village. He was clearly interested in the possibilities of some capital improvements in his mill. "Would you like to look at our mill?" Mr. Van Lang invited. "It is small but is in good repair."

I agreed, and the four of us walked out the back patio gate, through the garden wall that closed off the ends of the building's U shape. Behind the villa compound was an open, unplanted field. On the far side was the rice mill. Workshop paraphernalia lay about the yard outside the wooden building. I noticed two odd-shaped structures at the edge of the field to the right of the villa. Their function was not, immediately, apparent.

Van Lang walked us through the mill with Sergeant Khe translating, as if he really knew something about milling rice. It was as the miller had said—small, efficient, and in good repair. We returned to the patio.

KC asked. "What can we do to help you?"

Khe translated for Van Lang. "I would like to expand my operation in some way."

I asked him what the little buildings on the south side of the field were.

"I make bricks there. This villa is now all brick," said Lang with noticeable pride.

That got my attention. "Bricks? Do you make and sell bricks?"

"Yes, we make bricks, but not very fast, and do not make much money because they are expensive for me to produce."

I launched into the information that Jake Ledbetter had given me on my last visit. A USOM brick-making machine could have great potential right here in Vung Liem, and we spent the rest of the afternoon discussing the possibilities. By the end of the visit I had explained more than I actually knew about brick making and the marvelous little brick machine that could answer the demand for building materials that self-help projects would need to implement the Vung Liem Civic Action plan.

We left Ong Van Lang's home excited. "I'd say that went rather well, wouldn't you?" KC beamed.

I smiled. "I'd say, Captain Flint, that brick making is going to be *your* contribution to little ol' Vung Liem."

★★★

Time began to really drag for me. I was a short timer, now. But, the excitement of going home, and then on to graduate school, was being offset by the realization that I would be leaving my team. I would miss all the possibilities and excitement that lay ahead. Of course, KC had invited me to his wedding, which would be taking place as soon as KC got home next summer. And, I was determined to show up in Pittsburgh as an usher, no matter what it took. But as for the other men, it was unlikely we would ever meet again. That was not a happy thought, but this was the army, and the idea of extending my tour of duty never entered my mind.

In seven days I would be on the flight home. I would leave the district in four days, spend the night in the MAAG House at Province, fly the next day to Saigon, spend the night in Saigon—and then it was home free to a hero's welcome by a wife, a family, and a grateful nation. All the angst that had crept up on me during R & R was nearly forgotten. I was flush with pride in my team and their accomplishments.

KC poured out the brandy. He handed over the glass as he sat down across from me and the chessboard. We sipped quietly. Neither of us made a move at the board. I looked up at the poster KC had made shortly after my return from R & R. We had hung it on the back wall of the living room.

After another sip of my drink, I read the poster out loud: "Mission: to stop the advancement of Communist forces and guide American economic aid into productive projects."

I looked back down at my friend. "Are we accomplishing our mission?"

KC thought about it a moment. "Technically, yes … in Vung Liem, anyway. I can't answer for the rest of the country. But in reality …"

"In reality, what?"

"Well, I don't know. Things are quiet now, almost too quiet. But we know they are out there, and they are moving around. Yeah, a lot seem to be moving north, but there are still VC moving around in this district."

KC let his voice trail off and turned his attention to the district chief now up on the porch. "Come on in, *Daui*. Have a nightcap with us." He did not wait for a reply but went into the dining room to pour the Chief a brandy.

The Chief sat down. "Good evening, my American friends." KC handed him the brandy, which he graciously accepted.

I brought the Chief in on the discussion of our mission statement hanging on the wall. The Chief turned and began to read. "Do you think we are accomplishing our mission, or do you even think that is our mission?"

The Chief continued to study the poster. Then he sipped his brandy. All three of us sipped our brandy.

Finally, the Chief spoke. "I think that is *my* mission statement." KC and I exchanged a look, both clearly surprised at that response and not sure why. The Chief went on: "You think this war is about Communism against democracy or capitalism. Maybe for you that is true. But for Vietnamese it is not so much. The North thinks that there is only one Vietnam, to be run by Marxist Communism. The State owns everything.

"The South believes there are two Vietnams. In the South we have private ownership and private enterprise. Our government is imperfect and corrupt, with a very poor record on human rights; but it is ours, and we are protecting what is ours even as we learn to govern in the modern world. Our leaders are new and untrained. Look at my staff … how young and inexperienced. Do you know that the North sent teams into the Delta in the late '50s to assassinate hundreds of midlevel government administrators in order to seed dissention and disorder?"

KC and I sat in silence, digesting the Chief's remarks. The Chief finished his brandy and stood. "Yes, I think we are accomplishing that mission on your sign." He smiled modestly and walked over to his bedroom door. From there he waved good night as he entered his sanctum.

★★★

I paused beside the window. Master Sergeant Santana, Staff Sergeant Kuntz, and Private First Class de Groot waited in the courtyard for me to come out of the villa. Ong Than stood a little distance to their rear and waited unnoticed by anyone.

I took one last look around my sleeping area. It looked good to go. I threw my duffel over my shoulder and snatched up the overnight bag. Captain Flint was on the porch when I walked out. "Well, this is it, partner." KC gave a lame smile and grabbed the overnight bag as I came out onto the porch. I could see the troops lined up to say good-bye, and it choked me up a bit.

When I came down the steps, Ong Than suddenly skirted in front of the three enlisted men. He grabbed my duffel off my shoulder and hurried away to the jeep. He placed the duffel, which was nearly as big as he was, into the back of the vehicle and then steadfastly remained beside it.

I had to laugh. It was genuinely funny, and the act broke the tension of embarrassment for everyone. I grabbed Peter's hand and began shaking hands down the line, making nervous banter along the way. As I finished with Santana, I turned back to all and saluted them. And they returned it for the last time.

I quickly moved to the jeep. KC was already at the wheel with engine running. I reached out to Ong Than to take his hand, but the little man grabbed my hand in both of his and bowed from the waist. I could see the tears in the old man's eyes as he let go and stepped back. I couldn't talk myself, so I saluted Ong Than who instantly snapped to attention and returned the gesture with a perfect hand salute—palm forward. It would have made any French legionnaire proud.

The jeep pulled out onto the road toward the soccer field. I was talking to myself: It was easy to forget that Ong Than was a soldier.

KC spoke. "I'd like to have known Ong Than in his fighting days; one tough cookie is my guess." He looked at his watch. "You sure Province said ten hundred hours?"

There was no sign of a chopper, and it was nearly pickup time. "That's what they said, and they said it wouldn't wait."

KC and I had spent the last five days visiting all the self-help projects so that each of us could give up-to-date progress reports as part of a command turnover ... a sort of benchmark for the start of Captain Flint's command. We were halfway to the soccer field when I thought I heard a *lawn mower* engine at the side of the road. "Stop the jeep." I listened; it sure sounded like a lawn mower. "Back up a bit." KC backed up about fifty feet. The sound was louder.

I stepped out of the jeep. Without waiting for KC, I walked up a narrow trail through head-high vegetation. When I reached the top of a sandy dike, the sound of the engine was very clear. A few more feet further on, I came into a clearing. Under a lean-to squatted a skinny Vietnamese man administering to a gasoline engine. It was a two-stroke Briggs & Stratton—just like a lawn mower engine in the suburban USA. Next to the man squatted a not-so-skinny Vietnamese woman watching him run her stalks of sugarcane through the wringers being turned by the engine.

KC came up from the rear. "I'll be a monkey's uncle. Would you look at that?" The woman was catching the squeezing in a crockery jar. The two Vietnamese turned their faces our way. Both Vietnamese smiles were toothless, and I was grinning from ear to ear.

The sound of a chopper broke into the scene. I waved to the Vietnamese, and we both ran for the Jeep. This was the perfect end to the tour. You can't beat these people's entrepreneurial spirit. A guy invests in a two-stroke engine and rigs it to a couple of rollers, and he's in the service business of pressing out Mama-san's garden cane. And it was mobile to boot. Some story.

The chopper was on the ground as we pulled into the field. KC grabbed my duffel and walked with me to the aircraft. "See you in the summer. I'm counting on you."

"I'll be there. Got to warn that poor girl about what she's signing up for." From on board, I flipped KC a salute as the aircraft lifted out. Captain KC Flint held his return till the plane was well into its climb.

★★★

Tra Vinh airstrip looked a lot different from the day I had arrived. It was paved over with asphalt and appeared to be a few hundred feet longer. Ground transportation was waiting. Two officers I didn't recognize greeted me, as they climbed aboard the chopper. I jumped down, returned their greeting, and pulled off my gear.

I headed to the jeep. "Morning, Tom."

"*Chau, Daui*," said the driver. On the way to the MAAG House we chatted a little. Tom seemed to like the new province team chief, but did not appear too impressed with the new operations officer. "Ramsey Hartmann, good guy. I miss."

I recalled my first field trip with Ramsey. Yeah, he was a good guy. Men bond quickly under fire.

We pulled into the drive. Tom unloaded my bags onto the veranda. I went directly into the house. Major Steadman was in the dining room, bent over a cup of coffee. He stood as soon as I walked in. "You must be Captain Ed Skillman … Paul Steadman." He held out his hand. "Grab a cup of coffee. Have a seat."

I took his hand. Major Steadman was a tall, gaunt-looking man, fortyish, with thin lips and eyes set close together. He had an intense look. I poured a cup of coffee, and looked around for a cookie. There were none.

"Tell me what's going on in Vung Liem these days," said Steadman.

I began to recount in detail what KC and I had pulled together on our last rounds. All the villages had completed the self-help schools, and were almost done with the aid stations. I went on to describe the success of Sergeant Santana's sick call program. I suggested that Jake Ledbetter should order the brick-making machine, and I told the story about the Briggs & Stratton sugar press. As an afterthought, I mentioned that the third iteration of the ESL classes would start at the end of the month.

Major Steadman sat expressionless, and without comment. So I continued my report. There had not been any violent incidents since the hamlet operation at Ap Lin village. "The VC seem to be moving north, but we know there is still cadre operating in the district. They attempt recruiting, and still have enough muscle to tax the rice farmers. We can't gauge how successful they are. Security is still a problem, no matter what it looks like."

Steadman asked a few questions, and then the reporting slowly drifted into conversation on the team turnover, and the relative state of progress in the province. There were now, district advisor teams in five of the nine districts in the province, and, from the conversation, it seemed they were experiencing much the same things I had reported, although the new teams had more security problems, and progress was slower on the self-help stuff.

A couple of the new officers pulled in for lunch; the conversation expanded into banter. It was hard for me to get into the table talk. These were not the guys who had brought me on line. I didn't have much to say to them, and they didn't have much to ask of me, other than the camaraderie of men-at-arms.

"What's the movie tonight? I asked.

"*Bridge on the River Kwai*," said someone.

"What's it about?" said someone else. Several versions were thrown out with varying degrees of accuracy.

I looked around the table. "It's about a British Army colonel who gets so caught up in the process of building a bridge as a prisoner of the Japanese, that he forgets what his real mission is—to destroy the enemy. It's a good movie."

Everyone scattered to the winds after lunch. So, I struck out to find the bunk where Tom had stowed my bags. Peter had slipped me two Louis L'Amour Westerns which were in the duffel. Maybe before volleyball and happy hour I could finish the one I had started.

★★★

I watched the four men pull supplies off the Caribou. This plane was the milk run from Saigon, and I would be making the circuit today: from here to Bac Lieu, stopping at Soc Trang on the way, and then west to Ca Mau. If I was lucky, the plane would head straight back to Saigon. If not, I would visit Rach Gia and Long Xuyen, and not be in Saigon until around 1800 or later.

As it turned out, I was lucky, today. The Caribou touched down in Saigon at 1630 … 4:30 p.m. civilian time. I was already beginning to think again in the twelve-hour clock. This early arrival gave me plenty of time to drop by the tailors, and pick up the new uniform. I was excited -- less than twenty-four hours till the freedom bird. I sat in the kamikaze cab thoroughly enjoying the bob and weave through traffic that had been so terrifying a year ago. The cab pulled up in front of the tailor shop. I jumped out and tipped the cabby outrageously, just because.

The tailor saw me coming, and by the time I hit the door, the gentleman had the uniform laid out for the final fit. I stood in front of the mirror. It was perfect. I turned sideways. The fellow had done a magnificent job; it checked out from every angle. The tailor was obviously pleased with his work and pleased that I was happy.

We both stood looking at the image in the mirror. I was proud of the job he had done this year. For myself, I had seen nine new schools up and running, five aid stations manned, and a maternity clinic delivering one or two babies a week. We had kept the road open to Saigon (only one half-day exception) and the VC out of any new villages. I had dodged three known assassination attempts—who can guess how many I didn't even know about. And there was the economic impact of sugarcane and the hog market and now the potential of brick manufacturing. More than fifty Vietnamese had taken English lessons. Yeah, the image in the mirror looked like a winner.

As I came out of the dressing booth, I handed off the uniform, and signaled him to wrap it up. I counted out the cash we'd agreed to a year ago. The tailor literally bundled the uniform in brown paper and tied it with string. Evidently coat hangers and clothing bags were not big items of equipment in Vietnam. We shook hands and said our final salutations, one in Vietnamese and one in English, and we understood. I walked back to the Majestic Hotel.

⭐⭐⭐

I had that last night all planned out. I would find the French restaurant I enjoyed the first week in-country—La Petite Auberge? I would have a nice long meal and then return to the Majestic rooftop bar for a farewell drink—or two. Early to bed, early wakeup, then suit up in khakis for travel. After checkout through the army liaison office in the lobby of the hotel, I would catch the military bus to Tan Son Nhut Airport; board the plane; finish one Louis L'Amour novel, and into the arms of my wife and daughter. It was a good plan.

And the plan was working. Dinner was outstanding. I was again amazed that this fine French dining could be in Saigon. When I walked into the lounge on top of the Majestic, the bartender immediately reached for a brandy snifter. I was impressed and flattered that this man should recall my face, much less my drink, out of all the Americans who passed his way. We exchanged greetings as I slid onto the barstool, and waited for the songstress. Things were falling in line.

At the appointed hour, the boys in the band came out and warmed up the audience with a few rock-and-roll songs. Finally, what the predominantly male audience was waiting for appeared. She was so petite. She was nothing more than a big Barbie doll. She wore classic Vietnamese dress—a bit glamorized for showbiz, but quite elegant. The audience loved her.

"She speaks no English, you know," said the bartender.

"You're kidding?"

"No, it's true. She learns the music and the words by heart. She copies the gestures she sees the American performer make. While she knows what the song is about, she does not know the meaning of each word."

The beauty was singing Petula Clark's version of "Downtown." It was amazing. I wasn't sure whether I was impressed or disappointed. I was definitely entertained. The set ended with her rendition of "I Left My Heart in San Francisco." I had waited all year for this moment -- to hear this song and know that I was heading back to San Francisco in the morning. I finished the snifter. There was still a handful of funny money in my billfold, so I dumped it all on the barman, and bid the astonished man good night and farewell.

⭐⭐⭐

The wakeup call came at 0530. It was a little earlier than I originally planned, but I'd decided to get up early and put the brass insignia on the new uniform *before* I left.

I had decided to switch to the new uniform in San Francisco for the stateside leg. That would get me out of the summer khakis into the winter stuff which was still in season in the States. If I placed the insignia and shined the brass in the hotel room, I wouldn't have to do it in the airport restroom stateside. I showered and shaved, dressed in a fresh set of khakis, and packed everything but the new uniform.

I finished polishing my brass insignia and began to place crossed infantry rifles insignia on the lapel.

That's when it happened. There on this beautiful new tailor-made uniform. Right there, in the left lapel, was a *buttonhole*.

I couldn't believe it. How had I missed it?

The brass insignia I had so proudly polished, could not, would not, did not cover it, no matter how I tried. The whole lapel panel would have to be replaced, and I did not have the remnants. And a new panel would never quite match, and whatever I did, it would be expensive.

I was mad. Clearly, that tailor was a Vietcong subversive.

The *hell* with it, I was furious and abysmally disappointed; my own little personal project, took a whole year to set it up.

What a letdown. I stuffed the offending blouse into the duffel bag and followed it with the trousers. After I closed the bag, I gave it a couple of good swift, gratuitous hits. Mumbling to myself that I would cross that bridge when I got to it, I grabbed up my luggage and sailed out the door.

Right now I had a plane to catch. Waiting out there was a wife, and a family, and a hero's welcome.

EPILOGUE

Not Till the Fat Lady Sings

IN THE EARLY SPRING of 1965, the United States deployed conventional fighting forces to the nation of South Vietnam. Encouraging as that might have been from my point of view, the seeds of failure were sown domestically at nearly the same time. The feeling I had sensed six months ago, was no longer a matter of subtle attitudes; it had grown into outright ugly antiwar protests.

The Vietnam Day Committee (VDC) was a coalition of political groups, student groups, labor organizations, and pacifist religions in the United States that opposed the Vietnam War. On May 21, 1965, the VDC began a demonstration that lasted thirty-five hours and drew more than thirty-five thousand participants on the UC Berkeley campus. My homecoming was not quite the hero's welcome I expected from a grateful nation. It was disheartening and confusing.

In late October of the same year, air units of the Seventh Calvary, specially organized and trained for counterinsurgency, defeated North Vietnamese units in the Ia Drang Valley. It was the first large unit clash of conventional forces. It did not receive much favorable attention by the American press. And Americans never were given the chance to feel pride in the men who, so bravely, fought and met every criterion of heroism. Not until the book by Joe Galloway, *We Were Soldiers Once ... And Young* was released in 1992 did the public have the opportunity to witness the professionalism, and celebrate the raw courage of the American soldier.

In October 1965, doubt in the nobility of our purpose, began in the back of my subconscious mind.

In fact, the VDC planned and organized a nationwide demonstration to take place on October 15 and 16. VDC coordinated antiwar groups in two dozen cities to participate in the demonstration. Protest marchers made their way to the Oakland army terminal where men and material embarked to Vietnam. It disgusted and angered me. And worse, it crippled America's ability to morally support their fighting men who, so desperately, needed moral support in a dirty little guerrilla war.

By December of 1965 the American troop strength in-country reached almost two hundred thousand. At the end of 1966 that troop strength reached four hundred thousand, and a year later in 1967 it was nearly five hundred thousand.

General Westmoreland returned to the United States in the fall of 1967 and made every effort to sow optimism and build the morale of the American people on the home front. I watched along with a disheartened America as military victories over the next two years were turned into political defeats.

The fighting was hard and ugly, and did not make for good television entertainment in American living rooms. I could not reconcile what I was seeing on the news with what I had experienced. I knew from experience how CBS reported *their* news, but all the media seemed of one voice.

Draft card burning became the "in" thing, and skipping to Canada was the way out. For some people, that was a patriotic move. Somehow, in those days, the idea of patriotism got turned around.

It was as though public anger, which should have been focused on an enemy who had threatened to bury America, was, somehow, shifted onto the men and women who protected that America against that very threat.

Violence makes news, and pacification does not. Building infrastructure and stabilizing organizations were not newsworthy. And, they didn't seem to carry much weight in graduate school either. I had just earned a C and "see me" on a brilliant paper—if I did say so myself—on the merits of sound standard operating procedures in organizations. The grade really smarted because the paper was based on personal experience.

I reported to my professor. The man was in his late fifties and once upon a time had had wavy red hair but now sported a thinning, rusty gray comb-over. "You wanted to see me?" I had a chip on both shoulders as I stood in the open doorway of the small office.

"I did? What was it about?" The professor picked up the lit cigarette from his ashtray and leaned back from the desk.

The jerk didn't even remember the paper. "Your note on my paper on the value of sound operating procedures in organizations." I pointed out the C with the note.

"Oh yeah. Actually that was a pretty well-written paper."

Evidently not well enough. I was confused.

"And that's why I wanted talk to you personally. You need to know that *people* run organizations; not *organizations* run people. You don't have to believe me now, but you'll come to believe me someday. I'll change your grade to B-plus; can't give you an A because your premise is flawed."

I thanked the man and backed out of the tiny office. I was not sure if I felt pleasure or pain—pleasure for having the grade bumped or pain for being *flawed*. In retrospect, after working through denial of the truth, I concluded that pain was the stronger emotion. I am not particularly humble, and to acknowledge being flawed was painful. I guess the second lesson I learned was this: Sometimes the teacher you liked the least advanced your thinking the most.

In 1968 I was out of graduate school; and the Vietcong, in a high-risk gamble, launched what was known as the Tet Offensive. On 31 January the Vietcong, augmented with some North Vietnamese forces, attacked twenty-one towns and cities in a surprise move on the eve of Chinese New Year. After the initial successes of the surprise, the VC were defeated decisively by the American forces. In less than three days every major objective achieved by the Vietcong had been reversed. The North Vietnamese had only their horrendous losses to show for it: in one week forty-five thousand men. By the end of the month the number was fifty-eight thousand.

I was now, an instructor at the Army Management School just outside Washington DC. The job was to design and teach the new techniques of operations research and systems analysis—qualifications I had just accrued under the rubric of Master's of Science in Industrial Engineering at Georgia Tech. In the eyes of Army Human Resources, I was a full-blown expert, qualified to instruct Pentagon officials in the art of management—Secretary of Defense Robert McNamara–style.

It was spring 1968. The Tet Offensive had just been blunted, but the fog of war still hung over the battlefield. The attitude in the country, and in Washington, particularly, was decidedly negative toward the war effort.

I was lecturing in front of my 8:30 class. The students were at the end of their course. In a few weeks these senior officers of the American defense community would return to their jobs and assume new roles in the decision-making process. Most of them were colonels—a few lieutenant colonels and a couple of government civilians from the CIA and the State Department of similar pay grade.

A hand went up in the back of the room. I had just finished a teaching point on trade-offs for cost-effective decisions. I had used a simplistic analogy of choosing just the right size hammer for pounding a nail.

"What if we don't like the cost-effective choice, Major? What if the need to be effective is worth it at any cost? If you choose the 'most bang for the buck' solution, you may not get enough bang to do the job. When you haven't got enough hammer to really set the nail and drive it home, or when it takes so many strokes to do the job, you run out of time, then you either fail or fizzle."

I looked at the young lieutenant colonel. "The rules for professional behavior do not change just because you have some new tools for decision making. As a professional analyst, you have the responsibility to give the decision maker the best recommendation you can develop. It must be based on facts, your best analysis, and your experience. If the decision maker does not follow your recommendations, you as a professional owe him your best effort toward supporting *his* decision. Anything less than that is unprofessional and destabilizing to the mission.

Scream and holler all you want before the decision, but after the decision is made, you support it a hundred and twenty percent—or resign."

I looked around the classroom for any other comments, and then I turned back to the Marine lieutenant colonel. "By the way Colonel Williams, did you ever know a navy lieutenant by the name of Mack Williams?"

Colonel Williams hesitated a moment, then: "He was my cousin."

That stopped me in my tracks; it was such a surprise. I didn't know what I expected or even why I asked the question—maybe I was just rebuilding civility for a somewhat condescending answer to the colonel's challenge.

Now, the whole class was staring at me. I was not known for being short on words, but I was struggling with how to respond to the colonel; how to explain myself; so much emotion.

I eased to the center of the platform and tested the timbre of my voice. In the final few minutes of the class session I recounted the exploits of my friend Lieutenant Mack Williams, and how that heroic man lost his life in the service of his country.

Not everyone in America that day, had they heard my account of Mack Williams' bravery, would have seen it as a patriotic sacrifice.

Patriotism had always meant service and sacrifice and loyalty to America, but now, I was seeing it turned completely upside down. It became dissidence, and disruption of traditions and rituals, all in the name of freedom. Disrespect for authority and disobedience of the law, were declared acts of free speech and the new hallmarks of patriotism. I saw my patriotism under direct assault. Ugly doubts broke out of my subconscious after every newscast or headline. The act of patriotism was being redefined in "newspeak" thinking.

People were definitely running the organization, and the organization was changing. I watched the resounding U.S. military victory of the Tet Offensive transformed into a political defeat for America, and saw the meaning of patriotism twisted into domestic violence and civil disobedience, all in the name of free speech.

Years later, near the end of 1997, David Lamb in his book *Vietnam Now*, recorded his interview with the North Vietnamese General, Tran Do, who acknowledged that North Vietnam "in all honesty did not achieve [its] Tet objective." At the time of the battles the American press chose to interpret the outcome of the Tet Offensive quite differently. Domestic protests began to rise. With Tet, antiwar activists scored a strategic victory.

The North Vietnamese were quick to realize their good fortune, and were energized to renew the offensive. The conscription age was raised to forty, and a massive effort was begun to rebuild the Ho Chi Minh Trail.

"Without the Ho Chi Minh Trail, Hanoi's dream of uniting the two Vietnams might have remained only a dream, especially in the light of the heavy Tet losses in 1968." This line of communication facilitated the replacement of the decimated Vietcong Army with a new, North Vietnamese Army (NVA).

Yet, it was not until April of 1970 that President Nixon announced that American and South Vietnamese forces were now permitted to attack sanctuaries in Cambodia—through which the Ho Chi Minh Trail passed.

The antiwar crowd, with the sympathy of the American press, led our nation into self-doubt: to the point that on March 29, 1973, the last American troops were withdrawn from Vietnam. The South Vietnamese Army continued to fight successfully against an unseasoned and badly equipped North Vietnamese Army. Two years later the Congress of the United States voted to end all funding to Vietnam, terminating the pledge of military logistics and economic support to South Vietnam. South Vietnam lost its struggle. The American press ceased to report on events in Southeast Asia.

There was no end of critics against the war who came *after* the fact. These were the ones who never had the presence or professionalism to voice their doubts before the decision to stop the advance of world Communism. And, rather than resign, they continued criticism, and sewed dissention where unity of purpose was needed.

At best, these shapers of public opinion made it a point to portray the servicemen and women as victims of a bumbling military leadership and a misguided government. At worst, soldiers were assaulted and harassed for just answering their draft call.

Whatever the credibility of reports on the war's progress, and despite my nagging doubts on the nobility of our nation's mission, I always came back to what I had seen with my own eyes. With all it its shortcomings and delays, the establishment of a South Vietnam was in the best interests of the United States and the Vietnamese people. But, I had to be careful where and when I expressed support during the '80s and '90s.

Motives are important to a process, however, outcomes plot the course of history. After the journalists were no longer motivated to write about Vietnam, the historians began to sort out the facts. A different, more authentic, picture of the war started to take shape. Forty years later, outcomes became clear, and the plot of the true course of history became apparent. Time dampened the noise of the naysayers. The Gulf War renewed national pride.

By the late 1990s, evidence of my deep-seated convictions began to surface. In 1986, when the economy of Vietnam had been completely destroyed, thanks to a rigid Marxist view of Communism, and, after the revolutionary leaders were either dead or retired, the Sixth Party Congress instituted a program known as *Doi Moi* or *economic renovation*. Given the depths of Vietnam's desperation, it was a decision made out of necessity. Iit, also, reflected that the government was pragmatic enough to understand that slogans don't fill empty stomachs.

Doi Moi was designed to introduce a free market economy, to encourage private enterprise, and to free the entrepreneurial spirit of the Vietnamese. The capital to feed this economic renovation came, for the most part, from the South Vietnamese *boat people* scattered though out the world after the collapse of Saigon. The spark of capitalism rekindled first in the South.

In 2005 I looked back at the record, through the filter of forty years. History showed, clearly, that Communism ceased to expand after President Kennedy drew the line in Indochina. Though the attempts continued, from that day forward, no new nation fell under the control of a Communist regime. That was the kind of security, intended by the United States with its stand in Vietnam. At long last I felt vindicated.

Viewed through the prism of time, I saw a free market economy emerge in Vietnam. That, too, was an intended outcome from the American stand in Indochina. I watched, with pride, as Vietnam entered the global economy. With multiple growing seasons, Vietnam is right behind Thailand as the second-largest exporter of rice in the world. Making construction brick and poultry farming are commercial industries in Tra Vinh Province.

And sugarcane is a cash crop.

Author's Notes

The Vietnam events in this book actually occurred. The sequence is a function of my memory and the dramatization of the story, but the activities do track with the historical events of the times. In scenes where I was not a direct participant, the accounts are developed from third parties and my deductions. The battle scene at the chicken ranch is fictionalized for dramatic impact. The chicken ranch did exist, we did run an operation there, and the environment was distinctly hostile, including the attitude of the Vietnamese rancher.

The characters on the province team are composite personalities with fictionalized backgrounds to support the personalities presented, and the environments they came from. General Westmoreland and Raymond Burr did visit the province team for the reasons described. The staff sergeant with a French foreign legion background did come through Tra Vinh on his way to Cau Ke, but I could only surmise his background and his motives. All the CIA activity is accounted for as it happened.

The names of the Americans on the district team have been fictionalized to preserve the privacy of the individuals. Their backgrounds have been disguised to protect anonymity, but mostly because I have forgotten many of the actual details. I did go to KC's wedding, which was a fine affair, but as he soon reverted to his primary branch, our careers never crossed again. I never, again, saw or heard from the enlisted men.

My relationship with Navy Lieutenant Mack Williams was dramatized to emphasize the impact that the death of one American could have on the small advisor community when it occurred. He and his crew did exist, and we did meet. His swift boat was ambushed along a canal in the Mekong Delta, and he was killed. Men bond quickly in moments of danger; death has an accentuated impact.

Jake Ledbetter, his wife Letha, and Miranda Meadows were heroic representatives of the State Department. Miranda's home economics program, including her hog, was cancelled by a new director who arrived in late 1965. From my perspective it had been a very successful program.

The role played by Vietnamese Buddhism was not fully understood by the press or by military analysts and certainly not by us advisors. All I knew, at the time was that wherever there was trouble, a monk seemed to be in the wings.

As I researched the Buddhist movement for this book, I learned that in late 1963 the Vietnamese monks began concerted and determined efforts to undermine the South Vietnamese government, and those efforts continued until mid 1965. Historians strongly suspected that these very byzantine activities included collaboration with the National Liberation Front, the political arm of the North Vietnamese.

In this book I created a history for individual monks in order to capture the facts of the Buddhist activities of the day: the history of Japanese occupation, the riots in Hue, the convention in Saigon, the monk suicides by self-immolation. The blind monk did exist, as did his young assistant, and they did live in the town of Vung Liem. Other unidentifiable monks came and went. The names are fictitious, but the dramatized backgrounds of Tien Van Quan and Duc To Ngoc reveal the known history of the Buddhist movement in that special time from 1963 to 1965.

Bibliography

PRIMARY SOURCES

Butterfield, Fox. *The Vietnam War Almanac*, by arrangement with World Publications. 1985. New York: Barnes and Noble, Inc. 2005.
Karnov, Stanley. *Vietnam—A History*. New York: The Viking Press. 1983.
Lamb, David. *Vietnam Now-A Reporter Returns.* New York: Public Affairs. 2002.
Moyar, Mark. *Triumph Forsaken*. Cambridge, England; New York: Cambridge University Press. 2006.
Tanham, George et al. *War Without Guns—American Civilians in Rural Vietnam*. New York: Frederick A. Praeger, Inc. 1966.
Vietnam Business Forum. February, 2007. http://vibforum.vcci.com.vn

SECONDARY SOURCES

Smith, Adam (Andrew Skinner, ed.). *Wealth of Nations.* New York: Penguin Books. 1986.
Biddle, Stephen. "Seeing Baghdad, Thinking Saigon." *Foreign Affairs*. Vol. 85, No. 2. New York. March/April, 2006.
Pillar, Paul. "Unheeded Intelligence." *Foreign Affairs*. Vol. 85, No. 2. New York. March/April, 2006.
Prophet, Elizabeth Claire. *The Lost Years of Jesus Christ*. Livingston, Montana. 1987.
Rayburn, Joel. "How The British Quit Mesopotamia." *Foreign Affairs*. Vol. 85, No. 2. New York. March/April, 2006.